WOMEN, MEDIA, AND POLITICS

Women, Media, and Politics

EDITED BY

PIPPA NORRIS

Sponsored by the Joan Shorenstein Center on the Press, Politics and Public Policy, John F. Kennedy School of Government, Harvard University

New York Oxford
OXFORD UNIVERSITY PRESS
1997

Oxford University Press

Oxford New York
Athens Auckland Bangkok Bogota
Bombay Buenos Aires Calcutta Cape Town
Dar es Salaam Delhi Florence Hong Kong
Istanbul Karachi Kuala Lumpur Madras
Madrid Melbourne Mexico City Nairobi
Paris Singapore Taipei Tokyo Toronto

and associated companies in
Berlin Ibadan

Published by Oxford University Press, Inc.
198 Madison Avenue, New York, New York 10016

Library of Congress Cataloging-in-Publication Data

Women, media, and politics / edited by Pippa Norris.
p. cm.
"Sponsored by the Joan Shorenstein Center on the Press, Politics, and Public Policy, Kennedy School of Government, Harvard University."
Includes bibliographical references and index.
ISBN 0-19-510566-4 (cloth : alk. paper). — ISBN 0-19-510567-2 (pbk. : alk. paper)
1. Women in politics—United States. 2. Mass media and women—United States. I. Norris, Pippa. II. Joan Shorenstein Center on the Press, Politics, and Public Policy, Kennedy School of Government, Harvard University.
HQ1236.5.U6W6665 1996
305.4—dc20 95-52162
CIP

1 3 5 7 9 8 6 4 2

Printed in the United States of America
on acid-free paper

Contents

Tables

Figures

Preface

A flourishing body of research in political science has focused on the obstacles and barriers facing women in elected office, the gender gap in voting behavior, and the development of the women's movement. Another rich literature in communication studies has covered women's roles as journalists and broadcasters, and the portrayal of women in popular culture. The aim of this book is to bring together these separate disciplines to provide a comprehensive and systematic understanding of the relationship between women, the media, and American politics. Since this subject is open to multiple approaches, chapters draw on a plurality of methods—surveys of voters and campaign managers, personal interviews with journalists and broadcasters, focus groups and experiments to see how people react to different media messages, and historical archives, content analysis, and more qualitative readings of the nature of press coverage. We involved established and younger scholars in the project, to encourage a new research agenda which could be developed further in future. We are aware that we have only started to unravel some of the puzzles about the complex interaction between sources, journalists, and the audience, within the broader political culture and political system, which produces media coverage of gender politics in America.

The project started with a conference at the Joan Shorenstein Center on the Press, Politics and Public Policy, at the Kennedy School of Government, Harvard University, in August 1995. All the contributors were able to exchange ideas and draft chapters at this conference, which greatly aided the overall integration of the volume. A second conference was held in the Press Club in Washington, DC, in spring 1996, bringing together policymakers, journalists, and scholars to discuss the implications of this work. Meetings to discuss further research will be held in conjunction with the American Political Science Association (San Francisco, 1996) and the European Consortium of Political Research (Bern, Switzerland, 1997).

This project would not have been possible without the generous funding and continued support provided by the Ford Foundation. In addition, we would like to thank Marvin Kalb and Fred Schauer for their constant encouragement, Edie Holway, who organized the conferences with impeccable efficiency, Nancy Palmer and Jennifer Quinlan for helping with the arrangements, and all colleagues, fellows, and students at the Joan Shorenstein Center and the Kennedy School of Government who have supported this project at different stages. We would also like to thank Oxford University Press for its faith in this volume.

Pippa Norris

Harvard University

Notes on Contributors

STEPHEN ANSOLABEHERE is Assistant Professor in the Department of Political Science at the Massachusetts Institute of Technology. He is the author, with Shanto Iyengar, of *The Media Game* and *Going Negative.*

MAURINE H. BEASLEY is Professor of Journalism at the University of Maryland-College Park. A former staff writer for the *Kansas City (Mo.) Star* and the *Washington Post*, she holds a doctorate from George Washington University. Her books include *Taking Their Place: A Documentary History of Women and Journalism* and *Eleanor Roosevelt and the Media: A Public Quest for Self-Fulfillment.* She has been president of the Association for Education in Journalism and Mass Communications.

RICHARD BRAUNSTEIN is a doctoral student in Political Science at the University of Colorado, Boulder. His research interests include the cohesiveness of group voting and the access of organized interest groups to judicial decision making.

HEIDI BERGGREN is a doctoral student in Political Science at the University of Colorado, Boulder. She previously studied at the University of California at Berkeley and the University of Texas at Austin.

SUSAN J. CARROLL is Associate Professor of Political Science at Rutgers University and Senior Research Associate at the Center for the American Woman and Politics (CAWP) of the Eagleton Institute of Politics. Her research interests have focused on women as candidates, voters, and elected officials, producing publications on *Women as Candidates in American Politics*, *Reshaping the Agenda: Women in State Legislatures*, and *The Impact of Women in Public Office: An Overview*. Her current research focuses on the impact of women representatives in the 103rd Congress.

ANNE COSTAIN is Professor of Political Science and director of the Keller Center for the Study of the First Amendment at the University of Colorado, Boulder. Her primary research interests are gender politics, interest groups, social movements, and civil rights and liberties. She has published *Inviting Women's Rebellion: A Political Process Interpretation of the Women's Movement*, and articles and chapters on topics ranging from interest group politics to the electoral gender gap. She is currently writing a book on the mobilization of the women's movement and the gender gap in voting.

ANN GORDON is a doctoral student in the Department of Political Science at Arizona State University. Her interests include political psychology, the role of the mass media in the American political process, and women and politics.

LEONIE HUDDY is an Associate Professor at the State University of New York at Stony Brook. She has published several articles on gender stereotypes and women candidates. She is an editor of *Research in Micropolitics*, an annual series of volumes concerned with new developments in political psychology. Her current research interests concern the underpinnings of public support for the women's movement.

SHANTO IYENGAR is a Professor of Political Science and Communications Studies at the University of California, Los Angeles. He is the author of *News That Matters: Television and American Opinion* with Donald R. Kinder; *Is Anyone Responsible: How Television Frames National Issues*; *The Media Game: American Politics in the Television Age*; *Explorations in Political Psychology* and *Hitting the Spot: Campaign Advertising and American Politics.*

MARION JUST is Professor of Political Science at Wellesley College. She has held visiting fellowships at Harvard University and Massachusetts Institute of Technology. She is coauthor of *Crosstalk: Citizens, Candidates and the Media in the 1992 Presidential Campaign*; *Common Knowledge: News and the Construction of Political Meaning*; and *Coping in a Troubled Society*, as well as being the author of journal articles and book chapters on political communications and electoral behavior.

KIM FRIDKIN KAHN is an Assistant Professor of Political Science at Arizona State University. She is the author of *The Political Consequences of Being a Woman: How Stereotypes Influence the Conduct and Consequences of Political Campaigns.* She has published a series of articles examining how the media influence the electability of women candidates.

Her current work focuses on how competition affects the dynamics of U.S. Senate elections.

MONTAGUE KERN is Associate Professor of Communications at Rutgers University. She is the author of *Thirty-Second Politics*, and is coauthor of *Crosstalk: Citizens, Candidates and the Media in the 1992 Presidential Campaign*. She was a coinvestigator of the *Democracy '92* study, and a fellow of the Joan Shorenstein Center.

ANDREW KOHUT is Director of the PEW Research Center for The People & The Press in Washington, DC. In 1989 he founded Princeton Survey Research Associates, an attitudinal and opinion research firm specializing in the media, politics, and public policy studies. Kohut was president of the Gallup Organization from 1979 to 1989. He is a frequent press commentator on the meaning and interpretation of opinion poll results. He is coauthor of *The People, The Press and Politics*, and has written numerous polling articles for magazines, journals, and leading newspapers.

EVERETT CARLL LADD is executive director and president of the Roper Center for Public Opinion Research, and director of the Institute for Social Inquiry at the University of Connecticut. His principal research interests are American political thought, public opinion, and political parties. Among the books he has written are *American Political Parties: Ideology in America*; *Transformations of the American Party System*; *Where Have All the Voters Gone?* and *The American Polity*. His current research is on American ideology.

KAY MILLS has been a journalist for thirty years, working for the *Los Angeles Times*, *United Press International*, the *Baltimore Evening Sun*, and the *Newhouse News Service*. Since 1991 she has been a freelance journalist and writer. She is author of *A Place in the News: From the Women's Pages to the Front Page*; *This Little Light of Mine: The Life of Fannie Lou Hamer*; and *From Pocahontas to Power Suits: Everything You Need to Know about Women's History in America*.

PIPPA NORRIS is Associate Director (Research) of the Joan Shorenstein Center on the Press, Politics and Public Policy and teaches at the Kennedy School of Government, Harvard University. She has published *Political Recruitment: Gender, Race and Class in the British Parliament*; *British By-elections: The Volatile Electorate*; *Politics and Sexual Equality*; *Comparative Democracies*; *Women and Politics*; *Different Voices, Different Lives: Women and Politics in the United States and Europe*; *Gender and Party Politics*; and *Electoral Change Since 1945*.

KIMBERLY PARKER is assistant research director at the PEW Research Center for The People & The Press. She is a doctoral candidate in American government at Georgetown University. She has published in the fields of public opinion and media coverage of Congress.

RONNEE SCHREIBER is a graduate research assistant at the Center for the American Woman and Politics, Rutgers University. Her research interests include women's health care, abortion, and welfare; she is currently engaged in a major project analyzing the policy impact of women in the 103rd Congress.

ADAM F. SIMON is a doctoral candidate in Political Science at the University of California, Los Angeles.

NICHOLAS VALENTINO is a doctoral candidate in Political Science at the University of California, Los Angeles.

DAVID H. WEAVER is the Roy W. Howard Research Professor at Indiana University's School of Journalism. He received his Ph.D. in mass communication research from the University of North Carolina in 1974, after working as a newspaper journalist in Indiana and North Carolina. He has taught at Indiana since 1974, mainly in research methods and political communication. His books include *The American Journalist*; *Newsroom Guide to Polls and Surveys*; *Videotex Journalism*; *The Formation of Campaign Agendas*; *Media Agenda-Setting in a Presidential Election*; and *Contemporary Public Opinion*, as well as numerous articles and chapters about journalists, media agenda-setting, voter learning from media, and foreign news coverage.

BETTY HOUCHIN WINFIELD is Professor of Journalism at the University of Missouri. She has published *FDR and the News Media* and *The Edward R. Murrow Heritage: A Challenge for the Future*, as well as articles in *Media Studies Journal*, *Presidential Studies Quarterly*, and *Journalism History*.

WOMEN, MEDIA, AND POLITICS

Introduction
Women, Media, and Politics

Pippa Norris

Gender is one of the primary fault-lines running through contemporary American politics. For the last thirty years feminists have challenged conventional assumptions about the role of women in society. The revived New Right and the women's movement have been struggling to define the terms of the public debate in "culture wars." The political agenda has become deeply polarized by issues such as affirmative action, abortion rights, and welfare reform. The "gender gap" has split women and men more sharply along party lines. Record numbers of women have been running for, and winning, elected office in the 1990s. Recent American elections have been defined, accurately or not, in terms of the "Year of the Woman" and the "Year of the Angry White Male." In short, gender politics, once regarded as marginal, has emerged as one of the core dividing lines defining the identity of politicians, parties, issues, and voters in America.

In this context, not surprisingly, the way the media cover gender politics has become a matter of contention. The issue at the heart of this book is whether, as critics suggest, media coverage of women in America reinforces rather than challenges the dominant culture, and thereby contributes toward women's marginalization in public life. If so, it can be argued, journalism fails to meet its minimum professional standards. At the outset we need to be clear about the appropriate criteria which can be used to judge media performance.

Journalists can be evaluated against a number of benchmarks (for a discussion see chapter 13 by Beasley; also McQuail 1992b; Siebert et al. 1956). The most widely accepted account of journalistic principles, underlying guidelines like the American Society of Newspaper Editors' *Canons of Journalism*, is provided by social responsibility theory. As summarized by McQuail (1992a, 116–18), this holds that the media should accept certain obligations to society. These can be met by setting high professional standards of informativeness, truth, accuracy, objectivity, and balance. The media should be pluralist, reflecting the diversity of society, giving access to various points of view, and avoiding giving offense to minority groups. The question discussed in subsequent chapters is whether journalists meet the criteria set by their own professional bodies when covering women in public life.

The problem with assessing media performance is that some stories involve clear and simple "facts" about which there is little disagreement. The standards of "accuracy" and "truth" are self-evident. But few issues are clear-cut. Nor are these standards used to evaluate a single story, but rather a systematic pattern of coverage in a variety of electronic and print outlets concerning a wide range of subjects, which together constitute political communications. Most news stories involve subtle and complex questions of interpretation and balance, especially on issues where the social construction of reality is under challenge. Basic "facts" require a news narrative, or "frame," to make sense as a coherent story.

Framing Gender Politics

One common way to understand the news process is through the theory of framing, introduced by the sociologist Erving Goffman (1974). Defined fairly narrowly, in social psychology the concept of framing refers to subtle issues of presentation. In surveys, for example, even small changes in the wording of question choices have been found to produce different preferences among respondents (Iyengar 1991). Such effects have been detected in experimental and survey studies across a wide range of subjects. This book adopts a broader understanding, which defines news frames as interpretive structures that set particular events within their broader context. In this sense, news frames give "stories" a conventional "peg" to arrange the narrative, to make sense of the facts, to focus the headline, and to define events as newsworthy. Frames provide contextual cues giving order and meaning to complex problems, actions, and events. Frames guide the selection, presentation, and evaluation of information, for journalists and readers, by slotting the novel into familiar categories (Entman 1991, 1993a; Gitlin 1980, 1994). In Gitlin's words:

> Media frames are persistent patterns of cognition, interpretation, and presentation, of selection, emphasis, and exclusion, by which symbol handlers routinely organize discourse, whether verbal or visual. (Gitlin 1980, 7)

Some simple examples of news framing make the concept clearer. Within election campaigns the familiar "horse race" frame (who is ahead, who is behind) dominates coverage of the primaries (Hallin 1990). There are many alternative topics which could serve as the focus for stories in the primary season: the policies of the candidates, their records in office, their background and experience. Out of all these, the "horse race" is frequently adopted, because it provides all the criteria of newsworthiness: a simple and dramatic headline about "breaking" events focused on personal drama. For other examples of framing, in discussing Vietnam, Americans who refused to serve in the war were commonly referred to as draft "evaders," rather than in their own term, as draft "resisters" (Tuchman 1978b). In covering the student protest movement, activists were widely depicted as scruffy, flag-burning, radical extremists on the streets contrasted with calm, reasonable-sounding authorities in the studio (Gitlin 1980; Small 1994; Entman 1993b). In reports of complex acts of "terrorist" violence the victim-perpetrator frame simplifies the attribution of responsibility (Cohen and Wolfsfeld 1993). The black–white "race riot" frame often shapes coverage of civil disturbances, such as in Los Angeles, even where the conflict involves a complex range of diverse ethnic groups (Smith 1994). The developing world has long criticized the framing of news about countries only in terms of "coups, earthquakes and disasters" (Mowlana 1985). International conflict often used to be explained by a "Cold War" frame identifying friends and enemies, until this broke down following the fall of the Berlin Wall (Norris 1996d).

To clarify framing theory we can briefly compare three examples of the way framing has influenced the gendered interpretation of recent American elections in the media. This is apparent if we consider treatment of the "gender gap" in the early 1980s, the "Year of the Woman" in 1992, and the "Year of the Angry White Male" in 1994.

Framing the Gender Gap

After the 1982 elections there were a slew of articles about the gender gap in the electorate. The story originated from the National Organization of Women (NOW), who developed the phrase as a dramatic and simple way to publicize the women's vote (Bonk 1988). The story first broke with Judy Mann, "Women Are Emerging as Political Force" in the *Washington Post* (16 October 1981), based on a briefing pamphlet developed by NOW. The story was picked up again in a lengthy, front-page article by Adam Clymer in the *New York Times* in June 1982, who throughout focused on the change among women rather than men:

> The political habits of women appear to be undergoing deep changes that worry the Republicans and raise long-range hopes of the Democrats. A variety of newly available statistics show that women, who in the past have voted at a lower rate than men, are now voting at roughly the same level. These statistics also show that women, whose political attitudes used to be barely distinguishable from those of men, are beginning to take positions on issues that sharply differ from those taken by men.

By October, the gender gap had become one of the major stories in the campaign, an issue discussed by campaign managers and pollsters. Throughout the focus remained on how women's voting behavior had shifted, speculation about the possible reasons for this, and reaction by party strategists. The story took off dramatically in the analysis of the midterm results (Borquez, Goldenberg, and Kahn 1988), where the gender gap was treated as one of the most significant developments in the election, indeed the basis for a possible realignment. The extensive coverage of the gender gap in 1983 and 1984 provided leverage which prioritized women's issues, and strongly influenced the choice of Geraldine Ferraro as Vice Presidential candidate in the Democratic party.

Why was the 1982 election framed in terms of the gender gap? Was it because this was the first time there had been a significant difference in the voting preferences of American women and men? No. During the 1950s, Gallup surveys indicate there was a consistent gender gap (see Figure 1), with women leaning toward the Republicans (Stanley and Niemi 1994, 105), but this received minimal coverage in the news. Ladd suggests that if we adopt an even longer-term perspective, gender differences in the early twentieth century on issues such as Prohibition and Progressivism could have been as large as those found on "moral" issues today (see chapter 6). Moreover, as an alternative frame, the story about gender differences in voting during the 1980s could have been framed in terms of a strong Republican shift among men, as shown in Figure 1, yet this was far less common. Stronger Democratic support among women, although one interpretation among differing meanings, rapidly became the conventional frame to cover this story.

Framing the "Year of the Woman" in 1992

In the same way, the 1992 election was widely framed as the "Year of the Woman." Why? Four new women won Senate seats. Twenty-four new

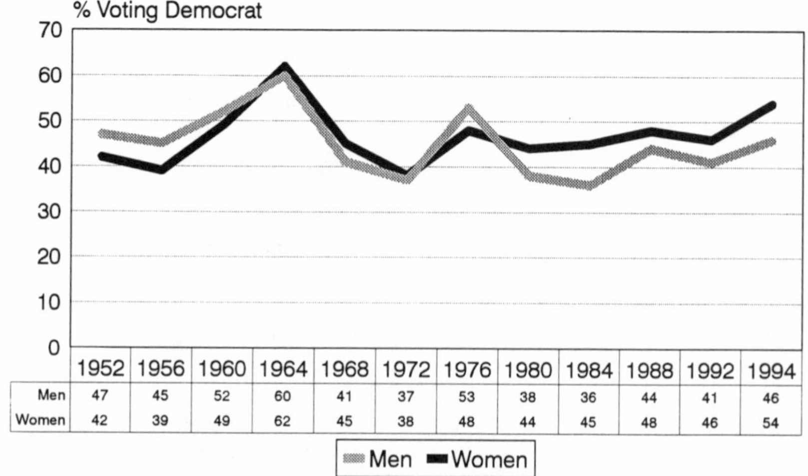

	1952	1956	1960	1964	1968	1972	1976	1980	1984	1988	1992	1994
Men	47	45	52	60	41	37	53	38	36	44	41	46
Women	42	39	49	62	45	38	48	44	45	48	46	54

Figure 1 Gender Gap in Voting, 1952–94. (Gallup Polls)

women were elected to the House, raising the number of women there from twenty-nine to forty-seven. Women continued to increase their numbers in state legislatures. But women remained far from parity. Nearly all women who challenged House or Senate incumbents lost, often by large margins. Moreover, it was not the year for all women: few who won were Republicans. Women's representation in Congress remains low compared with legislatures in many established democracies. If we compare the proportion of women in the House with comparable legislatures, there are twice as many women elected in Canada, Austria, and Germany; three times as many in the Netherlands and Denmark; four times as many in Sweden, Norway, and Finland. The advancement brought America up to the world average, no better. In this context, the election could have been framed equally accurately as the year where women's gains in the United States were much as might be expected from worldwide secular trends. Or the year where America did much worse than many comparable countries. But, no, the frame overwhelmingly emphasized the positive news of "dramatic" gains. Similar trends in the 1992 British general election, where women MPs increased from 6.2 percent to 9.6 percent, were covered by the press in one or two articles at most, and were regarded by women activists as relatively disappointing. Therefore the frame offered one meaning to the outcome, out of many alternatives.

Framing the 1994 "Year of the Angry White Male"

As Ladd discusses later, the 1994 midterm congressional elections were framed as the "Year of the Angry White Male," on grounds which are strongly open to challenge. In a *Lexis/Nexis* search of the major newspapers since 1990, the first use of this phrase came in an article by Richard Morin and Barbara Vobejda on 10 November 1994 in the *Washington Post*. In the next two weeks the phrase "angry white male voter" was rapidly picked up all over the country in the postmortem of the election results, in the *Atlanta Constitution* (November 12th), the *Houston Post* (November 14th), the *Los Angeles Times* (November 15th), the *Boston Herald* (November 15th), *USA Today* (November 18th), and so on. Interviews rapidly located people who had started to describe themselves as "angry white men." Some journalists challenged the framing, but most went along. By the end of November, the following example in *The Plain Dealer* was typical coverage:

> Democratic and Republican leaders, meeting separately to rehash the election, agreed on one conclusion: Angry white men fuelled the GOP landslide and could consign Democrats to long-term minority status.
>
> The Democrats, meeting at Walt Disney World in Florida to figure out what went wrong, talked about winning back independents, increasing their margin among union members and finding some way to become competitive in

> the South. They conceded, with some discomfort, that all of these categories were a manifestation of a problem that has been building for a generation: White men increasingly don't vote Democratic. (Peter A. Brown, *The Plain Dealer* 27 November 1994, 8)

The gender gap story was turned on its head. The *Lexis/Nexis* search revealed no recent references to angry white men voters in the major American papers prior to 10 November 1994. By the end of the year, thirty-two stories had appeared about this, with the number escalating to 208 stories in spring/summer 1995. Therefore in successive elections, first the Democratic edge among women, then the Republican edge among men (angry or not), became the conventional interpretation of gender differences in voting behavior, the dominant frame which could be adopted in a flexible way to cover stories about different regions, candidates, or party strategies. As shown in Figure 1, the basic gender difference between women and men voters had not substantially altered, but the media frame switched with the suddenness of a roller coaster.

The research presented in this book suggests that journalists commonly work with gendered "frames" to simplify, prioritize, and structure the narrative flow of events when covering women and men in public life. That is to say, gender can be one central element relevant to the way the story is presented and interpreted. Frames can be gender-neutral or gender-relevant: about middle-class problems with childcare facilities, or women's problems with childcare facilities; about the difficulties of fundraising for Senate challengers, or the difficulties of fundraising for female Senate challengers; about the problems of crack cocaine for the African American community, or the problems of crack cocaine for African American men. Stories about Janet Reno, for example, can be framed around the role and responsibilities of the Attorney General, such as the Waco decision. Or about initiatives on crime introduced by the Democratic administration, and the consequences for public policy. Or, as when she was first selected, stories can be framed as the appointment of the first woman Attorney General. Frames bundle key concepts, stock phrases, and conventional images to reinforce common ways of presenting developments (Tuchman 1978b; Gitlin 1980). Events are open to multiple interpretations, but some frames become the conventional way to treat developments. The essence of framing is selection to prioritize some facts, events, or developments over others, thereby promoting a particular interpretation (Entman 1993a). Reporters can "tell it like it is" within sixty seconds, rapidly sorting key events from surrounding trivia, by drawing on reservoirs of familiar stories to cue readers. Frames provide "pegs" which make events newsworthy. Whether stories are framed as gender-neutral or gender-relevant is itself part of the battle over cultural politics.

Gender is such a central part of our social identity—like race, age, and nationality—that implicit references to gender are ubiquitous throughout the news. What has changed in recent decades is that the heightened salience of gender politics on the American agenda means that news frames have become increasingly gendered on an explicit basis. That is, gender has come to be seen as a relevant peg for the story line whether covering candidates running for office, voters at the ballot box, international leaders, or policy debates about welfare reform, abortion, and affirmative action. Coverage of the 1992 California Senate race between Barbara Boxer and Bruce Herschensohn, for example, could have been framed in terms of a contest between a far right, flat-tax, conservative Republican and a liberal, anti–Gulf War Democrat. Boxer's record, after all, has been termed "by some measures the most leftist in the House" (*Almanac of American Politics* 1994, 85). Or stories could have framed the election as a contest between a former member of the Board of Supervisors from Marin County, San Francisco's trendy suburb, versus a Los Angeles television and radio commentator, Nixon speechwriter, and Reagan enthusiast. Or the story could be framed, as it commonly was, as a breakthrough for women in the U.S. Senate. This peg provided the story with wide appeal, creating news headlines of interest to readers of the *Chicago Tribune* and the *Miami Herald*, as well as the *Los Angeles Times*. The use of a frame where gender is regarded as relevant to the description of candidates, issues, or leaders may help or hinder women's participation in public life, depending upon the broader context. But the labeling process involved in gendered framing is likely to have significant consequences for cultural politics.

The Origin of News Frames

Where do news frames come from? Following Gans (1979), we can suggest that frames are located within a particular culture and are the product of the complex interaction between sources, media, and audiences.

The political *culture* determines the overall values and norms in society, such as attitudes toward the role of women within the family, the workplace, and public life. Since news is a product of a particular time and place, we can expect coverage of gender politics to reflect broader social attitudes. A report on the election of a woman President or Prime Minister, for example, is reported with certain common themes in different countries, but also with significant cross-cultural differences (see chapter 8).

The political system provides a range of *sources*, notably the communication strategies of politicians, parties, and social movements. As Costain et al. explain in chapter 11, groups within the women's movement try to shape the definition of issues such as affirmative action and sexual harassment, and the interpretation of developments such as the gender gap in voting behavior or the appointment of Ruth Bader Ginsburg to the Supreme Court. As discussed in chapters 3 and 4, women candidates may try to capitalize on "female" issues where they are perceived to be most effective, such as child care and reproductive rights, by prioritizing these issues on the electoral agenda.

Frames are also produced by the way the *media* routinely handle stories. Once frames are established, Tuchman (1978b) suggests they are institutionalized by news organizations, including news "beats" and "pack" journalism. Frames can be reinforced by professional training, journalistic practices, and news cultures which strengthen a common interpretation of events. The background and experience which journalists bring to newsrooms also have the potential to shape the way stories are interpreted. Chapter 1 by David Weaver and chapter 2 by Kay Mills explore whether women journalists frame stories in different ways, by prioritizing different issues, interviewing different sources, and bringing different concerns to the newsroom.

Lastly, gender frames in the media can be influenced by the dominant norms and values of the *audience* in the wider society. In their chapters Iyengar et al., and Kern and Just consider how pervasive sex stereotypes among voters shape perceptions of candidates. If voters hold strong views about the strengths and weaknesses of women and men politicians, candidates may seek to reinforce or neutralize these through their campaign communications, and in turn the media coverage may reflect the candidate's messages.

We need to be careful to clarify the relationship between the concept of "gender framing" and the concept of "sex stereotypes." These are related, since gendered news frames may combine and thereby reinforce a range of sex stereotypes. But "frames" can be understood as the broader narrative within which sex stereotypes may be located. The concept of *stereotyping* means evaluating individuals on the basis of characteristics assumed to be shared by social groups, irrespective of the individual's personal qualities, abilities, or experience. For example, a woman candidate may be perceived by voters as more knowledgeable about childcare policy than a man. Journalists may assume that a feminist is antifamily. A woman Senator may be seen as a less experienced politician, and more honest, than her male colleagues. We might expect a female Prime Minister to be more reluctant to deploy military force than a male leader. Yet these may be wholly erroneous and inaccurate judgments about individuals. A woman candidate for Congress may have more interest in the military and defense expenditure than in childcare policy. Many feminists strongly value family life. Margaret Thatcher, Golda Meir, and Indira Gandhi displayed little hesitation in using force where necessary. And so on.

Sex stereotypes relate to both political issues and the personal characteristics of politicians. In terms of *issues*, as discussed in subsequent chapters by Kahn and Gordon, and Iyengar et al., a well-established body of literature has found that sex stereotypes about women's "compassionate" nature and men's "aggressiveness" has led people to expect women and men to have different areas of competence in public life. Women in elected office are seen as more expert on issues of child care, poverty, education, social policy, and the environment. In contrast men in public office are seen as more competent on issues of foreign policy, defense spending, foreign trade, crime, and some aspects of the economy (Huddy and Terkildsen 1993b; Sapiro 1981; Norris and Lovenduski 1995). In addition, sex stereotypes affect expectations about the *personal characteristics* of women and men leaders, in terms of their competence and integrity (see chapter 3 by Kahn and Gordon). Women in politics are commonly seen as compassionate, practical, honest, and hard-working, while men are seen as ruthless, ambitious, and tough leaders (Norris and Lovenduski 1995).

Stereotypes are widespread because we all have views about groups, whereas we often lack perfect information about individuals. It is a short step to jump to the conclusion that individuals share group characteristics. For example, we commonly fit candidates to issues, assuming that a Democrat favors Medicare, that a representative from Iowa favors farm subsidies, or that a woman supports abortion rights. Sex stereotypes can be expected to prove particularly influential where journalists lack detailed knowledge and direct experience, because they provide an information shortcut. We would also expect more reliance on stereotypes in tabloid news, because these conventions provide a simpler and more familiar story for readers.

As studies within this book suggest, the effects of framing may be positive, negative, or neutral for women, depending upon the broader political context. Stories about a woman running for the Senate, for example, may be framed as a breakthrough for an "outsider," someone who can bring a more honest, caring, and fresh approach to politics as usual (the "Mom in tennis shoes"). This frame may maximize support for women candidates if voters are unhappy with Congress and want to rid themselves of incumbents. Yet conventional frames which reinforce sex stereotypes may also prove an electoral liability, if women are framed as inexperienced outsiders, and if voters feel that they need practiced leaders to deal with serious problems of the federal deficit or international security. This book therefore strongly suggests that the political context influences whether frames act as an obstacle or a resource for women.

Yet in general, since news frames can be expected to reflect broader social norms, political minorities challenging the dominant culture are most likely to prove critical of the way they are portrayed. Journalists and their readers or viewers are likely to regard news frames as "just common sense" where the mass media are addressing a broad audience, and society shares a common cultural consensus. The situation is more complex where local television stations or newspapers are targeting a specific subculture of society, for example, a Hispanic newspaper written for the ex-Cuban community, a militia newsletter distributed among the libertarian right, or even *Ms.* magazine for feminists. Within these subcultures, news frames are also likely to coincide with the norms and values of their audience, although cultural minorities will be more aware of the framing process, since they can listen to both mainstream and specialized media. Major disputes about news frames arise when the mass media aim to reach a wide audience which is deeply divided by cleavages of gender, race, and class, such as America today, where the interpretation and depiction of news are matters of cultural dissonance. The battle over news frames is itself a political process when cultural minorities challenge the creation and portrayal of social reality.

Understood in this way, it becomes clearer why the conventional gender lens in the media has often been criticized by women. During the last thirty years the women's movement has sought to challenge the dominant culture and social norms in America. Periods of major social change—like the transformation in women's and men's lives since the 1960s—highlight awareness of frames. Traditional gender roles, once taken for granted, come to be seen as out of touch with social reality. If journalists are unaware of these developments, projecting images of women which are no longer appropriate, their portrayal of the sexes may no longer be seen as meeting journalistic standards of accuracy, balance, and diversity. The process of social change requires journalists to be sensitive to slow, subtle, grinding shifts in the tectonic plates of society. Despite some social change, newsrooms continue to be disproportionately white, male, and middle class (see chapter 1). Based on their own experience, therefore, journalists may not understand why traditional gender frames are no longer appropriate in a more diverse society.

The criticisms of gender framing most commonly heard in the past relate to issues of the selection, presentation, and evaluation of news coverage. The question is whether these criticisms are valid. In terms of the *selection* of news, are women now increasingly visible as news reporters and correspondents, editorial columnists, and television news anchors? Does the headline news continue to exclude or downplay issues which concern women? In terms of *presentation*, does news coverage continue to depict women most commonly as wives, mothers, and victims, but rarely as policy experts, authorities, and leaders? Does the portrayal of women in office focus on their appearance rather than their achievements, their personalities rather than their policies, their sex rather than their status? Lastly, in terms of *evaluation*, does the overall balance of coverage on television, radio, and in newspapers provide a negative picture of women politicians, feminism, and the women's movement, a more positive portrayal reflecting the liberal leanings of reporters, or more ambiguous and schizophrenic messages? Despite long-standing concern about these issues, and much speculation, little comprehensive and systematic research has examined these questions.

An extensive body of research in communications has explored gender roles in popular culture such as in drama, children's programs, advertising, movies, and music videos (see, for example, Creedon 1993; Dines and Humez 1995; Press 1991; Gunter 1995; Tuchman et al. 1978; Baehr and Dyer 1987; Craig 1992; Brown 1990; Douglas 1994). There are many studies of women's role as journalists, columnists, and media executives (Braden 1993; Beasley and Gibbons 1993; Mills 1990; Eddings 1980; Robertson 1992; Epstein 1978; Sanders and Rock 1988; Schilpp and Murphy 1983).

From the beginning of the second-wave women's movement, feminists have expressed strong criticisms about sex stereotyping in popular culture, the way the news media cover women's roles, and the portrayal of policy issues of concern to organized feminism (Friedan 1963; Faludi 1991; Sommers 1994; Howell 1990). Official reports have repeatedly expressed concern about images of women and men in the media which reinforce cultural barriers and traditional sex roles (U.S. Commission on Civil Rights 1977, 1979; UNESCO 1980, 1989; Council of Europe 1984; United Nations 1995b). Yet surprisingly little work has looked at how the American media frame gender politics, from a systematic perspective, with a multimethod approach. The aim of this book is to rectify this gap to see whether the media frame gender politics "with a different eye," which hinders women's participation in public life.

The following chapters explore how the media frame gender politics, and how far these frames reflect the realities of women's and men's lives today. The chapters examine these issues using a variety of methods—survey data, personal interviews, focus groups, content analysis, and experiments. We start by looking at the role of women and men as journalists, then go on to consider how framing influences the coverage and support for women candidates, the portrayal of women in power, and the reporting of feminism and the women's movement.

Women as Journalists

The first section considers women's participation in the journalistic work force and its impact. One long-standing criticism of the media involves the barriers to entry and promotion which women have faced in newsrooms, as correspondents, reporters, editors, broadcast anchors, commentators, producers, news executives, managers, and publishers. Women's organizations within and outside the media have pressured communications organizations to employ more women, especially in decision-making and management positions. By the 1990s some of the barriers have diminished, as women journalists have increased their presence (Mills 1990; Lont 1995, 9; Beasley and Gibbons 1993, 32; Weaver and Wilhoit 1991). Nevertheless, as in other spheres of employment, the proportion of women diminishes at the higher levels of decision making. Vertical and horizontal occupational segregation continues (Beasley and Gibbons 1993; Marzoff 1977; Lont 1995). Building on this foundation, **David Weaver** compares changes in the background, managerial responsibilities, and perceptions of roles among women and men journalists during the last two decades. Based on major surveys of working journalists in weekly and daily newspapers, radio, television, wire services, and news magazines, Weaver examines gender differences in the newsroom. The chapter considers three issues: has the background and experience of women and men journalists become more similar in recent years; have women made significant gains in terms of their managerial responsibilities and editorial freedom; and do women and men differ in their perceptions of the role, news proprieties, and ethical standards of journalists?

A closely related question is whether the growth of women in the newsrooms has influenced the content of news coverage. Do women journalists have different styles of journalism and news agendas? Do they write and speak in a "different voice"? Or are professional norms and values so pervasive that women journalists and broadcasters are essentially similar to men in their news priorities, style, and tone? **Kay Mills** examines this issue, based on interviews with editors and writers, broadcast and print. The chapter argues strongly that women have made a difference, not in *how* they cover events or people, but in *what* they often choose to cover, especially in terms of issues historically underplayed by the media. In the 1990s, coverage of a wide range of stories—such as problems of child care and sexual harassment, domestic violence, women's political representation, and abortion—are routinely covered as headline news. Women's roles within journalism, acting in conjunction with the women's movement, have helped bring about this radical shift in news values.

Campaign Coverage of Gender Politics

Many feminists have long been critical of the dominant portrayal of political women, arguing that this encourages sex role stereotyping, and thereby perpetuates women's powerlessness. Women are seen as less credible by the media, especially on traditionally sex-typed issues like defense or crime, although at the same time they may be perceived as more credible on "compassion" issues like the family, welfare, and education (Huddy and Terkilsen 1993a, 1993b). We might expect gender stereotypes to be particularly pronounced in the political arena, given the minority status of women officeholders. We might also expect that media coverage during campaigns has important consequences for evaluations of the electoral viability of women and men candidates, and for how these candidates present themselves in elections (Kahn 1991b, 1993, 1994a, 1994b).

The third chapter, by **Kim Fridkin Kahn** and **Ann Gordon**, examines how women and men candidates chose to present themselves in campaigns for the U.S. Senate. Based on a telephone survey of campaign managers for major party candidates, the authors analyze the strategies of men and women candidates in the 1988, 1990, and 1992 campaigns. The chapter investigates whether men and women emphasize similar or different campaign issues than their opponents; whether men and women differ in their assessments of the news media's treatment of their campaigns; and finally, whether men and women differ in their attitudes toward various campaign techniques such as political advertisements and personal contacts. This analysis, building on previous research, illuminates the types of campaigns men and women choose to run. The chapter concludes that in elections to the U.S. Senate, women and men present alternative agendas to voters, but they deliver these distinct messages in a remarkably similar fashion.

In the next chapter, **Shanto Iyengar** et al. consider the effects of campaign coverage on the electoral prospects of women and men candidates. This work builds on innovative experimental studies which have demonstrated the impact of television news and political advertising on agenda setting and framing (Iyengar and Kinder 1987; Iyengar 1991; Ansolabehere et al. 1993). This chapter demonstrates that media attention to "women's" issues (such as sexual harassment or abortion) strengthens women candidates. The research shows that women maximize their electoral support when they advertise on issues over which they can claim "ownership." Playing to, rather than against, sex stereotypes is the most effective strategy for candidates.

Montague Kern and **Marion Just** go on to use focus groups based on the 1990 North Carolina Helms/Gantt Senate race to simulate the campaign, showing voters news and advertising, and monitoring the response. The study examines whether men and women construct different images of politicians, whether they react differently to negative advertising, and whether, in particular, women and men bring different experiences to the political discourse about the campaign.

Lastly, in chapter 6 **Everett Carll Ladd** looks at media coverage of the gender gap. Ever since the territory of Wyoming became the first place to provide for suffrage for women as well as men, vying for the women's vote has been an important part of regular, democratic politics. Today in the United States women are more than half the electorate. Any group this large is likely to be highly diverse and to resist easy characterization. There are interesting and important elements of sociopolitical outlook that distinguish women and men. These elements probably loom larger today than they did in U.S. politics from 1924 through the 1960s. The gender gap has grown in the modern era, and it may still be growing. This said, the gender gap is limited and subtle.

The sledgehammer characterizations which have predominated in the media typically distort more than clarify. Party leaders acting on these assumptions may go astray in ways harmful to their cause and, what is troubling, to the country. In 1994 there were presumably some white males who were angry, but this characterization, like many of its predecessors, almost entirely lacked empirical foundation. The myth, created by the *New York Times* interpretation of the 1994 exit poll data, became so ubiquitous it came to be repeated by President Clinton when justifying review of affirmative action policies.

The way the media frame election results can have important consequences. The media hyped the gains for women in 1992, but 1994 was framed as a backlash by white males. The interpretation of the electoral mandate may influence changes in policies from welfare reform to affirmative action. Therefore this chapter considers how journalists interpret election results in terms of gender, and why the press exaggerates these differences to make them appear "brighter and sharper" than they actually are in reality.

Changing Images of Women in Power

How do the media portray women leaders once they are elected? Previous research on news programs has commonly found a consistent pattern of exclusion and stereotyping in terms of both sources and subjects (Lont 1995; Gunter 1995; Craig 1992). There is some evidence that the dominant frame has shifted over time, but this remains a matter of controversy. Research for the *U.S. Commission on Civil Rights* (1977) found the following tendencies:

- Newsmakers in evening news programs comprised 78 percent white men, 10 percent white women, 8 percent nonwhite men, and 3.5 percent nonwhite women.
- Women newsmakers were commonly portrayed in a narrow spectrum of roles, usually either as helpless victims or supportive wives and mothers, and rarely as public officials, corporate executives, or expert commentators.
- Few news stories (1.3 percent) dealt with "women's issues."

The question is whether this pattern continues two decades later, despite changes in women's lives, or whether women are now recognized as playing a more significant role as political leaders. To examine these issues, in this section **Susan Carroll** and **Ronnee Schreiber** consider how the media frame women in Congress. The amount of media attention devoted to women candidates for Congress in the 1992 elections was unprecedented. The women who were elected to Congress in the so-called Year of the Woman were frequently portrayed by the media as agents of change. This chapter examines the media coverage which women representatives received after they entered the 103rd Congress to see whether these women continued to receive unprecedented levels of attention and whether they continued to be portrayed as agents of change.

The study focuses in particular on the coverage women members of Congress received on two major areas of legislation—women's health and crime. These issues were chosen because health represents a policy area in which women are usually assumed to be engaged and competent, while crime represents a policy area where women are commonly viewed as having little expertise or authority. The study compares what women in Congress actually did in these two policy areas with the coverage they received. Lastly, the chapter also examines coverage to ascertain how far gender stereotypes are evident in media coverage.

This research draws upon two data sources. *Lexis/Nexis* is used to analyze press coverage. The actual involvement and actions of women members of Congress on women's health and crime legislation are assessed through in-depth interviews, congressional hearings, and other documents collected as part of a major project on the impact of women in the 103rd Congress conducted by the Center for the American Woman and Politics.

The study concludes that the "Year of the Woman" meant that women elected to Congress for the first time in 1992 clearly received more media attention than one would normally expect for first-term members. Most of the coverage was positive, portraying women in Congress as agents of change who were making a difference on issues of women's health, abortion, and sexual harassment. Yet the coverage was also partial, there was little reporting that women were important players on other legislation, such as their role in foreign affairs, international trade, or regulatory reform. In short, the coverage was largely gender-framed.

Pippa Norris compares the way the media have treated women as world leaders. The chapter focuses on three questions: do female leaders receive less coverage than their male counterparts; are women leaders described in sex stereotyped ways, in terms of issues and personal characteristics; and is there a gendered frame common in coverage of women in public life? Certain commentators like Jeane Kirkpatrick (1995) have suggested that women leaders experience a process of dequalification when acting in what is perceived as a man's world of diplomacy, foreign affairs, and international security. This process consists of undermining or underestimating a leader's capabilities and experiences by focusing on gender-based evaluations of her dress and demeanor rather than the substance of her decisions and actions. Yet others suggest that coverage of women leaders depends, in large part, on their personality, character, and style; it can be argued that few stories portrayed Prime Ministers Golda Meir, Indira Gandhi, or Margaret Thatcher in stereotypical feminine ways.

Worldwide there have been twenty-three women elected as Presidents or Prime Ministers. The chapter uses selected international news sources to analyze coverage of twenty world leaders. Ten women were chosen as powerful Prime Ministers or Presidents with a significant impact on world politics, although with strikingly different personalities and styles of leadership, and drawn from divergent political systems and national cultures. The study uses a matched pair design to compare these women leaders with their immediate successors or predecessors in office.

The study concludes that male Presidents and Prime Ministers received slightly more coverage than their female counterparts, although the difference was not great. There was little evidence that women leaders were reported in sex stereotyped ways in terms of personal qualities or issue coverage. Nevertheless, a gendered news frame prevailed in many stories which stressed certain common themes: the breakthrough for women into positions of leadership, women leaders as outsiders, and women leaders as agents of change. So long as women remain a distinct minority in positions of political leadership, these themes are likely to continue to resonate as newsworthy for reporters and readers.

Turning to American first ladies, **Betty Houchin Winfield** focuses on how press coverage has evolved from Martha Washington to Hillary Rodham Clinton. Framing conventions in newspaper reporting of first ladies can be classified into four main categories. The earliest frame depicts the first lady mainly as the "escort" of the President: the wife is mentioned by virtue of accompanying her spouse. The next most frequent theme describes first ladies in their "protocol" role: the leader of fashionable society at ceremonial and social functions. In the early twentieth century the press came to place increasing emphasis upon the first ladies "noblesse oblige" role: charitable works compatible with women's voluntary work in the community. Lastly, the press has also covered the first ladies more controversial "policy" role: influencing the development of political issues. The chapter goes on to consider how the news framing of first ladies has changed, focusing on Martha Washington, Abigail Adams, Dolley Madison, and first lady-to-be Rachel Jackson in the earliest period, then turning to the preinaugural coverage of Eleanor Roosevelt, Jacqueline Kennedy, and Hillary Rodham Clinton in the twentieth century. The question is whether the media continue to expect first ladies to fulfill the escort, protocol, and noblesse oblige roles, but whether coverage is more critical if first ladies also try to adopt the policy role. The chapter concludes that media coverage denotes the boundaries of acceptable behavior for first ladies, and the roles expected for women in public life.

Coverage of the Women's Movement and Policy Issues

The debate about how the mass media framed the women's movement has been revived in the 1990s (Howell 1990; Creedon 1993a). Susan Faludi (1991) has argued that journalism popularized the backlash against feminism, depicting the problems women experienced as the fault of the women's movement. To examine these issues, **Leonie Huddy** looks at the ways newspapers have framed the terms "feminist" and "feminism" over the last thirty years. The chapter considers three core questions: what is the image journalists have conveyed of feminists since the inception of the modern women's movement; how accurately have they portrayed the diversity within feminism and the varied goals of the women's movement; and to what extent has this portrayal kept pace with changes in the women's movement over time?

The chapter concludes that the press has defined "feminist" and "feminism" fairly narrowly, rather than portraying the great diversity of people, organizations, and issues inherent within the women's movement. In particular, the terms are reserved for a small group of media spokespersons, such as Betty Friedan, and organizations such as NOW. In addition, the feminist agenda is associated in the press most strongly with women's concerns about changing domestic roles and the issue of reproductive rights, rather than issues about the expansion of women's roles in the labor force. This suggests a narrow framing of the women's movement by the press, which may have limited its appeal. The use of the term "feminist" in the media meant that the supporters were largely portrayed as an educated or professional elite that excludes ordinary working women, housewives, and mothers.

In a closely related chapter, **Anne Costain, Richard Braunstein,** and **Heidi Berggren** go on to consider further issues of media framing of the women's movement. Because of the longevity of the contemporary American women's movement, its public face has undergone a number of transformations, from civil rights–based protest movement in the sixties and early seventies, to mobilized pressure group in the late seventies and early eighties, to electoral bloc in the eighties and nineties. This chapter examines long-term trends in media coverage of the women's movement, as well as detailed analysis of how the language describing the women's movement has altered over time, both responding to, and stimulating, changes in the movement.

Like all social movements, the women's movement is highly dependent on media coverage to attract new recruits and to spread its views. The women's movement seems to have received coverage in the early years by fitting into a civil rights frame. This frame grew out of media reporting on the black struggle for civil rights, which was itself in decline by the late 1960s. Reporters were discovering new movements which shared much of the rhetoric and inspiration of the civil rights movement. The women's movement fitted comfortably into this type of coverage with its focus on an Equal Rights Amendment to the U.S. Constitution. When first lady Betty Ford took women's rights as her theme and President Jimmy Carter's election in 1976 moved these issues from "first lady" politics to presidential politics, women appeared to be a national constituency worthy of wooing. The press, in this period, featured women as power brokers within the Capital working for "their" bills. More recently, the women's movement is seen either as producing the consciousness behind the gender gap in voting or, alternatively, as spurring the "backlash" vote which led white male voters to cast ballots for Republican congressional candidates in the 1994 midterm elections.

This chapter emphasizes the transitions in media coverage. To what extent did changes in the politics of the movement precede or follow media coverage? Do the images of the women's movement alter during this time period? How does the descriptive language vary? Is there a movement from a civil rights frame, to one of pressure politics, to a focus on electoral politics and the "horse race"? Has the language and perspective of the women's movement influenced press coverage, or does it seem that the different stages of the movement have simply been incorporated into the standard analysis of that type of political activity? Because of the tight linkage between movements and the media, this chapter explores how each influenced the other.

In the next chapter **Andrew Kohut and Kimberly Parker** look at the role of talk radio, which has mounted a serious attack on the women's movement in recent years. Who participates in talk radio? Who listens? How much coverage is given to "women's" issues? And how balanced is this coverage? The chapter combines *Times Mirror* survey data analyzing the listenership of talk radio with a content analysis of two shows, by Rush Limbaugh and Susan Bray, to explain why talk radio has become such a male-dominated medium. The chapter concludes that the gender gap in talk radio is a function not of the medium but rather of the format, content and tone. Women are not drawn to American talk radio such as the *Rush Limbaugh Show* because they tend to be less conservative in their values, less hostile toward government, and less interested in discussing Washington politics.

Lastly, **Maurine Beasley** considers how media coverage of women could be improved, and she suggests guidelines for good practice. She argues that present news values are outmoded. The rhetoric of newswriting frames issues in terms of conflict and controversy, winning and losing, power and domination—language that often does not reflect the reality of women's experience. Codes of professional practice have started to recognize the need to avoid sex stereotyping in journalism, but further steps could be taken to improve good practice. The conclusion will outline guidelines for journalists, the media industry, and women in public life.

Part I

WOMEN AS JOURNALISTS

1

Women as Journalists

David Weaver

Journalism, like many other professions in the United States, has been dominated by men for much of this century. But during the past few decades, women have entered the U.S. work force in dramatic numbers (Fuchs 1988). In 1960 there were about twenty-three million working women who made up about one-third of the nation's work force. By the mid-eighties, there were nearly fifty million women—about 45 percent of all workers—holding jobs in the United States (Berger 1986; Lafky 1991). And by 1991 the U.S. Bureau of Labor Statistics estimated nearly fifty-seven million women working in the country, 45.4 percent of the civilian work force (Almanac 1993:55).

In recent decades the proportion of women journalists also rose significantly—from about one-fifth of the profession in 1971 (Johnstone et al. 1976) to just over one-third in 1992 (Weaver and Wilhoit 1996). What difference has this trend made? During the last twenty years, have women and men journalists become increasingly similar, or do they continue to differ, in their social background, experience, and careers? Have women made significant gains in terms of their managerial responsibilities and editorial autonomy? And do women and men differ in their perceptions of the role, news priorities, and ethical standards of journalists?

Many previous studies of women as reporters, columnists, and media executives have considered these issues (see Beasley and Gibbons 1993; Braden 1993; Creedon 1993a; Eddings 1980; Epstein 1978; Mills 1990; Robertson 1992; Sanders and Rock 1988; Schilpp and Murphy 1983). But these studies are not based on large, nationally representative samples of journalists working for the mainstream print and broadcast news media in the United States. This chapter aims to consider these questions based on findings from the three most comprehensive large-scale surveys of U.S. journalists, conducted in 1971, 1982–83, and 1992.

Data and Methods

The results reported here come from major national telephone surveys of U.S. journalists carried out in 1971 (Johnstone et al. 1976), 1982–83 (Weaver and Wilhoit 1986), and in 1992 (Weaver and Wilhoit 1992).[1] The findings for 1992 come from forty-five-minute telephone interviews with 1,156 U.S. journalists working for a wide variety of daily and weekly newspapers, radio and television stations, and news services and news magazines throughout the United States. Journalists in the main probability sample were chosen randomly from news organizations that were also selected at random from listings in various directories.[2]

Population. As in the earlier studies, the population of our main sample may be defined as all full-time editorial or news people responsible for the information content of English-language mainstream general interest news media in the United States. In other words, we are concerned in this study only with journalists who work for news media targeted at general audiences rather than special-interest or ethnic groups. These mainstream news media include daily and weekly newspapers, news magazines, radio and television stations, and general news or wire services (such as the Associated Press) based in the United States. They do not include literally thousands of magazines specifically aimed at women (for which many women work) that are not classified as news magazines. The sample means the numbers of women journalists reported here are likely to be considerably lower than if all magazine journalists were included.

Definition of a Journalist. Following earlier studies, we defined journalists as those who have responsibility for the preparation or transmission of news stories or other information—all full-time reporters, writers, correspondents, columnists, photojournalists, news people, and editors.[3] In broadcast organizations, only those in news and public affairs departments were included.[4]

The Social Background and Experience of Journalists

Women in the Journalistic Work Force. Trends in Table 1.1 show that the proportion of women rose from 20 percent of journalists in 1971 to 34 percent in 1982–83, but after this period the figures stabilized, so women remained about a third of all journalists in 1992. More women have entered the profession: 45 percent of all full-time journalists hired in the four years before our 1992 study were women. Nevertheless negligible growth in full-time journalism jobs during the 1980s, and a pattern of interrupted careers, has hindered any further rise in the overall proportion of women journalists.

Table 1.1
The Proportion of Women Journalists, 1971–92 (Percentage)

	Journalists			*U.S. Civilian Labor Force*		
Gender	*1971*[a]	*1982–83*[b]	*1992*	*1971*[c]	*1981*[d]	*1989*[e]
Male	79.7	66.2	66.0	66.4	57.5	54.8
Female	20.3	33.8	34.0	33.6	42.5	45.2

Sources:
[a]From Johnstone, Slawski, and Bowman, *The News People*, p. 197.
[b]From Weaver and Wilhoit, *The American Journalist*, p. 19.
[c]U.S. Department of Labor, 1971, table A-2, p. 28.
[d]U.S. Bureau of the Census, *Statistical Abstract of the United States, 1982–1983*, 103d edition, p. 379.
[e]U.S. Bureau of the Census, *Statistical Abstract of the United States, 1991*, 111th edition, p. 392.

In the U.S. labor force women represent 46 percent of all managerial and professional positions (*Statistical Abstract of the United States* 1992, 392). Nevertheless women are better represented in journalism than in some other professional occupations. In the early 1990s women were only about 27 percent of U.S. college faculty, 22 percent of attorneys, 9 percent of dentists, and 18 percent of physicians (Russell et al. 1991, 133; Nasar 1992, 10).

News Medium. The proportion of women journalists varies considerably by news medium, as Table 1.2 indicates—from about one-fourth in the wire services and television to nearly one-half in weekly newspapers and news magazines. But overall, there is not as much variation as there was in 1971, when only 5 percent of radio journalists were women, compared with nearly a third of those working for news magazines. The biggest increases of women during the 1980s were in news magazines

Table 1.2
Women Journalists in Types of U.S. News Media, 1971–92 (Percentage)

News Medium	*1971*[a]	*1982–83*[b]	*1992*
Radio	4.8	26.3	29.0
Television	10.7	33.1	24.8
Wire services	13.0	19.1	25.9
Daily newspapers	22.4	34.4	33.9
Weekly newspapers	27.1	42.1	44.1
News magazines	30.4	31.7	45.9

Sources:
[a]From Johnstone, Slawski, and Bowman, *The News People*, p. 198.
[b]From Weaver and Wilhoit, *The American Journalist*, p. 21.

and, to a lesser extent, in the wire services. Despite the appearance of more female TV news announcers during the 1980s, women actually lost ground as a percentage of all journalists working in television newsrooms and held steady in daily and weekly newspapers.

Race. Ethnic minorities constitute 18.6 percent of the total U.S. labor force (*Statistical Abstract of the United States* 1992). The increased emphasis on hiring ethnic and racial minorities has doubled their overall percentage in journalism—from about 4 percent of all journalists in 1982–83 to just over 8 percent in 1992. If only those journalists hired during the decade from 1982 to 1992 are considered, the percentage of minorities is notably higher (about 12 percent).

Women comprise a third of all journalists, but 52.5 percent of all Asian journalists, 53.2 percent of blacks, 48.1 percent of Hispanics, and 42.9 percent of Native Americans. Some have suggested this is because media managers are interested in getting credit for hiring both a racial minority and a woman in the same person. But minority women—especially African Americans—are more likely to finish college than are men, and more likely to major in journalism (Collison 1987; Giddings 1984, 325–35), both increasingly necessary conditions for being hired as a full-time journalist in the United States (Weaver and Wilhoit 1986, 1992). Women of color in the United States historically have been more likely than white women to be paid workers (Goldin 1990, 27). Unlike women in general, who were most well represented in weekly newspapers and news magazines in 1992, minority journalists were most likely to work for radio and television stations.

Family Life. The gender of U.S. journalists continues to be related to their marital status and family situation. Women journalists in 1992 were less likely to be married (48 percent) than men journalists (65 percent), and much less likely to have children living with them (28 percent) than men (44 percent). It should be noted, however, that the proportion of married women in journalism increased from 43 percent in 1982–83 to 48 percent in 1992. The percentage of married men also increased slightly. This suggests that more journalists are managing to balance personal and professional lives. The difficulty of combining career and family is greater for women than for men, although there are some signs that this is slowly changing.

Education. In 1971 women journalists were less likely than men to be college graduates, as Table 1.3 shows. By 1992, there was no significant gender gap in education, and women journalists were as well qualified as men. There has been steady growth in the proportion of women in U.S. college and university journalism programs, where women outnumbered men for the first time in 1977 (Beasley and Theus 1988).

Table 1.3
Education of U.S. Journalists, 1971–92 (Percentage in each category)

Highest Educational Attainment	*1971[a]*		*1982–83[b]*		*1992*	
	Men	*Women*	*Men*	*Women*	*Men*	*Women*
Some high school	2.0	1.3	0.6	—	—	0.3
High school graduate	10.6	18.4	6.2	10.1	3.6	5.4
Some college	27.4	29.5	19.1	16.3	15.0	11.0
College graduate	41.4	32.6	53.6	57.3	63.4	66.5
Some graduate training	10.2	11.6	8.3	9.2	6.3	5.9
Graduate degree	8.4	6.6	12.1	7.1	11.7	11.0

Sources:
[a]From Bowman, *Distaff Journalists*, p. 132.
[b]From Weaver and Wilhoit, *The American Journalist*, p. 166.

Age. The largest increase in women journalists during the 1980s was in the youngest age category (under 25), and the only decline was in the 45–54 age bracket. A cohort analysis suggests a pattern of interrupted female careers: middle-aged women were most likely to leave journalism during the decade from the early 1980s to the early 1990s, perhaps for family or professional reasons, or both (Table 1.4). The proportion of women in the youngest category slightly exceeds that for the total U.S. labor force in 1989, the first time this has happened. The increase in

Table 1.4
Women Journalists in U.S. Media and U.S. Labor Force by Age Group (Percentage of women)

	Journalists			*Total Labor Force*		
Age Group	*1971[a]*	*1982–83[b]*	*1992*	*1970[c]*	*1981[d]*	*1989[e]*
Under 25	25.5	42.0	48.9	40.9	46.5	47.6
25–34	17.9	35.1	37.9	32.3	42.5	44.5
35–44	15.5	28.6	30.6	35.6	42.6	45.7
45–54	22.5	33.0	30.6	38.4	41.8	45.2
55–64	25.5	24.7	27.6	36.8	40.1	42.9
65 and older	9.1	31.2	35.3	32.8	38.7	41.5

Sources:
[a]From Johnstone, Slawski, and Bowman, *The News People*, p. 198.
[b]From Weaver and Wilhoit, *The American Journalist*, p. 22.
[c]U.S. Department of Labor, 1971, Table 328, p. 211.
[d]U.S. Bureau of the Census, *Statistical Abstract of the United States, 1982–1983*, 103d edition, p. 379.
[e]U.S. Bureau of the Census, *Statistical Abstract of the United States, 1991*, 111th edition, p. 392.

women in late middle age signals a return to journalism after a career change or interruption.

Work Experience and Career Patterns. When the proportion of women in U.S. journalism is analyzed by years of experience, Figure 1.1 indicates that this proportion steadily declines with number of years in journalism, suggesting that fewer women were hired in earlier times or that women do not stay in journalism as long as men, or both. The average number of years of journalism experience was fifteen for men and twelve for women. Men are considerably more likely than women (40 percent vs. 27 percent) to have more than fifteen years experience in journalism, lending some support to the idea that women in general have not stayed in journalism as long as men. This does not seem to be a matter of age alone, because Table 1.4 shows a higher percentage of women in the oldest (65 and up) category, whereas Figure 1.1 shows a steady decline in the proportion of women by years of experience. This suggests that some older women work in journalism after other careers, or return to journalism after interrupting careers.

Income. In our 1982–83 study we found that the salary gap between men and women had decreased somewhat since 1970 (Weaver and Wilhoit 1986, 83). From 1981 to 1991, that gap decreased even more than in the previous decade. Overall median salaries for women in 1991 were

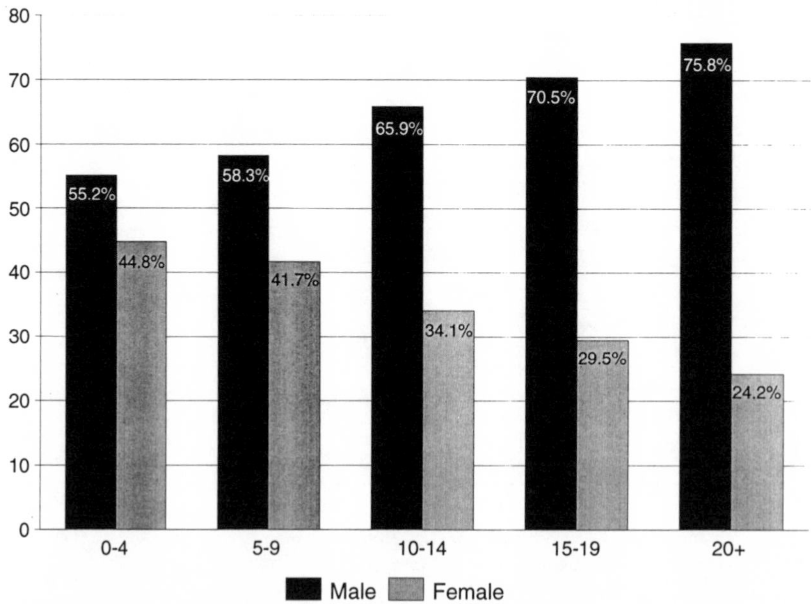

Figure 1–1 Experience of Journalists by Gender.

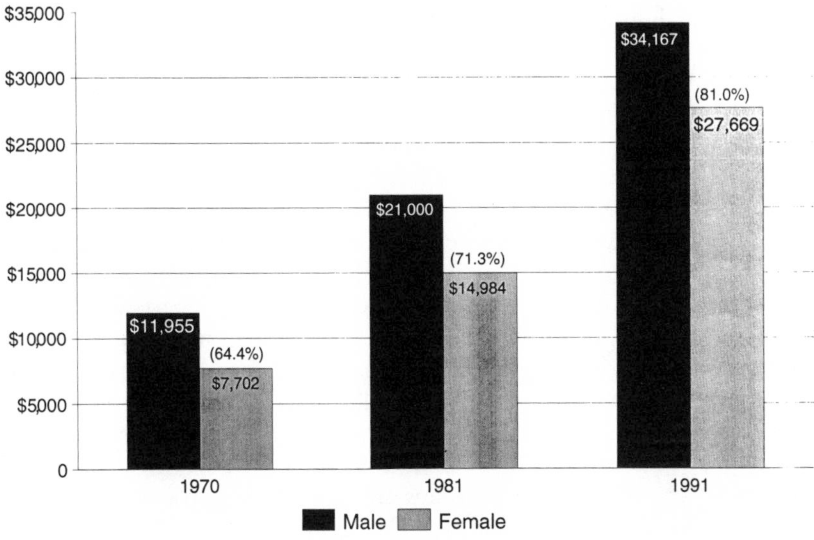

Figure 1–2 Income of Journalists by Gender.

81 percent of those for men, compared to 64 percent in 1970, as Figure 1.2 indicates. When years of experience in journalism is considered, the gender gap in income nearly disappears. Women with four years or less experience tend to work for slightly smaller news organizations than do men, helping to explain the small salary gap of nearly $1,800 between the most recently hired men and women journalists.

When a variety of predictors of income are controlled statistically (such as professional age, type of medium, size of news organization, managerial responsibilities, race, ownership of news organization, presence of a journalists' union, region of country, and education level), in a multiple regression analysis gender predicts less than 1 percent of the variation in pay. There is no income gap by race of journalist, except for Native Americans, who make substantially less than others primarily because they work for very small news operations. The strongest predictors of U.S. journalists' income are number of years experience, size of news organization, type of news organization (with news magazines and wire services at the top, and weekly newspapers and radio at the bottom), and holding a managerial position.

Managerial Responsibilities and Editorial Autonomy

Managerial Responsibilities. As more women have entered the profession, have they increased their influence on the news? In recent decades the surveys found that women journalists have gained managerial responsibility, which makes it more likely that they are in positions to influence news coverage. In 1992, 41 percent said they supervised news or editorial employees, compared to 43 percent of men. In addition, 18 percent of women journalists were owners, publishers, or upper-level managers (city editor or news director and higher) compared with 22 percent of male journalists. And 32 percent of women journalists were lower-level managers (desk editors, assignment editors, or assistant editors) compared with 30 percent of men. Despite greater parity in status, women newsroom managers were less likely than their male counterparts in 1992 to think they had a great deal of influence on hiring and firing new employees, especially in radio and television. Table 1.5 shows that there have been notable increases in women perceiving great influence on hiring since 1982, but only in the print media are women managers nearly as likely as men to perceive this influence in 1992. These figures clearly suggest that radio and television newsrooms are more likely to be controlled by men than by women, but this difference is not so clear in the print media of daily and weekly newspapers and news magazines.

The results indicate that as women become more numerous in various news media, they also gain more authority as managers. This is likely to be true especially in weekly newspapers and news magazines, where women are approaching parity with men in numbers. In these news media, especially, women seem to be in positions to influence news coverage.

Editorial Autonomy. Women journalists equaled and even surpassed men in the amount of editorial control they thought they had, in both print and broadcast news media, in the early 1990s. Table 1.6 shows that women journalists in broadcast media in 1992 were more likely than men to say that they could almost always select the stories they worked on, whereas in 1982–83 men in radio and television newsrooms were significantly more likely to claim this. Table 1.7 indicates that women journalists were notably more likely to do a great deal of editing in 1992 than a decade earlier, especially in the broadcast news media. When comparing men with women, it is clear that women were more likely to claim almost complete freedom in deciding story use in 1992.

Perceptions of the Roles, Priorities, and Standards of Journalism

Job Dimensions. How do journalists see their role? Men and women have been equally likely to rate freedom as very important during the past two decades. Women consistently have been more likely than men to prioritize helping people, with 68 percent women and 57 percent men saying this was very important in 1992.

Table 1.5
Newsroom Managers' Influence on Hiring by Gender (Percentage in each category)

	1982–83				1992			
	Print		Broadcast		Print		Broadcast	
Influence	*Men* (n = 242)	*Women* (n = 111)	*Men* (n = 96)	*Women* (n = 19)	*Men* (n = 253)	*Women* (n = 128)	*Men* (n = 74)	*Women* (n = 33)
A great deal	47.1	27.0	37.5	10.5	39.9	35.2	40.5	21.2
Some	17.8	20.7	25.0	10.5	20.9	22.7	20.3	27.3
A little	12.8	16.2	12.5	26.3	18.2	16.4	25.7	27.3
None at all	22.3	36.0	25.0	52.6	20.9	25.8	13.5	24.2

Table 1.6
Editorial Autonomy by Gender (Percentage in each category)

Frequency of Being Able to Select Story Worked on	*1982–83*				*1992*			
	Print		*Broadcast*		*Print*		*Broadcast*	
	Men (*n* = 370)	*Women* (*n* = 225)	*Men* (*n* = 132)	*Women* (*n* = 67)	*Men* (*n* = 583)	*Women* (*n* = 328)	*Men* (*n* = 172)	*Women* (*n* = 63)
Almost always	60.3	60.0	67.4	44.8	47.5	46.0	44.8	54.0
More often than not	27.3	26.2	23.5	28.4	37.7	36.6	43.0	39.7
Only occasionally	11.4	12.4	8.3	22.4	14.1	16.8	11.6	6.3
Don't make proposals	1.1	1.3	0.8	4.5	0.7	0.6	0.6	0.0

Table 1.7
Editing by Newsroom Managers by Gender (Percentage in each category)

	1982–83				*1992*			
	Print		*Broadcast*		*Print*		*Broadcast*	
Amount of Editing	*Men* (*n* = 489)	*Women* (*n* = 264)	*Men* (*n* = 168)	*Women* (*n* = 71)	*Men* (*n* = 585)	*Women* (*n* = 329)	*Men* (*n* = 173)	*Women* (*n* = 63)
A great deal	35.8	33.0	23.2	19.8	39.1	42.6	20.8	34.9
Some	36.0	34.4	51.2	56.3	37.1	29.5	60.1	41.3
None at all	28.2	32.6	25.6	23.9	23.8	28.0	19.1	23.8

Pay and fringe benefits are also becoming more important aspects of work for women, with increasing numbers rating them as very important over time, whereas for men the figures do not change much. But compared to other aspects of journalistic work—such as editorial policies, the chance to help other people, job security, and autonomy—pay and fringe benefits are lower on the list of priorities for both men (22 percent and 33 percent in 1992) and women (20 percent and 38 percent in 1992). Whereas men were more concerned than women about chances for advancing in 1971, there was no significant difference between men and women on this dimension of work in 1992.

Job Satisfaction. In 1971, even though women journalists in the United States received less pay and were less numerous and influential, they were more likely than men to say that they were very satisfied with their work (Bowman 1974). By 1982–83 this was no longer true—women did not express any less satisfaction than men, and both groups were equally likely to want to stay in journalism—with 84 percent of women and 82 percent of the men saying they would like to be working for a news organization in the next five years (Lafky 1991, 176). In 1992 there were again no significant differences in overall job satisfaction of men and women, with 27 percent of each group claiming to be very satisfied. Women were slightly less likely than men (75 percent vs. 79 percent) to say they would like to be working in the news media in five years. But overall, there was a significant drop in the percentage of U.S. journalists saying they were very satisfied—from 49 percent in 1971 to 40 percent

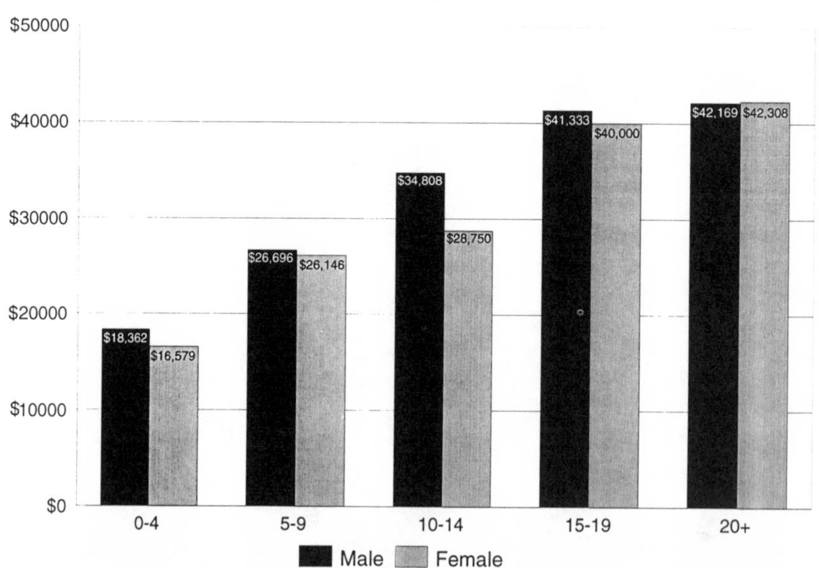

Figure 1–3 Income of Journalists by Gender and Experience.

in 1982–83 to 27 percent in 1992, and a significant increase in the percentage saying they would like to work outside the news media in five years—from 7 percent in 1971 to 11 percent in 1982–83 to 22 percent in 1992 (Weaver and Wilhoit 1986, 96).

Some have dismissed these trends as being generally true in the U.S. work force, but a comparison shows that the proportion claiming to be very satisfied in other occupations is considerably higher—44 percent in a national survey of 1,517 adult workers by the National Opinion Research Center in 1991 and 43 percent in a national survey of 1,008 American office workers in 1991 by Louis Harris (NORC 1991; Harris 1991). These figures do not vary much during the 1980s. This suggests that there is a special problem with declining job satisfaction in American journalism that is not common to other occupations, but it does not seem to be related to gender. A more in-depth look at this decline identifies three major problems: management policies, low salaries, and inadequate opportunity for advancement (Wilhoit and Weaver 1994, 32).

News priorities. In 1982–83 women and men journalists responded in mostly similar patterns in rating various news media stories. Men were less likely than women to consider it extremely important to avoid stories with unverified content, and women were a little more likely than men to rate providing entertainment and relaxation as extremely important. (See Table 1.8.) But women were just as likely as men to think it was extremely important to investigate government claims and to get information to the public quickly, and were equally unlikely to rate being an adversary of government or business as extremely important. These perceptions did not change much a decade later. The ratings of general media priorities by men and women journalists were quite similar, except that women were considerably less likely to consider providing entertainment and relaxation as extremely important (as compared with a decade earlier, and to a lesser extent with men) and somewhat more likely to value getting information to the public quickly.

Overall, there was little change in men's and women's news media priorities—and very little difference in how these roles were rated by gender—suggesting that women and men journalists have similar and stable views of the general role priorities of the news media. These findings also suggest that women journalists are not any more likely than men to shy away from the tougher stories about government wrongdoing or to downplay analysis of problems and discussions of national policy. Nor are women journalists less likely than men to highly value an adversary role.

Ethical standards. Much public debate about journalism focuses on the ethics of various reporting practices, such as using hidden cameras or microphones, paying for information, and not revealing that one is a journalist. In 1982–83 we asked about seven questionable reporting practices and found much disagreement among journalists as to whether certain

Table 1.8
Amount of Freedom Men and Women with Editing Duties Have in Deciding Story Use (Percentage in each category)

	1982–83				*1992*			
	Print		*Broadcast*		*Print*		*Broadcast*	
Amount of Freedom	*Men* (*n* = *350*)	*Women* (*n* = *178*)	*Men* (*n* = *126*)	*Women* (*n* = *56*)	*Men* (*n* = *428*)	*Women* (*n* = *230*)	*Men* (*n* = *138*)	*Women* (*n* = *48*)
Almost complete	42.3	34.8	49.2	37.5	15.9	21.3	24.6	41.7
A great deal	25.7	25.8	23.0	37.5	33.9	33.0	30.4	37.5
Some	21.7	23.0	23.0	12.5	35.3	28.3	37.0	16.1
None at all	10.3	16.3	4.8	12.5	15.0	17.4	8.0	4.2

practices might be justified on occasion or would not be approved under any circumstances. In fact, the only practice that U.S. journalists overwhelmingly agreed on (95 percent) was that divulging confidential sources should not be approved under any circumstances. For the rest of the practices, the percentages ranged from 20 percent to 67 percent who thought that they might be justified on occasion (Weaver and Wilhoit 1986, 127–28). Taken together, there were not significant differences between men and women journalists in 1982–83 regarding whether these controversial reporting practices might be justified, but older and more experienced journalists, especially those working for radio, were less likely to approve. Those journalists working for larger news organizations and making higher salaries were more likely to see these reporting practices as sometimes justifiable.

In 1992 the percentages of journalists saying that the various practices might be acceptable did not change much from 1982–83 for five of the seven methods—getting employed to gain inside information, badgering unwilling informants to get a story, paying for information, claiming to be somebody else, and disclosing confidential sources. But there was a dramatic increase in those saying that using confidential business or government documents without authorization might be acceptable (from 55 percent to 81 percent) and in those saying that using personal documents such as letters and photographs without permission might be justified (from 28 percent to 47 percent). Again, as in 1982–83, there were almost no significant differences between men and women journalists regarding the acceptability of these controversial reporting methods, suggesting that women journalists are not likely to be more or less aggressive than men in pursuing news stories.

Instead, the major differences occur by news medium and by minority status. For example, in 1992 daily newspaper, news magazine, and wire service journalists were significantly more likely than others to justify the use of unauthorized documents, as were Asian journalists. Weekly newspaper, radio, and Native American journalists were least likely to approve of the use of documents without permission, perhaps because they are likely to work for smaller news organizations in more cohesive communities where journalists and news sources more regularly interact.

Another striking demonstration that gender is less important than newsroom environment and minority status in ideas about reporting ethics comes from one of the three reporting practices we added in the 1992 study. Disclosing the names of rape victims has been a controversial topic during much of the 1990s, made even more salient by the William Kennedy Smith rape trial in Palm Beach, Florida, and the furor over protecting the identity of the victim. Even though U.S. journalists in 1992 were nearly evenly split on whether it could be considered justifiable to disclose the name of a rape victim (43 percent said it might), they were not split by gender as one might expect. Exactly the same proportion of men and women journalists said it might be justifiable on occasion

(Weaver and Wilhoit 1992, 13–14). Native American journalists were much less likely to agree (21 percent), as were news people from television (34 percent) and radio (28 percent).

On the other hand, when we asked about using hidden microphones or cameras, television journalists were most likely to give a qualified approval (90 percent) and weekly newspaper journalists least likely (45 percent). Among minorities, the proportions varied from 59 percent for Native Americans to 72 percent for Asians. The proportions of men (61 percent) and women (59 percent) in the overall sample did not differ significantly.

This same pattern of greater differences by news medium and race or ethnic background than by gender emerged for all the controversial reporting practices we asked about in 1992, suggesting again that newsroom environment and community/cultural setting are more powerful influences on the ethical values of journalists than gender.

Conclusions

Taken together, the series of major national studies of U.S. journalists conducted in 1971, 1982–83, and 1992 suggest considerable progress for women in American journalism during the past two decades, with a few setbacks, and a few areas of little change.

Social Backgrounds, Experience, and Careers. By the early 1990s women journalists were clearly as educated as men at both undergraduate and graduate levels, and more likely to be married than ten or twenty years ago. But they were still much less likely to be married than men and much less likely to have children living with them, suggesting more difficulty for women than men journalists to combine careers and families.

Women were also more likely to work full time for a wide variety of news media in 1992 as compared with the past, and were better represented in journalism overall than in other professional occupations such as college or university teaching, dentistry, law, and medicine. But the overall representation of women in U.S. journalism did not increase from 1982–83 levels, even though the proportion of women under twenty-five increased notably, primarily because women have not stayed in journalism as long as men. Many women have experienced a career break, leaving journalism before their midthirties and returning in later years, resulting in fewer total years of experience than men who have stayed on the job without taking a leave. Women actually lost ground in television news, dropping from one-third of all TV journalists in 1982–83 to about one-fourth in 1992. They held steady in daily and weekly newspapers, and made the largest gains in news magazines and wire services.

The income gap between men and women continued to decrease, from 64 percent of men's salaries overall in 1971 to 81 percent in 1991.

When years of experience, size of news media organization, managerial responsibilities, and several other predictors were held constant, the gender gap in income virtually disappeared by the early 1990s.

Managerial Responsibilities and Authority. Women also made significant gains in managerial responsibility, especially in the print media, and in amount of editorial control, although there seemed to be a decrease in perceived autonomy to select stories for both women and men during the past ten to twenty years. Women lagged behind men in perceived influence on hiring and firing, especially in radio and television news. Overall, the findings suggest that radio and television newsrooms are more likely to be controlled by men than women, but not so for the print media where women are more numerous. These findings also suggest that more women are in positions to influence news coverage in the 1990s than in previous decades. There was a notable drop in both the 1970s and the 1980s in the proportion of U.S. journalists claiming to be very satisfied with their work, but by the 1980s there were no significant differences between men and women on perceived job satisfaction. Women were slightly less likely than men to say they would like to be working in journalism in the next five years. Women were equally as unlikely as men to belong to a professional journalism association (slightly more than one-third claimed membership), and equally likely to rate their news organization as doing a very good or outstanding job of informing the public (nearly two-thirds said so).

In general, then, there were not many differences between men and women in job experiences or satisfaction, except in perceived influence in hiring and firing, where women were less likely to think they had a great deal of influence in the broadcast news media. There were suggestions that women journalists in the 1990s are more likely to exert influence over news policies and coverage than they were ten or twenty years ago.

Professional Roles and Ethics. Likewise, there were very few detectable differences between men and women journalists in their perceptions of which news media roles were most and least important, and in their opinions on which questionable reporting practices might be justified on occasion and which should not be approved under any circumstances. Instead, opinions on these topics were much more likely to vary by type of news organization (daily and weekly newspaper, news magazine, radio, television, and wire service) and by racial and ethnic background than by gender.

This finding suggests that newsroom and community environments are stronger influences on journalists' professional values (and probably on the kind of news content they produce) than is gender, raising the question of whether news coverage is likely to change much as more women enter journalism and assume positions of increasing responsibility. In our 1982–83 study, we found that factors in the organizational environment—as opposed to education and demographic background measures—were most predictive of journalistic role orientation (Weaver and Wilhoit 1986, 117). We also found that newsroom learning and family upbringing were the most often cited sources of influence on ideas about journalism ethics for both women and men (Weaver and Wilhoit 1986, 135). The same patterns emerged in 1992, with respect to both ethical and news values—journalistic training and newsroom learning were perceived as the most influential by the most journalists, both men and women. These findings suggest that a larger representation of women in journalism will not automatically result in changes in news coverage of politics or other subjects unless the culture of newsrooms, the structure of news work, and the traditions of journalism change.

This conclusion is supported by an additional analysis of our 1982–83 data by Lori Bergen, who correlated the individual and organizational characteristics of journalists with samples of their best work (and also with their open-ended descriptions of their best work in our survey). She found that organizational characteristics (income, years employed at organization, amount of editing, frequency of reporting, beat assignment, perceived autonomy, type and size of media organization, type of ownership, presence of a union, and size of city) were stronger predictors of the kind of stories journalists wrote than were individual traits (age, gender, education, college major, membership in professional organizations, political leaning, and role orientation), although neither were very strong influences on news content (Bergen 1991a).

In analyzing the stories that journalists sent to us as examples of their best work in 1983, Bergen coded topic of the story, news values evidenced (conflict, timeliness, proximity, prominence, unusualness, and impact), sources relied upon (gender, anonymous vs. named, documentary vs. person, institutional vs. private), event or issue orientation, role concepts (adversarial, interpretive, neutral disseminator), and cultural values (ethnocentrism, altruistic democracy, responsible capitalism, etc.) (Bergen 1991a, 53–65; Bergen 1991b). In every aspect of the stories analyzed, the organizational characteristics were consistently stronger predictors than the individual, but the small proportions of variance predicted by both suggested that there were other influences operating which were not included in this study, or that much of the difference in news content was idiosyncratic, or that more subtle aspects of news coverage were not measured.

Whatever the explanations, it seems clear from this analysis and from other studies such as those by Hirsch (1977) and Shoemaker and Reese (1991) that most journalists, even those with great freedom, work within the constraints of specific news organizations. As such, most realize that they must meet organizational, occupational, and audience expectations. In addition, the news organizations within which they work are influenced by external societal and cultural environments. Given these layers of influences, it is not too surprising that the individual characteristics of journalists do not correlate strongly with the kinds of news content they produce, but it would be a mistake to think that individual journalists have no freedom to select and shape news stories—or to change the nature of the news organizations for which they work.

In our analysis of 180 stories sent to us by journalists as examples of their best work, for example, we found that women journalists were somewhat more likely to include female sources in their news stories than were men, who were more likely to include male news sources. We also found evidence of a shift from more traditional government and crime news to news of personalities and human interest over the decades from the early sixties to the early nineties in this set of self-selected stories, with those written by women more likely to be concerned with social problems and protests, and less likely to emphasize timeliness (Weaver and Wilhoit 1996). Our findings from this analysis also suggest that journalists, especially women, may be stepping out of more conventional news beat systems and tapping ordinary people as sources more often. The increase in features in 1992 seems consistent with the shift in news sources found in this group of stories.

Thus in spite of the increasing similarities between men and women journalists from the 1992 survey, as compared with the two earlier studies in 1982–83 and 1971, there is some evidence in the stories sent to us in 1992 of differences in subjects and sources by gender of journalist. These are not a random sample of journalists' best or routine work, however, so care must be taken in generalizing from them.

There are other indications in this book that women in U.S. journalism can make a difference in news coverage of politics and other areas as well. In chapter 2, Kay Mills finds that as women have become more numerous in U.S. news organizations, they have broadened the definition of news to include issues of economic and educational interest to women, child care, women's health and recreation. Mills argues that women journalists have also made the climate for women's participation in politics "less chilly." Although we lack systematic evidence, the numerous examples that Mills presents suggest that women in U.S. journalism have made a difference in the news, even if some of their attitudes regarding roles and ethics do not differ much from those of men.

Changing the culture, structure, and values of news organizations, especially large ones, is not a simple or quick matter. As Mills notes in chapter 2, women at some newspapers and broadcast media lack the "critical mass" to alter definitions of news. And as Maurine Beasley points out in a quotation from Katharine Graham, chairman of the board of the *Washington Post*, there is "a difference between having the authority to make decisions and the power to make policy." In the last chapter, Beasley suggests some strategies for improving the media coverage of women. When more women attain higher levels of authority in news organizations, more fundamental changes in news coverage may be possible. But women, like men, will still be constrained somewhat by the economic realities, organizational structures and journalistic values under which they worked on the way up.

Notes

1. The 1992 study was intended to be a partial replication of the 1971 national telephone survey of 1,328 U.S. journalists by John Johnstone and his colleagues, and the 1982–83 national telephone survey of 1,001 U.S. journalists by myself and G. Cleveland Wilhoit. Accordingly we followed the definitions of a journalist used by these earlier studies, and asked many of the same questions although we added some items to reflect the changes in the news media environment from 1982 to 1992.

Moreover in 1992 we deliberately over-sampled journalists from the four main minority groups—Asian Americans, African Americans, Hispanic Americans, and Native Americans—to ensure adequate numbers for comparison with each other and with white journalists. We kept these over-samples of minority journalists separate from the main probability sample when making comparisons with the earlier studies.

2. These directories include the *1991 Editor & Publisher International Year Book*, *The Broadcasting Yearbook 1991*, the *1991 Gale Directory of Publications and Broadcast Media*, and the Summer 1991 *News Media Yellow Book* of Washington and New York. We used systematic random sampling to compile lists of 181 daily newspapers (stratified by circulation), 128 weekly newspapers, 17 news magazines, 28 wire service bureaus, 121 radio stations, and 99 television stations, for a total of 574 separate news organizations. (See Weaver and Wilhoit 1996, Appendix I, for more details.) The interviews were conducted by telephone from 12 June to 12 September 1992, by trained interviewers at the Center for Survey Research at Indiana University's Bloomington campus.

3. Our definition of journalists, as in the earlier studies, includes editorial cartoonists but not comic-strip cartoonists. We did not include librarians, camera operators, and video and audio technicians, because we followed the reasoning of the earlier studies that they do not have direct responsibility for news content in the various media. We did include photojournalists in this study, unlike the earlier studies, because they increasingly combine picture making and writing, and work independently from reporters. (See Weaver and Wilhoit 1986, 1996.)

4. The response rate for this sample was 81 percent, and the maximum sampling error at the 95 percent level of confidence is plus or minus 3 percentage points. Sampling error margin is, of course, higher for the individual media groups.

2

What Difference Do Women Journalists Make?

Kay Mills

News is new, that which we do not already know. A report of a recent event. Analysis of why Candidate X beat Candidate Y. Coverage of a murder trial. Even a forecast of summer movies. Much news, however, is actually "old," the same subjects repackaged with new names and new quotations. What happens when different people frame the media's view of the world—suggesting or assigning the stories, reporting them, editing them? Is new news added to daily print and broadcast journalism when women bring their experiences or different range of vision to the mix? As David Weaver suggests in the previous chapter, are newsroom and community environments stronger influences on journalists than gender, or have women helped change the definition, and therefore the coverage, of news?

"Very basically, women tend to live different lives," said Geneva Overholser, former *Des Moines Register* editor, seeking to explain some female journalists' and readers' different approaches to the news. She added:

> Women tend to be more involved with home and family issues. Much as women might have "passed"—seeking eagerly to cover the cops or to write on national security issues in order to be sure they're taken seriously—the result of women's different life patterns is an acute awareness that the press overemphasizes politics, cops and government at the expense of subjects closer to people's lives. Interestingly, those subjects that readers say they want more of—news of their own community, articles about personal finance, fitness or child care—are subjects women within the newspaper may be likely to care about as well. (Overholser 1989).

There are a variety of reasons why women may make a difference in news-gathering. Women who are journalists today may have had to struggle for attention in the classroom when they were in school. They may have had to feign lack of interest in schoolwork or in athletics, either to attract a boy or not to outshine one. They may have been denied jobs or promotions solely because they were women. They may have done more of the marketing, housekeeping, or childrearing than their spouses. They may be raising children alone. They clearly have some different health concerns. They bring these experiences to their jobs as journalists.

This different set of experiences means that some women write or broadcast different elements in stories than some men would write or broadcast about the same events. Men and women may dial their telephones the same way, type on their word processors the same way, and organize their stories similarly, but men and women often see different things while on assignment. Likewise, many female editors ask some questions that their male counterparts do not ask, and thus their editing may seem different even though both have the same training in the elements that make up a news story. Of course, not all women regularly write stories that detail the human condition; some women rarely do and some men always do.

To understand women's influence on the news-gathering process today, one must first know how their reporting has evolved. News used to be even more about presidents and police, tariffs and treaties, than it is today. Smoot and Hawley were men. Men were the people making the decisions, and men were the people being covered by the news media. In the past the idea that only men made news predominated. In a job interview with *Newsweek* in 1966, for example, I was told that the magazine's Chicago bureau needed a reporter who could go anywhere, cover anything. "And besides, what would you do if someone you were covering ducked into the men's room?" (Mills 1988, 1).

Few women reported anything but society or homemaking news until the 1960s. In colonial America, women in journalism were almost always widows of publishers of small newspapers. Nineteenth-century female reporters were "stunt girls" who committed themselves to hospitals and jails to report on conditions. One, Nellie Bly, raced around the world to see if she could beat the eighty-day "record" of Jules Verne's fictional Phileas Fogg. She did it. Later, women were "sob sisters" who covered lurid trials. While many of those women were fine journalists, rare was the Margaret Fuller who could write political commentary from Italy in the nineteenth century, the Dorothy Thompson who was the first foreign journalist thrown out of Hitler's Germany in the twentieth, or the Marguerite Higgins who shared a Pulitzer Prize for her coverage of the Korean War. Rarer still were women of color like Ida Wells-Barnett, fearless crusader against lynching.

Some inroads were made in Washington in the 1930s when first lady Eleanor Roosevelt decreed that only women could cover her news conferences (see chapter 9 by Winfield). Still more women entered newsrooms when American men went off to fight in World War II; newspapers hired women as reporters and sportswriters and promoted others into temporary editing jobs they had to relinquish at war's end. Not until more women entered the work force and until discrimination on the grounds of sex was outlawed did women move into the newsroom and onto the anchor desk in any numbers.

Even then the newsroom culture often made it difficult for isolated women to do anything more than cover the same stories men covered. By newsroom culture, I mean that journalism was almost totally led by middle-aged white men, and it reflected their interests, their biases, their backgrounds. There were fewer college graduates among them than there are among today's editors. More had served in the military and were accustomed to hierarchies. Their wives usually did not work outside the home. And these editors often had little contact with African Americans or other people of color except as maids, janitors, or waiters. Suggestions for stories were welcome, but more frequently assignments came from above. There were fewer news meetings (perhaps a blessing) but also fewer people making decisions. To get the attention of these editors, reporters had to do well what the editors themselves had done well. Then and only then might reporters be allowed to venture onto new turf.

Women had all they could do to win many of the traditional news assignments, as editors chivalrously protected women from working at night, seeing the dead bodies that they might encounter on the police beat, or entering the proverbial smoke-filled rooms where men (and it was always men) were making political deals. They certainly were not going to send women into war zones, although a few women were able to cross these male-imposed barriers. Faced with having to prove that they knew the difference between a political machine and a sewing machine, those few women on cityside news or metropolitan broadcasting staffs were not going to expend their hard-earned credibility on stories about women.

Far-sighted women's page editors like Dorothy Jurney of the *Miami Herald* and later the *Detroit News* and Vivian Castleberry of the *Dallas Times Herald* started covering financial or education issues affecting women in their sections in the 1950s and 1960s. Only then did female cityside reporters begin to venture into this territory as well. Even so, they put no more than a toe in the water, because the editors' reaction remained tepid. As more women started to raise their voices in political and social protest in the late 1960s and early 1970s, a few female reporters tried to find a handle for the story (see Costain et al. in chapter 11). News was still largely events, however, and there were few events to cover. Writing about a consciousness-raising session was like trying to nail Jell-o to the wall.

At that same time, women in American newsrooms realized that they faced the same discrimination on the job that they sought to cover in the outside workplace. Many a top editor said he thought simply hiring more women would solve any problems of discrimination within the newsroom, but women remained blocked at entry or midlevels. It took lawsuits against such media giants as the *New York Times* and the Associated Press in the 1970s, as well as strong commitment to affirmative action plans by media cautioned by those lawsuits, to bring more women into the journalistic work force. Not until they entered the newsroom in any numbers would women reach decision-making jobs and start changing the nature of the news that was covered.

Slowly, female reporters sought to convince editors that women might face different problems running for office or holding jobs, supporting families alone, or obtaining adequate health care—and that those problems might be news. Many of the women I have interviewed remember the glazed looks that came over editors' eyes when they suggested stories on child care or women in politics; one woman told me it was as if you were a space alien. Space aliens might, in fact, have garnered more attention in those days.

Forceful women on occasion could impress the merits of a story on their editors or simply add coverage of the women's movement to their existing beats because they recognized it as news. They were the exceptions. Among others, Eileen Shanahan of the *New York Times* saw that women's interests in entering the legal profession, passing an equal rights amendment, and moving more actively into politics or labor union leadership were elements of a developing movement. But she also knew that to cover these stories she would have to do so in addition to, not instead of, her economics and tax reporting.

When Shanahan first heard about upcoming ERA consideration in the House of Representatives, she told her editors, who assigned the story to another woman in the Washington bureau, Marjorie Hunter. Hunter preferred to continue covering an education bill so Shanahan said she would do it. It was the presence of Eileen Shanahan and several other women reporters (including Grace Lichtenstein and Judy Klemsrud), coupled with the emergence of legal and political issues that they could cover, that strongly contributed to the visibility of women's issues in the *New York Times* in this era, which Leonie Huddy describes in chapter 10.

Shanahan recalled that her editor was astonished that she wanted to cover ERA.

> I remember distinctly his saying to me, "Oh, well, you do not cover women." He didn't say, "You cover important things like the federal budget," but obviously that's what he meant. . . . Well, no editor is sorry when somebody volunteers for work, and so I was allowed to do it, though I was considered very strange for wanting to . . . I must have known even then that this was a matter of some importance. And so I covered it. I didn't have any concept of how important and how broad [it would be], nor did I know what was going to flow from it. (Mills 1988, 58–59)

Generally, however, it was not until there was a critical mass in the newsroom—and until more and more women were in the work force, seeking child care, speaking out about harassment, running for office—that women were able to make their different voices heard. "You have to have 'the rule of three' functioning before there will consistently be impact," said Glenda Holste, editorial writer and columnist for the St. Paul, Minn., *Pioneer Press.* "If there is just one woman in a story conference or editorial page meeting, you have to blend in. If there are two, you compete for attention. When there are three women, you reach a critical mass."[1]

Today, not only are some women helping make the political decisions (and presumably ducking into the women's room), but the news media also cast a wider net in determining what is news. Consider these headlines from early June 1995 on stories that would not have been taken seriously by most editors two decades ago:

—"New Clues in Balancing the Risks of Hormones After Menopause,' by Jane Brody, *New York Times,* 15 June 1995, p. A1.

—"American Girls Face Confidence Crisis," *Houston Chronicle,* 4 June 1995.

—"Increasing Shift Work Challenges Child Care," by Constance L. Hays, *New York Times,* 8 June 1995, p. B5.

—"Sexism Still Alive in Sacramento," by Cathleen Decker and Jennifer Warren, *Los Angeles Times,* 12 June 1995, p. A1.

—"Citadel Plan to Isolate Woman Is Rejected," by Reuters, *Los Angeles Times,* 8 June 1995, p. A20.

There are few studies documenting the impact of gender on news coverage on a more systematic basis. I surveyed two months' worth of front pages of the *New York Times,* January and February 1994, and the same months in 1964 to see what changes a generation has made. There are almost half as many stories on the 1994 front page as in 1964 yet seven times more women's bylines. Out of 407 bylines in the 1994 papers, 78, or 19 percent, were women's. In 1964, there were 777 front-page stories in January and February, with 21, or 2.7 percent, by women. More than half of those were economics stories from Washington by Eileen Shanahan. In those two months, only five individual women had front-page bylines.

On the 1994 front pages there were nineteen stories that might be considered of special interest to women (omitting the health-care debate and the Tonya Harding skating scandal), eight of them by women. Subjects included fertility research, popularity of women's colleges, sex education for the young, amniocentesis advances, caring for the elderly at home, harassment of lesbians in Mississippi, and worldwide abuse of women. In 1964 the front-page stories included announcement that Governor Nelson Rockefeller's wife, Happy, was pregnant, several articles on the engagement of Dutch Princess Irene, the visit of Lady Bird Johnson to Wilkes-Barre, Maine Senator Margaret Chase Smith's announcement of her presidential candidacy, and birth control help for welfare clients. One 1964 photo caption of presidential candidate Barry Goldwater identified the woman with whom he was speaking as "the widow of Senator Styles Bridges," as though she had no other name.

All news, however, is not headline news. The changing nature of front-page stories at a "paper of record" such as the *New York Times* hints that if students undertook a more thorough survey of entire newspapers in this same time period, they might see even more fully the change in the nature of news. Change has occurred on editorial pages as well. In the early 1980s, when I was the lone woman on the editorial page staff at the *Los Angeles Times*, I constantly heard jokes or grumbling from male colleagues when I suggested that the paper run an editorial on a spousal rape case in Oregon or support actions to increase the number of women fire fighters and police officers. Today, there are four women writing editorials at the *Los Angeles Times*, and they report a much different climate.

"Topics about women are no longer unique," said Gable Pollard Terry. These subjects carried greater weight once Janet Clayton became assistant editor of the editorial page in the early 1990s and should continue to do so after her appointment in 1995 as editorial page editor. She is the first woman—and first African American—to hold that job at the *Los Angeles Times.* With four women writing editorials, the page also benefits from "the diversity of opinions among women," Pollard Terry added. "We all have different takes on the world."[2]

The impact of critical mass takes many forms—on story decisions, editorial policy, assignments, even hiring. At the *Everett Herald* in Everett, Washington, in the 1980s, for example, the management team reached this critical mass when Joann Byrd was editor. Karen West, then the city editor, recalled helping interview a candidate for a top management position when the editing team doing the interviewing consisted of more women than men. The man under consideration made a comment about having to treat women differently. Asked what he meant, he said that "at certain times of the month women are more emotional, more sensitive." "There was a slight pause" [West said]. "There were four women managers in the room. The first voice was male, who said he thought that was ridiculous. The men were better feminists, and the women never had to say anything. At that moment, he lost any hope of getting that job. If he had been sitting in the room with all men, he might not have had that reaction. But the men at the *Herald* knew different because they worked with women" (Mills 1988: 290–91).

Women reporters also interview women for their stories; men do not always. When Connie Koenenn was editor of the daily arts section for the *Los Angeles Times*, reporters assigned to cover conferences about breaking into the film industry regularly returned with quotes from men only. "Weren't there any women there?" she would ask. "Sure," they would reply. "Why not talk to some of them?" she suggested. And they did (Mills 1988, 251).

And how many hospital stories have you read that never quote a single nurse? "In the stories I did several years ago about death and dying," said Melinda Voss of the *Des Moines Register*, "I quoted about twenty nurses and two doctors. That is highly unusual. I let the nurses speak out about what they felt and heard and saw. For that story, that made sense."

Who receives the assignment to do a particular story influences the way it is reported and written. Margaret Wolf Freivogel, the national and foreign editor for the *St. Louis Post-Dispatch*, says that when assignments are being made she throws some names into the hat that some other editors might not consider. "Sometimes I think just being in the room helps. The others may be just a little more aware of their assumptions as a result."

The differences can be as major as sending a female reporter to cover the murder of nuns in Liberia or as small as raising a point about a feature written for National Secretaries Day. Freivogel recalled that the story was about a woman who began her career taking dictation and working on a typewriter but who is now a whiz on computers. "I asked, 'Do we deal with the question of why she's not called an administrative assistant now that she knows so much about computers?'" Freivogel said. Administrative assistants earn more money. "There happened to be two or three other women sitting in on that meeting where this subject came up and they nodded. The reporter did go back and deal with those questions . . . There are so many subtle things that go into deciding the play of a story or how a story is handled. You can't put your finger on where the crucial decision is made but being part of the process is important. When you add it up, you can feel you made a difference."

Sometimes having a woman strategically placed in the news hierarchy determines whether an entire set of stories is done and, once completed, prominently displayed. When Linda Mathews was assistant national editor at the *Los Angeles Times* in the mid-1980s, she saw wide-ranging changes and problems for women in the work force. The mother of two children and pregnant with her third, she was living many of those changes. She raised the idea of a series of articles, lobbied to free staff members to do the reporting, and kept the project on track. She edited the last of the articles just days before her daughter, Kate, was born. Each of the ten articles began on page one of a newspaper that until then had not focused in any concentrated way on working women (*Los Angeles Times*, 9–18 September 1994).

Winning prizes is a powerful reinforcement for women's voices, and no prize is more treasured within journalism than the Pulitzer. Nan Robertson won hers about toxic shock syndrome the hard way: she became violently ill and had her fingertips amputated because of gangrene caused by circulatory damage from toxic shock. Robertson fought her way back to type herself her compelling *New York Times Magazine* article on her own illness and the efforts to track down the cause of the disease (Robertson, 1992). For that article, she won a Pulitzer in 1983. Even in her triumph, she was patronized by a senior editor at the *Times.* Congratulating her, he held her at arm's length and said, "What's a little bitty thing like you doing winning the Pulitzer Prize?" (Mills 1988, 77–78)

In recent years, more women have won these coveted awards and more have won them for stories that a decade or two ago would have been buried inside the paper, if covered at all. In 1991, Melinda Voss analyzed twenty-two years of Pulitzer Prize–winners for the *Journalism and Women Symposium* newsletter, a study triggered by the fact that nine women had shared in Pulitzers that year. That was a record, topping the previous high of four in 1986.

In 1991, "five of the women won for typically hard-news subjects," Voss wrote. "The other four won for stories that particularly touch the day-to-day lives of women and their families, for stories dealing with subjects that were not necessarily considered prizeworthy material in decades past." For example, Cheryl James of the St. Petersburg, Fla., *Times* won a Pulitzer for feature writing for a story on abandoned babies; Marjie Lundstrom and Rochelle Sharpe of *Gannett News Service* won the national reporting prize that year for stories on deaths from child abuse; and Jane Schorer of the *Des Moines Register* won the public service award for one woman's story of being raped (Voss 1991).

In July 1989 *Des Moines Register* editor Geneva Overholser had written a thoughtful column about whether newspapers should name rape victims. Victims of any other crimes are routinely named in news stories; failing to name a woman who has been raped may perpetuate the stigma attached to that crime, Overholser argued. She expressed the wish that newspapers could speak more openly about rape. At the same time, she acknowledged that in this case, newspapers had to honor women's wishes because the stigma remained a reality (Overholser, *Des Moines Register*, 11 July 1989). As one of the ranking female editors in the country at that time, Overholser's words carried special weight. It was probably a column only a woman could write; a male writer might have been labeled insensitive.

The article caught the eye of Nancy Ziegenmeyer of Grinnell, Iowa, and she called Overholser. She was willing to tell the story of her rape, and to let her name be used. Jane Schorer, a *Register* feature writer, who said that until then her best-known work "was a corny piece about an old farmer whose prize tomato plant was a candidate for *The Guinness Book of World Records*," was assigned the piece (Schorer 1991). Schorer worked for seven months on the story, learning about Ziegenmeyer's marriage, about the rape, about the effects of her trauma on her children, about the trial, about its aftermath. The first article in the series, "It Couldn't Happen to Me: One Woman's Story," ran in February 1990, names and all; the following year the *Register* won the Pulitzer for Schorer's articles.

In 1994 the *Dallas Morning News* received the Pulitzer Prize for international reporting for a series, "Violence Against Women," that had evolved in part from the women journalists' network there. Pat Gaston, assistant foreign editor, kept seeing items on the wire about violence against women and communicated with other women at the *News*, often electronically on the paper's computer system, about the issue. Then the United Nations announced that it would hold a conference in June 1993 on human rights. That announcement gave the women a peg and they sold the series idea to their bosses. Writers and photographers traveled to Egypt, Thailand, India, China, Bosnia, Kenya, Sweden, Brazil, Mexico, and Canada to do their articles. They focused on the personal stories of women who lived in rural villages and big cities and who had been beaten, raped, burned, shot, mutilated, and forced into prostitution (Loe 1994).

"I'm confident that if there weren't women in this newsroom and who had some standing, that series wouldn't have been done," said Pam Maples, who wrote about domestic violence in the United States for the series. Doing the articles "raised a lot of consciousness in the newsroom," Maples added. "Not long after the Pulitzer, we ran a story on the Sunday front about how a husband of a woman in Dallas doused her with gasoline and lit her, some people put her out, he relit her, and she died. That story was on the front page of the *Dallas Morning News.* I was here that Saturday. I didn't even have to mention it—the men put it on the front page. We do not put a lot of crime on page 1; I really think it was because of the sensitivity raised because of the project."

For whatever reasons—the Pulitzer, changing newsroom culture, changing definitions of news—Maples sees that "the men in charge are now more open to stories that particularly affect women than they used to be. They are willing to weigh them. They may not initiate them but they are willing to consider them."[3] Certainly that may be the case at many newspapers today where male editors are simply more sensitive to women's concerns and aware that they often are newsworthy. Not only are more men with working wives now entering the newsroom, said Patt Morrison of the *Los Angeles Times*, there are also more senior editors whose daughters are working and who may have encountered discrimination or harassment. "When it's daddy's little girl who's getting dissed, it sinks in in a way it never did before."[4]

One of the *Dallas Morning News'* Pulitzer team reported how her own thinking was affected by the project. "Working on this series changed me," said Gable Reaves. She went to Thailand to write about sexual slavery of young girls; she also reported on sexual assaults on Dallas women by policemen. "I had never made the connection that all these different forms of violence that we wrote about are points on a continuum, that these are related types of things that are all part of the attempt by men in patriarchal societies to control women" (Becker 1995).

Reaves had already been covering women's issues on a half-time basis for the *Morning News* in addition to working on special projects. While she has found that much of her reporting has been on abortion because

Dallas is such an active arena, pro and con, Reaves has also written about the high number of women in the Washington State legislature, about laws against stalking under consideration in the Texas legislature, and about various local women's issues. She also covered the international women's conference in Beijing.

Would she have sought the beat, and would she have been assigned to it ten years ago? Probably not, she said, even though she has been a feminist for a long time. She had tended to look at issues from a more personal standpoint than on a professional basis of how the news was covered. That changed when she helped found the Association of Women Journalists in the Dallas-Fort Worth area in 1987 and when she started attending annual meetings of a similar group, the *Journalism and Women Symposium.* The annual *Women, Men and Media* surveys, as well as one done locally by Association of Women Journalists, also influenced her thinking about how infrequently certain issues were being covered. In winning the assignment, it doubtless helped that she had won a prestigious George Polk reporting award for stories that appeared in 1990 about a drug war in south Texas. She had also reported on the political fight surrounding Texas' approval of parimutuel betting and assignment of licenses.[5]

Her experience was a world away from that of Eileen Shanahan, who, in the 1970s, considered proposing that she be assigned a national women's movement beat for the *New York Times.* She never did it, largely because she knew that as long as she was covering tax legislation, the budget, the Federal Reserve—"all that stuff that the male power structure respects"—she would be viewed as a true professional. She would be heeded when she suggested that a women's issue story belonged on page one. But if she covered the beat full-time, she felt that within six months she would be viewed as "crazy Shanahan who's always screaming and shouting and wanting to cover some silly-assed women's story" (Mills 1988, 60–61).

Two decades later, the changing climate at newspapers has also allowed women—and some men—to lobby for and be assigned to beats that focus on family issues. In 1995, for example, the Casey Journalism Center for Children and Families at the University of Maryland sponsored its annual week-long conference on child welfare issues, and three times as many reporters as there were fellowship spots applied to attend. More than two-thirds of those selected were women. In addition, Columbia University has announced plans to offer a new course, "Covering Children's Issues," at its graduate school of journalism (*The Children's Beat* 1995, 1).

In addition to enlarging the definition of news, women have also had an impact in shaping newspapers' political coverage and thus the climate of opinion in which women decide to run for office. Women as reporters helped bring women as candidates into the mainstream of coverage. Ruth Mandel, who headed the Center for the American Woman and Politics at Rutgers University for more than two decades and now directs the Eagleton Institute of Politics there, has spent hours on the telephone talking to reporters about women in politics. "There is no question in my mind that the intensity of interest is different for male and female reporters. That is not to say that some men aren't very interested and some women would rather not be doing the story." But as if by birthright, women in the media identify with the frustrations, the barriers, and the breakthroughs of women in politics because they have had similar experiences in their own newsrooms. "You didn't need a college degree to get it," she added.

"If we would announce a conference for women elected officials, the odds are it would be female reporters who would go to their editors and ask to go because they felt it was an important story," Mandel said. Interest translates into coverage. And in doing those stories, Mandel added, "While I would not say that women were entirely innocent of asking the question of women candidates, 'How do you do this and raise a family?' they are less likely to do that than the men" because they are living the answer themselves.

With coverage by women reporters and appearances of women as analysts on television, the climate for participation by women in the political arena has also become "less chilly," Mandel said. "If you are looking at a TV set with women journalists talking about politics, with women analyzing the news and commenting on it, that sends a message that this is not hostile territory."[6]

When law professor Anita Hill walked into what was clearly hostile territory—the Senate Judiciary Committee hearings on confirmation of Clarence Thomas to the U.S. Supreme Court in the fall of 1991, there nonetheless were female reporters aware that the issue that she raised of sexual harassment was a real one. Senators faced a barrage of questions from female reporters who were incredulous that these men were so dismissive of Hill's charges without even having heard them. Whatever they felt about the specific case, these women knew that sexual harassment happens. In a survey released a year later by the Associated Press Managing Editors, one out of every three women journalists among the 640 who had responded said she had been sexually harassed in the newsroom where she worked (*Media Report to Women* 1993, 2).

The Anita Hill–Clarence Thomas confrontation enlightened many male editors and reminded many female reporters that they encounter routine frustrations the men do not see. Patricia Sullivan, a reporter on *The Missoulian* in Missoula, Montana, recalled arguing with an editor about including as a source on a story about Hill's charges a female psychologist who said that all working women know someone who has experienced sexual harassment. "He thought that was over the top," so she told him that every woman in the newsroom had gone to the women's room and cried over some frustration, some difficulty of getting their point of view across. Astonished, he checked with another woman, who said, yes, that was so. "He still remembers that."[7]

Not only are there more women having more effect in the newsroom, there are also more women heading editorial page staffs and writing editorials and columns today than in the past, a change reflected in the subjects addressed. It took women longer to reach editorial writing posts than many other newsroom jobs because editorial writing was considered the purview of the most experienced journalists. Because they had been kept out of journalism, women were not the most experienced. As Jean Otto, formerly editorial page editor for the *Rocky Mountain News* in Denver, has written: "The result was—and is—that many editorial boards were composed of people who looked and thought just like each other—silver-haired or balding sages, up from the ranks, who had covered the same subject matter, spoken the same language, invested in the same philosophy and rarely challenged each other to different perspectives or new ideas. They meant well, but too few of these editorial oracles could see clearly beyond their own horizons" (Otto 1993, 159).

That is changing, albeit slowly. In 1992, the last year for which a survey was completed, women were editorial page editors at 62 papers, or 14.4 percent, up from 46 (10.3 percent) in 1986. Most of these women worked for papers of circulations of 100,000 or less (Wolfe 1993, 12–13; Jurney 1986, 4–7, 10). However, women edit the editorial pages of the *Washington Post*, *Los Angeles Times*, *Atlanta Constitution*, *Minneapolis Star Tribune*, *Seattle Times*, *Dallas Morning News*, and *San Antonio Express-News*, among others.

"Women absolutely bring a different perspective to issues addressed on the editorial page," Rena Pederson of the *Dallas Morning News*, told Jean Otto. "Without women's input, editorial pages would have been much slower to discuss battered women, child abuse, and rape," Pederson said. "It isn't that men didn't care, but it wasn't their primary interest" (Otto 1993, 163).

Women find increasing receptivity to their opinions in editorial-page conferences. When Pamela Moreland was an editorial writer at the *New York Daily News*, she recalled, she was always encouraged to write editorials that would interest women readers. This, at a tabloid with macho headlines, very much a guys' paper. "If there was a story about collusion in the infant formula industry to fix prices, I could do an editorial on it. I remember after one airline crash, there was a lot of focus on the need for child safety seats. I did a series of editorials on that. They were going after women readers; that was important to them."[8]

Lynell Burkett, editorial page editor at the *San Antonio Express-News*, would agree. "We are each so much a product of our experiences and that's what we have to contribute" to the news and editorial mix. "It helps us filter what we see. It's more than rhetoric for me when we talk about how diversity matters." At her newspaper, she said, family and children's issues now "are being considered prime beats where covering education or social services used to be a first beat."

Burkett went to the *Express-News* when its rival, the *San Antonio*

Light, folded. At *The Light*, where she was also editorial page editor, the paper made children's issues its chief 1992 editorial agenda. "Something simply had to be done to help turn things around for children," she said. A Rockefeller Foundation–financed study showed that editorial backing made a marked difference in local achievements that year. Burkett felt that had there been all men at the table considering that agenda, "not that they would have opposed it but it probably wouldn't have come up."[9]

This desire to attract and retain female readers illustrates that economics, not altruism, drives the news business. Female readers either feel they do not have enough time to read the paper, think there is nothing there for them, or would rather get their information from television, more specialized magazines, or other media. "If the same proportion of women as men read the newspaper today, the nation's newspapers would have nearly 4 million more readers today," according to the Knight Ridder Women Readers Task Force report in 1991. "Had we maintained our appeal to women equal to what it was in 1970, we would have 17 million more readers" (Knight Ridder 1991).

Surveying her own readership in planning for 1996, Barbara Henry, publisher of the *Great Falls Tribune* in Montana, said a panel of women had been invited in to talk about the newspaper. "One said that she would read the paper more 'if you run things that help me cope.' She subscribes to *Parenting* magazine and she reads that but she doesn't get the paper. She wants more information on things to do with her children in town, things about the schools and the education system which her kids are about to enter." Henry said that papers need to give people this local information—"not to the exclusion of hard news—but we have to be more selective with what we do with our features pages."[10]

Nancy Woodhull, one of the founding editors of *USA Today*, consults now with newspapers seeking to win women readers. She has discovered that while the business office may be convinced of the merits of her arguments because it sees the question in terms of circulation, "the debate comes in the newsroom." Male editors tend to see the issue as male vs. female. "I tell them to consider women a huge suburb you do not cover well and the lights go off in their head. If all women lived in one suburb, they'd get it."[11]

In this attempt to reach out to new readers, many newspapers are realizing that hiring diverse staffs can be good business. A white editor who may not have a clue what's going on in Hispanic East Los Angeles but needs to attract those readers may now have a colleague who knows—or knows how to find out. "If you are not white male," Pam Moreland, who is African American and is city editor at the *Independent Journal* in San Rafael, California, said, "newspapers now are saying, 'I want you to bring your un-white-maleness to the table now' as decisions on coverage are made."[12]

The millennium has not arrived, however. Women in any newsroom can give you a laundry list of stories showing that the more things change, the more they stay the same. There remain countless newsrooms where women still are underrepresented or where they feel reluctant to speak their minds, and those newspapers and news programs still feel less effect of women's experiences.

Newsrooms where some progress was being made on hiring more women and people of color now face tensions from white males who feel they are not getting the good jobs, the good assignments, although in many cases they still are. The top people at the major news outlets still are men. For example, the editors at the nation's four most prestigious newspapers—the *New York Times*, *Washington Post*, *Los Angeles Times*, and *Wall Street Journal*—all named since the late 1980s, are all men. No woman has ever headed a network news division. Only a handful of women are Washington news bureau chiefs.

Women of color remain poorly represented in membership and leadership of professional organizations, in key editing jobs and on Pulitzer juries. Television has done better in this regard with African American, Asian American, and Latina anchorwomen on local news broadcasts. That development did not occur, however, until after a Federal Communications Commission ruling against discrimination in hiring and news broadcasting.

With so few women in decision-making positions, there still is often no one to raise a red flag when egregious sexism appears in news stories. In 1992, for example, the *Los Angeles Times* profile of former Republican Party cochair Mary Crisp led with a description of her as "an unlikely hell raiser. A 68-year-old grandmother, she wears pearls, gold earrings and a red, white and blue suit." The *Women, Men and Media* survey reporting this story asked: "Would the media use a comparable lead in describing Ron Brown, Democratic Party chair?"

In discussing the "down side" of coverage of news about women, one sees both the above errors of commission and many of omission. Susan J. Carroll and Ronnee Schreiber report in their chapter that, since the hype of "The Year of the Woman," they have found little media coverage focusing on the range of issues tackled by those Congresswomen elected in 1992. That means readers and viewers may have a distorted view of what these representatives actually do.

Nor have women fared well in sports coverage. A study released in 1991 by the *Amateur Athletic Foundation* of Los Angeles documented scarcity of stories about women's sports in four newspapers. "Stories focusing exclusively on men's sports outnumbered stories addressing only women's sports by a ratio of 23 to 1. Even when all men's baseball and football stories were eliminated from the total number of men's stories, men's stories still outnumbered women's stories by an 8.7 to 1 margin . . . 92.3 percent of all photographs in sports sections were pictures of men" (*Amateur Athletic Foundation* 1991).

In sum, there have been breakthroughs and breakdowns. There remains no question in my mind that American news coverage is different today than it was when I began my professional career three decades ago. Different, but as these and many other examples I could cite illustrate, not different enough. I am hardly alone in my thinking.

Joann Byrd, until recently the ombudsman at the *Washington Post* and now a journalism professor at the University of Washington, told me when I first interviewed her in the mid-1980s that she did not think there was any difference between men and women on the question of news judgment. She was then editor of the *Everett Herald* in Everett, Washington. "I take it all back. Now I use that as practically the opening line of half the talks I give. In my first couple of years as an editor of a newspaper, I was practicing news judgment that I had learned from my predecessors, and of course they were all men. I knew what journalism was and I knew what news was. Several years later I said, well, hey, who says that's what news is? Why aren't those things that interest me news?" Day care, nanny problems, she said, would never have been considered news twenty-five years ago. "You know damn good and well sexual harassment never would have been considered news." A day or so before we spoke in 1995, the front page of the *Washington Post* carried a story about Prozac being used to treat premenstrual syndrome. "I suspect that ten years ago that would never have been on the front page, maybe not even in the newspaper," Byrd added.[13]

Patricia Sullivan of *The Missoulian* offered an apt metaphor for the change brought about by having more women in the newsroom who are covering more women's issues. You could compare the question of whether women make a difference to the movement of water heading downstream, she said. "It hits resistance and eddies around. But when it moves on, there's been change."

Notes

1. Glenda Holste interview, 30 May 1995.
2. Gable Pollard Terry interview, 15 June 1995.
3. Pam Maples interview, 25 May 1995.
4. Patt Morrison interview, 15 June 1995.
5. Gable Reaves interview, 13 June 1995.
6. Ruth Mandel interview, 13 June 1995.
7. Patricia Sullivan interview, 7 May 1995.
8. Pamela Moreland interview, 28 May 1995.
9. Lynell Burkett interview, 12 June 1995.
10. Barbara Henry interview, 13 June 1995.
11. Nancy Woodhull interview, 2 August 1995.
12. Moreland interview.
13. Joann Byrd interview, 9 June 1995.

Part II

CAMPAIGN COVERAGE

3

How Women Campaign for the U.S. Senate: Substance and Strategy

Kim Fridkin Kahn and Ann Gordon

At the Democratic National Convention in July 1992, women candidates for the U.S. Senate appeared to sound a common theme. "I am a mother and I am a grandmother, and I want to leave a legacy of clean water and clean air. . . . I want . . . a nation that cares for its sick and elderly," Jean Lloyd Jones told the crowd. Lynn Yeakel echoed her concerns, "I dream of an America where no worker is denied a job, no child goes hungry or homeless, no person is uneducated, and no one goes without health care." Dianne Feinstein warned, "Today, America's greatest national security threat is her domestic home front, and the battles are education; health care, including AIDS and breast cancer; jobs; infrastructure; the budget deficit; and the environment." These themes, together with a pro-choice stance, were embraced by many women candidates running for the U.S. Senate in 1992 (Nicolosi and Ceballos 1992, 127–29).

In addition to holding similar substantive concerns, women's campaigns share other commonalities as well. Specifically, women candidates often face questions about their effectiveness as campaigners (Tolleson-Rinehart 1994; Tolleson-Rinehart and Stanley 1994; Carroll 1994). For example, in a recent analysis of the 1992 Illinois race for the U.S. Senate, Jelen (1994) explained that Carol Moseley-Braun ". . . was regularly characterized by the news media as having a superficial grasp of important issues, and of 'sitting on her lead' by avoiding controversial statements. . . . On a tactical level, Moseley-Braun's campaign was often described as 'disorganized' and 'chaotic' " (Jelen 1994, 147).

This study aims to see whether women campaign differently from men substantively and strategically. With regard to *substance*, the 1992

Democratic National Convention speeches clearly illustrate similarities in the policy priorities of women candidates. However, are these priorities different from the policy concerns of their male colleagues? Furthermore, is the agenda articulated by women candidates in 1992 endorsed by women running in other election years? In terms of *strategy*, we will examine whether women are poorer campaigners than men. While Carroll (1994) identified some weaknesses in the campaigns of women candidates, she concludes that "lack of qualifications and inadequacies in campaigns are of limited utility in explaining women's rate of election" (p. 91). Given the persistence of concerns about women's abilities as campaigners, additional work is needed to analyze the relative skills of male and female candidates.

We will examine gender differences in both the campaign messages and the campaign abilities of male and female candidates, relying on a survey of campaign managers running U.S. Senate campaigns in 1988, 1990, and 1992 to explore these questions. We begin by discussing our hypotheses about gender differences in campaign messages and campaign strategy, and then describe our survey methodology. Next, we present the results of our analysis and conclude by talking about the implications of our findings.

Expectations about Campaign Messages

Female candidates may often bring a different perspective to the electoral arena. This perspective, which may be influenced by women's experiences as mothers, their position in the workplace, or their socialization as children, is likely to affect how women candidates campaign. For instance, some feminist theorists contend that women's unique experience as mothers affects their views on policy (Okin 1990). Women's traditional role as nurturer, for example, could lead women candidates to campaign for government programs designed to help others (for example, caring for the elderly, or assistance for the poor).

Similarly, women's fundamentally different experiences in the workplace can persuade women candidates to adopt particular policy priorities in their electoral bids. Women, for example, earn less money than men, are more likely to work part time, and often work without health insurance. These types of experiences may be shared by women candidates who believe that government should protect citizens from inadequacies in the workplace. Women candidates may want to ensure that all citizens have access to adequate health care, an optional family leave policy at their place of employment, and protection from sexual harassment.

Finally, men and women have different socialization experiences. From a young age, certain traits are encouraged among boys (such as assertiveness, leadership), while other traits (such as empathy, sincerity, understanding) are viewed as desirable for young girls (Graber 1989; Sapiro 1983). These socialization patterns, based on people's views about gender-appropriate behaviors, maintain sex stereotypes. These sex stereotypes lead people to view women as possessing expressive strengths (such as being emotional, understanding, gentle, warm, compassionate), while men are viewed as possessing instrumental strengths (for example, being independent, objective, ambitious, acting as a leader, aggressive, knowledgeable) (Ashmore and DelBoca 1979; Broverman et al. 1974; Deaux and Lewis 1984; Ruble 1983).

Issue Competence. As Huddy and Terkildsen (1993b) explain, stereotypes regarding women's compassionate nature and men's aggressiveness encourage people to view men and women candidates as having alternative areas of expertise. There is a large body of research demonstrating that voters view male candidates as better able to deal with foreign policy, the economy, defense spending, arms control, foreign trade, and farm issues, while female candidates are considered better able to deal with day care, poverty, education, health care, and civil rights (Huddy and Terkildsen 1993; Gallup 1984; Leeper 1991; National Women's Political Caucus 1987; Sapiro 1981–82).

While these studies demonstrate that stereotypes influence views about the abilities of men and women candidates to deal with a number of issues, gender differences do not pervade all policy domains. For example, evaluations of men and women's relative ability to deal with unemployment may depend upon the way the issue is framed (Huddy 1994). If a woman candidate talks about the issue of jobs by discussing her desire to end the hardship of the unemployed, people's stereotypes about women's compassionate nature may lead them to see the woman candidate as superior at handling unemployment issues. However, if a male candidate frames the issue of unemployment by talking about the candidate's experience with creating jobs in the private sector, then people's stereotypes about the greater competence of male candidates may produce an advantage for the male candidate.

Given the pervasiveness of sex stereotypes, documented with survey and experimental data (such as, Gallup 1984; Kahn 1994a; National Women's Political Caucus 1987; Sapiro 1981–82), women candidates may choose to play to stereotypes by emphasizing their perceived areas of strengths in their campaigns. Similarly, women candidates may concentrate on "female" policy areas if they hold these same stereotypes and believe their expertise lies within these policy domains. The prevalence of sex stereotypes could lead women candidates to emphasize certain issues (such as education, health care, the environment, day care), while ignoring others (such as the economy, foreign policy).

The expectation that women will emphasize certain types of issues in their campaigns is documented by recent research. Kahn (1993), looking at the televised political advertisements of U.S. Senate candidates in the

1980s, found that women candidates were more likely to stress issues like health care and education in their commercials, while male candidates spent more time focusing on the economy, defense, and foreign policy in their ads. In addition, several scholars have shown that women who have been elected to state legislatures and to the U.S. Congress have different agendas from their male counterparts (Dodson and Carroll 1991; Carroll, Dodson and Mandel 1991; Kathlene, Clarke and Fox 1991; Poole and Zeigler 1985; Thomas 1991). For instance, results of a survey of men and women legislators in twelve statehouses indicate that women are more likely to introduce legislation concerning rape, teen pregnancy, pay equity, day care, and domestic violence. In addition, women are more likely to work on legislation dealing with women's "traditional" areas of interest: health care, welfare of children, the elderly, housing, and education (Carroll, Dodson, and Mandel 1991).

While women may be more likely to stress their perceived strengths in their campaigns, the effectiveness of such a strategy is likely to be contingent upon the prevailing political climate. In particular, when characteristics of the electoral climate place a premium on women's stereotypical strengths, women will have an advantage. For example, if issues like health care dominate the political agenda, citizens are likely to be concerned with the issue (for a review of agenda-setting research, see Ansolabehere, Behr, and Iyengar 1993), and women candidates may be able to exploit existing stereotypes by emphasizing health care in their campaigns. In contrast, when the public is concerned with other issues—like defense policy during the Cold War— voters are likely to perceive women candidates as ill equipped in this policy area. Such evaluations, in a climate where defense issues are salient to voters, could hinder women's electoral prospects.

Personal Traits. In addition, gender differences could influence the relative emphasis placed on issues and personal characteristics. Reliance on sex stereotypes, for example, leads people to view women as less competent overall than men (Ashmore, DelBoca and Wohlers 1986; Broverman et al. 1972; Huddy and Terkildsen 1993b; Leeper 1991; Ruble 1983; Williams and Best 1990). Female candidates may therefore feel a need to emphasize policy concerns in their campaigns as a way of dispelling voters' doubts about their ability to handle issues.

When women choose to stress personal characteristics in their campaigns, they need to decide which types of traits to focus on. Scholars of voting behavior have found that citizens consider two types of trait dimensions when voting in elections: competence and integrity (Markus 1982; Miller, Wattenberg, and Malanchuk 1986). The *competence* dimension is defined by traits like "knowledgeable," "leadership," "experience," and "intelligence" while the *integrity* dimension is defined by "honesty," "moral," and "trustworthy."

Since voters consider women candidates to be more compassionate and honest, while they consider men stronger leaders and more knowledgeable, candidates can develop campaign strategies to accent or revise these stereotypes. Women candidates, a product of their socialization experiences, may choose to stress their warmth, empathy, and integrity in their campaigns, since they are likely to see these traits as their strengths. Benze and DeClerq (1985) find evidence for this expectation in their content analysis of 113 political advertisements for male and female House and Senate candidates. Specifically, the authors find that female candidates stress their compassion and warmth twice as often as their male counterparts.

However, this strategy of emphasizing their empathy and honesty may be problematic for women candidates. Research at the presidential level suggests that assessments of a candidate's competence and leadership are more influential than other trait assessments (Kinder 1983; Markus 1982; Miller, Wattenberg, and Malanchuk 1986). Similarly, Rosenwasser and Dean's (1989) experimental research shows that students rate tough and aggressive traits as more important than warm and expressive traits when asked to assess the qualities of a "good" politician. Furthermore, the possession of typical masculine traits appears to increase a candidate's perceived competence across a variety of different issues (Huddy and Terkildsen 1993b), while typical feminine personality traits, such as compassion and empathy, are considered less important for officeholders (Huddy 1994; Kinder 1983).

Given the greater importance assigned to "male" traits relative to "female" traits, women candidates may try to eradicate harmful stereotypes by stressing "male" traits in their own campaign appeals. In contrast to Benze and DeClerq, a more recent study examining more than seven hundred advertisements for Senate and gubernatorial candidates in the 1980s, demonstrates that women strive to reduce potentially damaging stereotypes by stressing their competence in their ads (Kahn 1994a). Women candidates focus almost exclusively on their leadership, experience, and ability in these commercials, talking about their competence much more often than their male counterparts.

In sum, we hypothesize that women's experiences, as well as expectations about "female" traits and issues, will influence the substance of women's campaigns.

- We expect women candidates to stress issues more than traits as a way of demonstrating their competence.
- In addition, when talking about issues, we expect women to focus more on "female" issues like education, health care, and the environment than on "male" issues like the economy and foreign policy.
- Lastly, with regard to traits, we expect that women will seek to revise damaging stereotypes by demonstrating their knowledge and experience in their campaigns.

Expectations about Campaign Strategy

The strategies candidates adopt in their electoral bids, in addition to the substance of their campaigns, may vary with the gender of the candidate. That is, women and men may differ in their ability as campaigners, in their assessments of various campaign techniques, and in their likelihood of pursuing particular campaign strategies. Gender differences in campaign strategy can be explained by three factors: the prevalence of sex stereotypes, the experience of the candidates, and gender bias in news coverage of campaigns.

First, sex stereotypes can affect the choice of campaign strategy. For example, people's stereotypical images of men and women can affect their decision to use positive or negative appeals. Trent and Friedenberg (1983) explain that since women are viewed as less assertive than men, they are expected to be less verbally aggressive in their electoral campaigns. Therefore, when women violate these expectations by initiating aggressive and forceful attacks, they are viewed negatively (Wadsworth et al. 1987). In particular, voters view women candidates who initiate aggressive attacks as "unfeminine, shrill, [and] vicious" (p. 115). In their experimental study of television advertising in the 1990 California gubernatorial campaign, Ansolabehere and Iyengar (1991) provide empirical support for this contention when they show that "attack" ads were significantly less effective for Dianne Feinstein than for Pete Wilson. Given people's preconceptions regarding "proper" female behavior, negative campaigns are likely to be problematic for women candidates and, therefore, women candidates may be less likely than men to wage campaigns featuring "attack" advertisements.

Women may also differ from men in their ability as campaigners. Women, in general, have less experience than men because they are much less likely than men to be incumbents. This lack of political experience may affect women's expertise as campaigners, including their ability to understand and respond to their opponents' campaigns and their ability to influence media coverage of their electoral contest.

In developing successful campaigns, candidates and their advisors make judgments about the utility of various campaign techniques. For example, they need to decide how much money to spend developing and airing televised political advertisements and how much effort to expend generating personal contact between the candidate and potential voters. We do not believe that the candidate's gender will directly affect assessments of various campaign techniques. Instead, we expect the status of the candidate and the competitiveness of the race to be more important. Incumbents, for instance, may value personal contact more highly than nonincumbents, since they have developed extensive casework networks during their tenure in office. Similarly, candidates in competitive contests may be more likely to value televised political advertisements, since they expect citizens witnessing a close electoral contest to pay more attention to commercials about the candidate.

Finally, candidates need to develop positive press attention during their campaigns as a way of increasing support among the electorate. We believe that men and women candidates will differ in their assessments of news coverage of their campaigns. In particular, women may view news coverage as less positive and less responsive to their campaign agendas. While women candidates may not be aware of systematic studies documenting gender bias in news coverage (Kahn 1994a), they are likely to be familiar with anecdotal stories describing reporters as preoccupied with the attire and hair styles of women candidates instead of their issue positions (Witt, Paget, and Matthews 1994).

Given the different experiences and constraints faced by men and women candidates, we expect some gender differences in campaign strategy. In particular:

- Women may view negative campaigning as less effective given common conceptions about feminine behavior.
- Similarly, women may be less likely than men to view press coverage of their campaign in favorable terms.
- Lastly, assessments of various campaign techniques as well as evaluations of the candidate's campaign ability are more likely to be explained by the candidate's political experience, status, and the closeness of the race rather than the candidate's gender.

Research Design

To assess whether men and women pursue campaigns that differ in their substance and strategy, we conducted postelection telephone interviews with the campaign managers of the major party candidates running for election to the U.S. Senate in 1988, 1990, and 1992. These surveys were undertaken between November 1991 and June 1993. Interviews were completed with 147 of the 194 campaign managers, yielding a response rate of 77 percent.[1] For the 47 campaign managers not interviewed, 36 could not be reached and 11 refused to be interviewed.

During the interviews, we asked the campaign managers to identify the main themes of their campaign as well as the types of issues and personal characteristics stressed during the election. In addition, we asked managers to report the campaign themes presented by their opponents. Finally, we asked the managers to rate the usefulness of televised political advertisements and personal contact as campaign techniques. In conducting the interviews, we used alternative interview schedules based on the status of the candidates and the outcome of the race.

Gender Differences in the Substance of Campaigns

Women's personal experiences, as well as their recognition of common sex stereotypes, may encourage women candidates to emphasize different themes than their male colleagues. Since women need to overcome damaging expectations regarding their competence, we expect women candidates to emphasize their issue priorities in their campaigns instead of focusing on their personal characteristics. By demonstrating their competence in various policy areas, women will try to dispel voters' concerns about their ability.

The Main Focus on Issues or Personalities

When campaign managers were asked to identify the main themes of their campaign, the managers of women's campaigns were significantly more likely than managers of male candidates to mention issues. For women's campaigns, 78 percent of the themes mentioned were concerned with policy matters, while 22 percent focused on personal traits. Campaigns for male candidates, in contrast, stressed issues only 61 percent of the time, while touching on traits 39 percent of the time. This greater emphasis on issues for women candidates is substantively large and statistically significant.

Furthermore, women's preference for issue themes is not explained by differences in the status or party of the candidates, nor differences in the competitiveness of the contest. As an illustration, among Democrats, issues make up 82 percent of the major themes of women's campaigns, while comprising only 61 percent of the major themes of male campaigns ($p < .05$). Similarly, in the most competitive contests, the managers of women's campaigns focus on issues 80 percent of the time, while the managers of male campaigns discuss issues less than two-thirds (65 percent) of the time ($p < .05$). Finally, among nonincumbents, women mention issues eight out of ten times, while men concentrate on these themes only three-quarters of the time.

Although women are more likely to make issues a major focus of their electoral bids, the campaign managers of men and women are equally likely to view the news media as unresponsive to the candidate's preferred agenda. Campaign managers of both men and women candidates see the news media as focusing less heavily on policy matters when compared to the candidate's own emphasis. Campaign managers for women candidates say the news media discuss issues less than two-thirds (63 percent) of the time, while the candidates focus on issues more than 80 percent of the time. For male candidates, campaign managers view the media as discussing the candidate's issue concerns less than half of the time (46 percent), while the candidate's own campaign focuses on issues more than 60 percent of the time. Campaigns for both male and female candidates see a 15 percent gap between the types of themes the campaign is issuing and the sorts of messages presented by the news media.

Type of Issues Emphasized

In addition to focusing more attention on policy matters in their campaigns, women are expected to discuss different types of issues when compared to their male colleagues. As discussed earlier, women's unique experiences at home and in the workplace, as well as their recognition or adherence to sex stereotypes, may lead women candidates to spend more time on issues like education, health reform, and child care. We expect male candidates to focus less extensively on these policy areas and to discuss issues which have traditionally topped the agenda in Senate races: economics and foreign policy (Kahn 1991a; Tidmarch, Hyman, and Sorkin 1984).

The data presented in Table 3.1 support our hypothesis. Campaign managers for women candidates consistently focus on "female" issues more frequently than the campaign managers of male candidates. These differences are robust and complement prior research examining the political advertisements of male and female senate candidates (Kahn 1993). The greater preference for "female" issues among women candidates persists when we control for the status of the candidates. For example, among candidates competing in open races, women are almost twice as likely as men to mention "female" issues as topics emphasized in their campaigns. Finally, the difference in the policy agendas of male and female candidates is not a reflection of partisan differences. Republican women talk about "female" issues almost half the time, while their male counterparts discuss these issues less than one-third of the time. Among Democrats, "female" issues account for almost two-thirds of women's issue themes, while comprising less than half of policy themes of male candidates.

These gender differences in campaign agendas may reflect authentic differences in the policy priorities of men and women candidates. Research examining the political attitudes of women candidates, officeholders, and voters suggests that men and women differ in their policy priorities (Carroll, Dodson, and Mandel 1992; Kathlene, Clarke, and Fox 1991; Poole and Zeigler 1985; Thomas 1991).

Men and women candidates may also target distinct policy areas for more strategic reasons. Since voters' priorities about issues are not stagnant (see Iyengar and Kinder 1987, for instance), candidates may try to manipulate these priorities during their campaigns. Women can capitalize on common stereotypes by emphasizing issues where voters believe they are more competent (environment, drugs, health, education, welfare, child care, civil rights), while male candidates may focus on their stereotypical strengths (foreign policy, defense, budget, taxes, farm policy). By stressing their perceived strengths in their political campaigns, candidates can make these issues more salient to voters, thereby increasing positive impressions of their candidacies.

While women and men clearly pursue different types of policy initiatives in their campaigns, the candidates do not believe the news media reflect their desired emphasis. When asked to identify the news media's

Table 3.1
Issue Agendas of U.S. Senate Candidates by Gender

	Percentage "Male" Issues[a]	*Percentage "Female" Issues*[a]	*N*[b]	*P-Value*[c]
All candidates				
Women candidates	39	61	(17;43)	$p < .05$
Men candidates	63	37	(130;307)	
Challengers				
Women candidates	39	61	(12;28)	$p < .05$
Men candidates	63	37	(47;121)	
Open race candidates				
Women candidates	38	62	(4;13)	$p < .05$
Men candidates	68	32	(25;65)	
Republicans				
Women candidates	55	45	(7;13)	n.s.
Men candidates	73	27	(68;172)	
Democrats				
Women candidates	35	65	(10;30)	$p < .05$
Men candidates	51	49	(62;135)	
Competitive races				
Women candidates	33	67	(4;12)	$p < .10$
Men candidates	56	44	(33;84)	
Somewhat competitive races				
Women candidates	33	67	(7;18)	$p < .05$
Men candidates	69	31	(48;121)	
Noncompetitive races				
Women candidates	53	46	(6;13)	n.s.
Men candidates	63	37	(49;102)	

[a]"Male" issues include foreign policy, defense spending, foreign trade, economic issues, and farm issues. "Female" issues include day care, welfare, education, health care, drugs, and the environment.
[b]Entries are the number of candidates followed by the number of issue mentions.
[c]The p-value is the difference in the proportions test.

coverage of issues during the campaign, campaign managers for women candidates saw the press as focusing on "female" issues only 40 percent of the time, while the managers said they focused on these types of issues 61 percent of the time. The campaign managers of male candidates also perceived an imbalance between the focus of news coverage and their own focus; however, the perceived imbalance was less striking for male candidates. The managers for male candidates mentioned "male" issues 63 percent of the time and they saw the news media focusing on these issues 51 percent of the time.

Ideology

Men and women not only present different policy agendas in their campaigns, they also have different ideological positions. To measure ideology, we asked the campaign managers to identify their candidate's position on a liberal–conservative seven-point scale (1 = very liberal to 7 = very conservative). Like prior work documenting greater liberalism among women candidates and officeholders (Poole and Zeigler 1985; Darcy, Welch, and Clark 1994), we find that women candidates are more liberal than male candidates. As the data in Table 3.2 show, female Republicans and female Democrats are significantly more liberal than their male counterparts. For example, Republican campaign managers rate their female clients, on average, as moderate (4.14), while Republican male candidates are considered somewhat conservative (5.11).

Gender differences in ideological placement persist when we control for potentially confounding variables like the status of the candidate, the candidate's political experience, and the competitiveness of the race. The results of the regression analysis, also presented in Table 3.2, show that while party is the most powerful predictor of the candidate's ideology, the gender of the candidate is substantively and statistically significant. Women, on average, are one point more liberal than their male counterparts.

Emphasis on Personal Traits

When candidates campaign for political office, they do not restrict their rhetoric to policy matters. Although campaign managers say they spend most of their time focusing on issues, managers nevertheless recognize the importance of trait discussion. According to the campaign managers surveyed, candidates often try to demonstrate their possession of desirable personality traits during their campaigns for the U.S. Senate.

While stereotypes about men and women lead people to view women candidates more favorably along certain trait dimensions (such as compassion, integrity), we believe that women candidates will ignore these stereotypical advantages and try to revise damaging stereotypes about their competence. Since people weigh assessments of a candidate's competence more heavily than other trait dimensions when developing overall impressions of the candidate (Huddy 1994; Huddy and Terkildsen 1993b; Kinder 1983; Markus 1982; Miller, Wattenberg, and Malanchuk 1986; Rosenwasser and Dean 1989), it makes sense for women candidates to try to assuage people's apprehension about their competence by demonstrating their experience and leadership in their campaigns.

Table 3.2
Ideological Positions of U.S. Senate Candidates by Gender[a]

A. Average Ideological Position

Republicans	
Women candidates	4.14 ($n = 7$)
Men candidates	5.11 ($n = 66$)
	F-Statistic = 5.12, $p < .05$ (one-tailed test)
Democrats	
Women candidates	2.70 ($n = 10$)
Men candidates	3.36 ($n = 67$)
	F-Statistic = 2.47, $p < .10$ (one-tailed test)

B. OLS Regression Predicting Candidate's Ideological Position[b]

	Unstandardized Coefficient	*(Standard Error)*
Gender of candidate	−.99	(.35)*
Experience of candidate	−.05	(.05)
Status	−.61	(.89)
Party	−1.74	(.27)*
Competitiveness	−.01	(.01)

$R^2 = .44$
Adjusted $R^2 = .40$ $N = 86$
*$p < .01$

[a]Ideological positions are based on a seven-point scale ranging from 1 = very liberal to 7 = very conservative.

[b]Gender of the candidate is coded 1 = female and 0 = male. Experience of the candidate is coded from 1 = no prior political experience, 2 = celebrities with no prior experience, 3 = local officeholders and appointive officeholders, 4 = state legislators, 5 = state legislative leaders, 6 = mayors of major cities, 7 = first term House members or statewide officials, 8 = House members or statewide officials who have served more than one term, 9 = governor. Incumbent is coded 1 = incumbent, 0 = non-incumbent. Party is coded 1 = Democrat, 0 = Republican. Competitiveness of the race is measured by the last poll conducted in the state. This variable ranges from 0 (i.e., no difference in support for two candidates) to 72 (i.e., 72 points separating two candidates).

Given Kahn's (1993) finding that women Senate candidates are significantly more likely than male candidates to highlight their competence in their political advertisements, we expected to find similar gender differences in the candidates' trait appeals. However, the data presented in Table 3.3 show that men and women are equally likely to focus on their competence in their campaigns. According to their managers, male and female candidates spend most of their time documenting their competence by discussing their experience, expertise, and leadership ability. Incumbents obviously have an easier time highlighting their competence because they can talk about their experience in the U.S. Senate, their important committee assignments, their service to their constituents, and their seniority. Nonincumbents try to compensate by showing how their background or career provides them with important and unique insights (for example, a medical doctor's experience may be helpful in developing ways of reforming health care, a successful entrepreneur may have useful insights for improving international trade relationships). These two categories—competence and career—make up more than half of all trait mentions for male and female candidates. Both men and women candidates spend considerably less time talking about women's perceived strengths: honesty and compassion.

Overall, these results suggest that men and women choose to talk about the same sorts of personal characteristics in their campaigns, while differing markedly in their choice of policy. While men and women both focus almost exclusively on their experience in their campaigns, women are more likely than their male colleagues to make issues a major focus of their campaign, they are more likely to talk about "female" issues, and they are more liberal than male candidates.

Finally, we examined whether the gender of the manager influences the substance of the campaign message. In our study, 77 percent ($N =$ 106) of the managers are men and 23 percent ($N = 31$) are women. Overall, male and female campaign managers do not differ significantly in their campaign emphasis. For example, male and female managers offer similar assessments of their candidate's ideology. Furthermore, the gender of the candidate and the gender of the manager do not interact to produce

Table 3.3
Trait Discussions of U.S. Senate Candidates by Gender

	Women Candidates[a] *(Percentage)*	*Men Candidates* *(Percentage)*
Experience[b]	40	38
Honesty	13	15
Compassion	0	2
Career	27	23
Personality	7	9
Ties to state	13	12
	(13;15)[c]	(118;210)[c]

[a]None of the gender differences in trait discussion reach conventional levels of statistical significance ($p <$ .10). We relied on the difference in proportions test to calculate statistical significance.

[b]The experience category includes mentions of the candidate's experience, constituent service, competence, knowledge, intelligence, effectiveness, leadership, seniority, committee assignments, and independence. Honesty includes mentions of the candidate's honesty, integrity, and trustworthiness. Compassion includes mentions of candidate's compassion and empathy. Career includes any mention of candidate's career, job, background, war record, and special life experience. Personality includes mention of candidate's personality, such as candidate is popular, candidate is "a nice guy." Ties to state includes mentions of candidate's roots in the state.

[c]Entries are the number of campaign managers followed by the number of responses given.

differences in judgments of the candidate's ideological position. As an illustration, women with women managers are not viewed as more liberal (or less liberal) than women with male managers.

We discovered one instance where the gender of the manager was related to the campaign content: women candidates with women managers emphasize "female" issues significantly more often than women candidates with male managers. The gender of the manager is not as important for male candidates: male candidates emphasize the same proportion of "female" issues, regardless of the gender of the manager. The importance of the manager's gender for the issue orientation of women's campaign is intriguing. However, given the limited number of women managers in our study, our findings are only suggestive.

Gender Differences in Campaign Strategy

We believe that some of the same factors that produce gender differences in the campaign messages of men and women Senate candidates will encourage men and women to adopt different campaign strategies. In addition, women's relative lack of experience could influence their ability to campaign. The women candidates in our study have significantly less experience than the male candidates. First, only one woman in our study was an incumbent, while fifty-eight of the men were incumbents. In addition, when we examine the political experience of nonincumbents with ordinary least squared regression, we find that women are less experienced than men.

Negative Campaigning

People's stereotypes about "proper female behavior" may lead women candidates to refrain from negative appeals, since such tactics may be viewed unfavorably by voters. When asked to identify the major themes of their campaign, campaign managers rarely identify negative messages. However, the managers of women candidates are slightly less likely to mention negative themes as compared to male candidates. Overall, only 7 percent of the themes mentioned by managers of women candidates are negative, while 11 percent of the male candidates' themes are negative.

The tendency of women candidates to limit negative appeals, while not dramatic, holds for all types of candidates (that is, for challengers, open race candidates, Democrats, Republicans, candidates running in competitive, somewhat competitive, and noncompetitive races). For example, in the most competitive contests, women candidates completely refrain from negative appeals, offering no negative messages, while 11 percent of the themes mentioned by competitive male candidates are negative ($p < .01$). Furthermore, gender differences in negative messages are most dramatic among challengers, the category which includes the vast majority of women candidates. For example, only 5 percent of the themes presented by women challengers are negative, while male challengers present four times (21 percent) as many negative themes ($p < .01$). These results indicate that women may be adjusting their strategy in response to citizens' stereotypes about preferred feminine behavior. Given recent experimental work (Ansolabehere and Iyengar 1991; see chapter 4) the preference for positive themes by women candidates is likely to produce more favorable electoral dividends than the launching of an aggressive attack strategy.

Assessment of News Coverage

We stated earlier that women may be less likely than male candidates to describe press coverage of their campaigns in positive terms. Many successful and unsuccessful women candidates have complained publicly about the press' preference for style over substance (Trent and Friedenberg 1991, 136). Similarly, Witt, Paget, and Matthews (1994) note the use of stereotypes by the prestige press in 1992. Lynn Yeakel of Pennsylvania was described by a *Washington Post* reporter as a "feisty and feminine fifty-year old with the unmistakable Dorothy Hamill wedge of gray hair . . . a congressman's daughter [with] a wardrobe befitting a First Lady . . ." (p. 181). The *New York Times* called Carol Moseley-Braun of Illinois ". . . a den mother with a cheerleader's smile" (p. 181).

In addition to anecdotal evidence, a systematic analysis of news coverage of U.S. Senate campaigns between 1982 and 1986 demonstrated that the press does cover women candidates less favorably than male candidates; this research showed that the news media spend less time talking about issues and more time talking about the viability of women candidates (Kahn 1994a). Furthermore, reporters were less responsive to the issue and trait agendas of women candidates when compared to their male colleagues.

While our earlier analysis comparing the candidates' preferred issue agenda with their perception of the media's agenda suggested that women's campaigns viewed the news media less favorably than the campaigns of male candidates, a more direct assessment of press coverage fails to find significant gender differences. Specifically, when campaign managers are asked to rate news coverage of their campaign from favorable(1) to unfavorable(3), the campaign managers for women candidates did not give the press a more negative rating (1.94) than other campaign managers (1.89). We also performed a regression analysis to see if gender is related to assessments of the news media when we include measures of the candidate's party, experience, status, and the competitiveness of the race. The multivariate analysis confirms the bivariate results: gender of the candidate is not related to judgments about the nature of campaign coverage. For a detailed discussion on how women in Congress are treated by the press, see Carroll and Schreiber (1996).

Assessment of Candidate's Ability and Campaign Techniques

We asked campaign managers to evaluate their candidate's effectiveness as a campaigner as well as their assessments of two common campaign techniques: television political advertising and personal contact. First, when we asked campaign managers to rate their candidate on a four-point scale ranging from very effective (1) to very ineffective (4), we failed to find any significant gender differences in the managers' assessments. Women receive an average score of 1.41 on the four-point scale, while men receive an average score of 1.25. Second, we developed a more indirect measure of campaign ability by asking managers to assess the campaign themes of their opponents. Again, the campaigns of women candidates are as effective as the campaigns of male candidates: the managers of women's campaigns correctly perceived 23 percent of their opponent's themes, while the campaigns of male candidates were correct 30 percent of the time.

Third, almost all campaign managers, regardless of the gender of their candidate, view televised political advertisements as extremely effective. The managers of male candidates gave a mean response of 1.25 on a four-point scale, while the managers of women's campaigns gave an average rating of 1.41. Finally, the campaigns of men and women candidates view personal contact as equally effective, with male campaigns giving an average score of 1.6 on the four-point scale and women's campaigns offering a mean score of 1.5.

Overall, the results of our survey show that campaign managers do not believe that men and women differ in their abilities as campaigners. Furthermore, their campaigns offer similar assessments of the news media's treatment of their campaign and are equally likely to consider political ads and personal contact as effective campaign techniques. With regard to strategy, we identified only one gender difference: women candidates are more likely to avoid negative campaigning. The managers of women's campaigns consistently emphasized negative themes less often than the managers of male candidates.

Conclusions and Implications

In races for the U.S. Senate, men and women present alternative agendas to voters, but they deliver these distinct messages in a remarkably similar fashion. Women are more likely than men to make issues a cornerstone of their campaign, they are more likely to focus on social issues, and their ideological perspective is more liberal than their male colleagues. However, the campaign managers view men and women as equally adept campaigners, as equally likely to receive favorable press coverage, and their assessments of various campaign techniques are virtually indistinguishable.

These results suggest that differences in the electability of men and women candidates are not due to differences in the campaign abilities of the candidates. Instead, the success of women candidates may depend more heavily on the alternative agenda articulated by women candidates. During times of economic turmoil and international uncertainty (such as, during the early 1980s), social issues like education, welfare, and health are less likely to resonate with the news media and voters. In contrast, during periods of economic prosperity and international peace (such as 1988), women's messages may be represented more faithfully by the news media and embraced more heartily by voters. Given the importance of the campaign context, women candidates may be well advised to consider public priorities when choosing among campaign themes.

Since women candidates emphasize different policy areas than their male counterparts, by electing more women to the U.S. Senate, the range of issues considered by Congress is likely to increase. For instance, by increasing the number of women Senators, we may increase the probability of passing significant legislation dealing with issues like health care, protection from sexual harassment, and the institution of adequate family leave policies. In addition to differences in policy priorities, men's and women's traditional roles in society could influence how women govern. Women's experience as mothers, for example, may produce women's greater sense of connection with others, their empathy, and their less decisive individuation (see Okin 1990). These qualities could lead women to adopt governing styles that are more cooperative, democratic, and inclusive than the governing styles employed by their male colleagues.

In future research, scholars should examine whether women and men differ in how they govern once elected. While some work has explored this question (for example, Thomas 1994b), given the previous paucity of women Senators, this issue has not been studied for this level of office. For example, in the U.S. Senate, do the different themes women emphasize in their campaigns become the subject of legislation? Similarly, how successful are women in putting forth an alternative agenda? Finally, do women receive the same type of press coverage as their male counterparts and does press treatment influence their ability to legislate?

While much research remains for scholars, Senator Patty Murray believes women have had an impact in the U.S. Senate. She told reporters, "There is absolutely no doubt in my mind that woman have dramatically changed both the agenda and the debate in the U.S. Senate. Women think about the world differently than men" (Westneat 1993, C8). Similarly, Senator Barbara Boxer (1994) observed, "The five Democratic women Senators taken together have already changed the center of gravity in the Democratic caucus and the Senate as a whole. The greatest impact has come, I believe, from presenting a different perspective—from putting a more sensitive, human-oriented focus on the real problems facing individuals, families, and our country" (Boxer 1994, 234). As Boxer predicted at the 1992 Democratic National Convention, women candidates have "cracked open the closed doors of the United States Senate."

Notes

1. The women candidates included in the study are Maria Hustice of Hawaii (1988), Jane Brady of Delaware (1990), Josie Heath of Colorado (1990), Kathy Helling of Wyoming (1990), Senator Nancy Kassebaum of Kansas (1990), Patricia Saiki of Hawaii (1990), Claudine Schneider of Rhode Island (1990), Christine Whitman of New Jersey (1990), Barbara Boxer of California (1992), Carol Moseley-Braun of Illinois (1992), Dianne Feinstein of California (1992), Charlene Haar of South Dakota (1992), Jean Lloyd-Jones of Iowa (1992), Patty Murray of Washington (1992), Gloria O'Dell of Kansas (1992), Claire Sargent of Arizona (1992), and Lynn Yeakel of Pennsylvania (1992).

4

Running as a Woman: Gender Stereotyping in Political Campaigns

Shanto Iyengar, Nicholas A. Valentino, Stephen Ansolabehere, and Adam F. Simon

Elective office in the United States is a male bastion. For decades, fewer than 10 percent of United States Senators, Representatives, and state governors have been female. The 1992 elections appeared to mark a turning point: following the dramatic Senate confirmation hearings of Justice Clarence Thomas, large numbers of women declared their candidacies, resulting in a campaign environment dubbed "The Year of the Woman." This new political activism resulted in a significant increase in the number of women elected to the United States House of Representatives and Senate. The female head-count increased to 7 percent in the U.S. Senate and 18 percent in the House of Representatives (Wilcox 1994).

The 1992 elections stimulated considerable interest—academic and journalistic—in the question of whether women and men candidates face any special advantages or disadvantages among voters. While there are undoubtedly many universal factors at work in electoral success, including financial capability and the caliber of the opposing candidate (see Burrell 1994, 1995; Jacobson and Kernell 1983), this chapter focuses on how gender stereotypes influence voters.

As Kahn and Gordon discussed in the previous chapter, there is an extensive and well-developed body of evidence that voters see candidates through the pervasive lens of gender stereotypes. American voters (both male and female) tend to see women as relatively liberal on a variety of issues (Sapiro 1981–82). Psychological evidence suggests that people view women as more compassionate and emotional than men (Ashmore and DelBoca 1979). These stereotypes may provide a signal to voters of a candidate's presumed policy preferences and effectiveness (Huddy and Terkildson 1993b). These stereotypes may have significant political implications both during campaigns and once women are elected. Williams (1994) demonstrates that women Senate candidates in 1992 used many of the same advertising techniques as males, but were more likely to emphasize "feminine" traits like compassion and empathy in their advertising appeals. [In the previous chapter,] Kahn and Gordon also discovered significant differences in issue foci: women candidates are more likely to emphasize social issues and tend to be liberal in their ideological approach. Finally, some evidence suggests that these differences do not disappear once a women takes office. Thomas (1994a) finds that women in state legislatures are more likely to focus on legislative activity in areas of particular interest to women, like child care and comparable worth.

How gender stereotypes affect men's and women's electoral fortunes depends upon the larger campaign context. National events may stimulate interest in issues which benefit female candidates. The Clarence Thomas Senate confirmation hearings of October 1991 focused attention on sexual harassment, an issue on which female candidates are likely to appear more credible and effective than males. On the other hand, an election focused on issues of tougher sentencing for criminals and national security could benefit male candidates. In addition, the level of office sought by candidates should moderate the use of group stereotypes. McDermott (forthcoming) has noted that in races with little other information about the contestants, like most subpresidential contests during the primary season, stereotypes play an important role in evaluating candidates.

This chapter focuses on the importance of gender stereotypes in influencing the ability of women and men candidates to win elections. We show that candidates have significant opportunities to capitalize on gender stereotypes during election campaigns. Women who campaign on stereotypically "female" issues, like education, and men who campaign on stereotypically "male" issues, like crime, will enjoy significant electoral advantages. In short, candidates are best advised to play on their "own" turf. These conclusions are based on two field experiments carried out during the 1992 California senatorial elections and the 1994 California gubernatorial campaign, both of which pitted a woman against a man. The experimental evidence demonstrates that women candidates were strengthened when their campaigns were organized around the issues of women's rights, unemployment, and education, and weakened when they addressed crime and illegal immigration.

The Resonance Model of Campaigns

Our analysis of female candidates' campaigns rests on a view of campaigns as constantly evolving and interactive information environments. Candidates select a particular set of issues or themes on which to campaign. They then strive, either through the use of paid or free messages, to focus voters' attention on these particular issues. The premise of the resonance model is that campaign communication is most persuasive when it plays upon—or interacts with—voters' prior predispositions. A woman candidate who enjoys presumed competence on a particular issue should initiate significant advertising addressing this issue. Her opponent is then left with a choice between changing the subject and bringing forward some alternative issue on which the opponent is not at a disadvantage, or becoming engaged in a dialogue on the female candidate's issue.

In the context of American politics, partisanship is the most essential of voters' prior predispositions. Most Americans acquire a sense of party loyalty at an early age, and this psychological anchor remains with them over the entire life cycle (Jennings and Niemi 1981; Sears 1983). The importance of voters' partisan predispositions goes beyond the mere fact that self-identified Democrats are more likely to vote Democratic and self-identified Republicans are more likely to vote Republican. Voters are also socialized to expect stable differences between the political parties and the candidates who run as Democrats or Republicans. Democratic candidates, for instance, are considered responsive to the interests of the working person and racial minorities, while Republican candidates are expected to exhibit a strong sense of fiscal responsibility, opposition to big government, and a tough posture on crime (Baumer and Gold 1995; Petrocik 1996; Ansolabehere and Iyengar 1994).

Culturally ingrained expectations about the strengths and weaknesses of candidates serve as important filters for interpreting and understanding campaign communication. The typical voter lacks the motivation to acquire even the most elementary level of factual knowledge about the candidates and campaign issues (Popkin 1991; Buchanan 1991). In low information environments, expectations based on visible cues—including a candidate's gender—take on special importance (McDermott 1995). Messages that confirm rather than cut against these expectations are more likely to be noticed, assimilated, and retained. Campaigns that resonate with or reinforce voters' expectations are thus more likely to be effective. A Democrat should be better off using advertisements that emphasize his or her intent to reduce unemployment, while a Republican should promote his or her support for a balanced budget. In general, the resonance model suggests that political campaigns should be fitted to the candidate's distinctive attributes and what voters might expect based on these attributes. Defense and military issues will be especially persuasive as campaign material when the candidate is a male war hero; sexual harassment, child care, and matters of educational policy will resonate well with voters' beliefs about a female candidate.

Identifying issues as more or less gender-relevant is, by nature, imprecise. Some issues, such as sexual harassment or child care, convey *manifest* gender cues. In races contested by women and men, these cues are likely to be the dominant bases for evaluating the candidates. Other issues, such as unemployment, crime, or education, provide only *latent* connections to gender. People need to infer that women, because they are assumed to be compassionate, are less responsive on stronger criminal sentencing and more so on education (Huddy and Terkildsen 1993b). On these issues, gender competes on a more even footing with alternative characteristics such as the candidates's age, ethnicity, or occupation. Thus a dichotomous categorization can be defined. In this paper we compare the effectiveness of manifest vs. latent gender issues in advertisements by female and male candidates. If voters link message content with a candidate's gender to inform their vote choices, then we expect support for candidates to be highest when they emphasize issues which resonate with gender stereotypes.

We designed two studies to test the predictions of the resonance model as it applies to advertising on the issues by women candidates. In Study 1, we examined the success of U.S. senatorial candidates Barbara Boxer and Dianne Feinstein when they broadcast a campaign advertisement that dealt with either crime, unemployment, or issues of particular relevance to gender. We found that campaign advertising on gender-related issues was optimal for Boxer and Feinstein. Conversely, they gained little by advertising on crime. Study 2 moved beyond the examination of a woman candidate's advertising to focus on the campaign "dialogue" between the advertisements of gubernatorial candidates Kathleen Brown and Pete Wilson. Here the results indicated that Brown fared best when both candidates converged on the issues of education or unemployment. When the campaign agenda swung toward crime and immigration, however (as they did over the course of this campaign), Brown's prospects were doomed.

Research Design

We rely on experimental methods to assess the effects of campaign advertising. The advantages and disadvantages of experimentation are well known. Unlike surveys, experiments yield precise causal inferences. Because the researcher manipulates the phenomenon under investigation, he or she knows that the experimental participants either were or were not exposed to it. In the case of campaign advertising, an "experimental" group is given a particular ad, and a "control" group is not given the ad. Because participants are assigned to the two conditions on a purely random basis, the researcher can be confident that the conditions will be no different from each other in composition. These two basic features of the experiment—the ability to exercise physical control over the experimental stimulus and the use of comparison groups that are equivalent in all respects but the presence of the experimental stimulus—provide researchers with the all-important ability to attribute any observed difference between the experimental and control groups to the effects of the experimental stimulus.

This paper involves two types of experiments which address different aspects of campaign communication effects. The first type focused on a single advertising message from a female candidate, while the second pitted a female candidate message against a male candidate message. The objective of our one-ad design was to assess the effects of a single attribute of campaign advertisements. In our first study, for instance, we used the one-ad design to manipulate the gender of the candidate sponsoring the advertisement. In one of our studies, for example, we produced an advertisement on the subject of crime. Against the backdrop of burned and looted stores, the announcer described the sponsor's commitment to battle urban crime.

> April 29, 1992. Los Angeles burns. Three days of riots leave 58 dead, 2,400 injured, 17,000 arrested. Gangs and lawlessness have ruled our cities for too long. As a U.S. Senator, ________ will fight for additional police protection, tougher sentencing, and the strengthening of our criminal justice system.

This very same advertisement was presented on behalf of Senate candidates Barbara Boxer and Dianne Feinstein, and their opponents Bruce Herschensohn and John Seymour. Because the advertisements were replicas of each other (with the exception of the name and party of the sponsoring candidate), any differences in the effectiveness of the advertisement can be attributed only to the attributes of the sponsor.

In addition to crime, we also used the one-ad design to examine the relative effectiveness of messages dealing with unemployment and women's issues. Thus, the identical advertisement on unemployment or sexual harassment was aired on behalf of several different candidates including males and females.

The two-ad design (which was used in our second experiment) expanded the scope of the manipulation to include two advertisements, one from each of the candidates. Within this "paired" arrangement, we varied the issue agenda of the campaign. Thus, the spots addressed particular issues which, once again, were more or less stereotypically "masculine" or "feminine" in nature. Gubernatorial candidates Kathleen Brown and Pete Wilson each advertised on crime or immigration (male issues) or on unemployment or education (female issues). Participants were thus exposed to campaign advertising that centered on either male or female issues, or advertisements that switched from male-oriented to female-oriented issues.

1992 California Senate General Elections

Due to a variety of unusual circumstances, both of California's U.S. Senate seats were contested in 1992. The race for the "short" seat (to fill the two years remaining on Pete Wilson's term) was between the former mayor of San Francisco Dianne Feinstein and Pete Wilson's appointed successor, Senator John Seymour (formerly a state legislator from Orange County). The race was one-sided from the outset; Feinstein, who benefited from having lost a close gubernatorial election to Pete Wilson in 1990, established a commanding lead that proved immune to Seymour's campaign efforts. She won election easily with 54 percent of the vote.

The race for the "long" seat pitted Marin County Democratic Congresswoman Barbara Boxer against Bruce Herschensohn, a staunchly conservative southern California broadcaster. Boxer enjoyed a wide lead in the polls when the race began. Herschensohn went on the attack immediately, pointing out that Boxer had "bounced" several checks at the House bank and that she epitomized a corrupt Washington establishment. This barrage of attacks reduced the Boxer lead significantly, and by mid-October the race had tightened. The Boxer campaign retaliated with its own attack advertisements, and Barbara Boxer eventually won by a narrow (4 percent) margin.

In both Senate races, the lingering economic recession was the dominant campaign issue. Boxer and Feinstein both championed additional federal support for job retraining programs and federal subsidies for "conversion" of defense-related installations. In the aftermath of the Los Angeles riots, the Senate candidates also addressed issues of crime and urban disorder. Of course, the presence of two women candidates and the lingering controversy over the hearings to confirm Justice Thomas made gender-related issues such as sexual harassment and abortion rights especially relevant. Both women candidates' advertisements made frequent reference to the Hill–Thomas hearings and their opponents' opposition to a woman's right to choose.

The 1994 California Gubernatorial Election

Kathleen Brown, the state treasurer, emerged as the Democratic nominee for governor. On the Republican side, incumbent Pete Wilson easily won renomination, turning back a conservative challenge in the primaries. Given the state's continued precarious economic condition, Brown campaigned aggressively on the issue of unemployment and economic mismanagement by the incumbent. She also attempted to hold Wilson accountable for the declining quality of the state's public schools. Wilson's campaign was centered around the emerging issue of illegal immigration. The governor highlighted his support for the controversial (and widely publicized) Proposition 187, which would cut off all forms of state social welfare and public health assistance to illegal immigrants. Wilson also reminded voters of his steadfast support for tough anticrime legislation including the "three strikes and you're out" measure.

Brown's campaign was plagued by frequent organizational conflicts and turnover. Following her hard-fought primary victory over John Garamendi, she dismissed her campaign manager and key advisors and hired Clinton Reilly, a consultant with limited experience in running statewide campaigns. Reilly's strategic planning proved disastrous; the Brown campaign ran out of campaign funds and was unable to purchase advertising time during the crucial last days of the campaign. Governor Wilson was reelected handily by a margin of 55 percent to 41 percent.

The Experimental Advertisements

During the dual 1992 Senate races, we created advertisements dealing with crime, unemployment, or sexual harassment and aired them on behalf of the different candidates contesting the Senate races. The condition of the state's economy and the significant loss of jobs (unemployment had reached 10 percent in September) was the overriding issue in both Senate races. Our experimental advertisement on unemployment, aired on behalf of all four candidates, took the following form.

> Since 1990, California has lost 2.5 million jobs. The state now has the highest unemployment rate in the nation. California needs elected officials who will end the recession. ______ will work to bring jobs back to our state. As a U.S. Senator, ____ will introduce legislation to increase government funding for job training programs and to provide California companies with incentives to modernize and expand their factories and plants.
>
> California needs ______ in the U. S. Senate.

In addition to the state's precarious economy, the Los Angeles riots propelled issues of "law and order" into the spotlight. Our experimental advertisement (described earlier) replayed the devastation caused by the riots and called for tougher law enforcement and sentencing of offenders.

Finally, the presence of two women candidates and the widespread interest in Senate hearings to confirm Judge Clarence Thomas made sexual harassment a potent issue in 1992. Our advertisement on the subject featured scenes from the Senate confirmation hearings and described the commitment of the sponsor to gender equality.

> The Senate Judiciary Committee. Professor Anita Hill testifies that she was repeatedly subjected to sexual harassment by Clarence Thomas. The Senators reject Hill's testimony; some even question her sanity. ________ believes that sexual harassment is a real problem and it is time to stand up for the rights of women. ⟨Candidate's sound bite.⟩ Elect ________ U.S. Senator.

In the 1994 gubernatorial campaign, our experimental manipulations relied on advertisements that were actually aired by candidates Pete Wilson and Kathleen Brown. These advertisements addressed unemployment, education, crime, and illegal immigration. The Brown advertisement on the economy highlighted California's massive job losses and Governor Wilson's inability to stem the exodus of companies from the state. Wilson countered with an advertisement describing his successes in cutting red tape and providing tax incentives for industry. On the subject of education, Brown used an advertisement that pointed to the declining quality of the public schools and the candidate's efforts to develop "high tech" classrooms. For his part, Wilson pledged to preserve state funding for the public schools.

Crime and illegal immigration were the mainstays of the Wilson advertising campaign. Wilson's advertisements on crime highlighted his backing of "one strike" legislation for major crimes and his opponent's opposition to the death penalty. Brown joined the debate on crime by decrying the rise in youth crime and violence in the schools and calling for "boot camps" to deal with juvenile offenders. Finally, our study utilized a pair of Wilson advertisements dealing with immigration and the governor's consistent support for measures that would deny state services to illegal aliens.

Data and Results

We conducted three separate experiments during the 1992 senatorial campaigns in which the experimental manipulation was a single campaign advertisement bearing either on crime, unemployment, or sexual harassment. We pooled the three studies (which were administered between late August and early October) to compare the effects of the differing issue environments on candidate preference. After pooling, the total sample size was 1,070 respondents.

Voter Choice. The analyses utilized three indicators of candidate preference to gauge the effects of campaign messages. The most telling indicator, of course, is the respondent's intended vote choice following exposure to a campaign advertisement. In all cases the vote choice variable was keyed to the candidate sponsoring the advertisement. That is, respondents who viewed a Boxer or Herschensohn advertisement reported their preference between these candidates, while those in the Feinstein/Seymour conditions chose appropriately. For respondents assigned to the control or baseline conditions (in which there was no campaign advertisement), the vote choice indicator was defined as the average margin by which the female (Democratic) candidate was favored in the two Senate races. As a result, the effect of the experimental manipulation measures the difference between the lead of either Democratic female candidate and the average lead of both female candidates in the absence of campaign advertising.

Trait Rating. The second indicator of candidate preference was a summary trait rating scale. In each study, respondents were asked to rate how well various words described the candidates on a scale that ranged from "extremely well" to "not at all well." Favorable responses (for example, claiming that the term "hardworking" described a candidate "extremely well") were coded as +2, while the most negative responses ("not at all well") were scored as −2. Responses in between were either scored +1 or −1 and those with no opinion were coded 0. For negatively valenced terms such as "devious" or "arrogant," the scoring was reversed. Thus the final trait rating scale ran from −2 to +2 points.

In order to make the trait rating indicator a measure of comparative preference, the trait ratings for the Republican candidate in each Senate race were subtracted from the ratings of the Democrat. This "net trait rating" variable was also keyed to the race in question so that it consisted of the Boxer–Herschensohn or Feinstein–Seymour score depending upon the condition to which participants were assigned. Once again, the net trait rating was defined as the average "lead" of the female candidate in the two races among participants in the control conditions.

Affective Likes. Our third and final indicator was based on open-ended responses to the question, "Please tell us what you most like or dislike about each of the candidates listed below." As in the case of the net trait rating, we subtracted negative comments about a particular candidate from positive comments about that candidate. The Republican candidate's net score was then subtracted from his opponent's net score. In the control condition, the net likes score was defined as the average preponderance of positive over negative comments for both the female candidates.

Effects of a Campaign Agenda Focused on Women's Issues

We began the analysis by testing the hypothesis that the gross issue content of campaigns influences support for female candidates. Does campaign communication that addresses particular issues lead to greater support for women candidates regardless of the source or form of the information? If particular issues play into the hands of women, then news reports or advertisements by *any* candidate about these issues should boost the prospects of women candidates.

Figure 4.1 presents the results of this test. Respondents were classified into particular issue groups based on their exposure to news coverage or advertising on the "target" issue (as indicated at the bottom of each panel). The control group was composed of respondents who watched no campaign advertisements or relevant news reports. Using the control group as the baseline, we found that respondents exposed to messages about crime were not more likely to support the female candidate. As the focus of the campaign shifted to unemployment, the female candidate's share of the two-party vote increased, but very slightly (by 1.8 percent). A much larger shift of 8.3 percent occurred when the campaign focused on women's issues.

VOTE SHARE

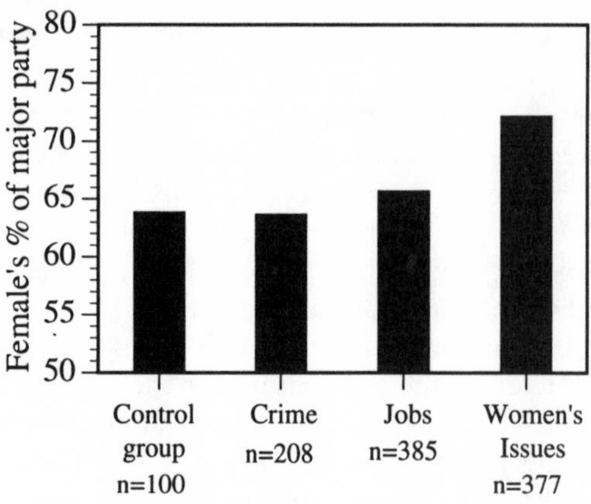

NET TRAITS[1]

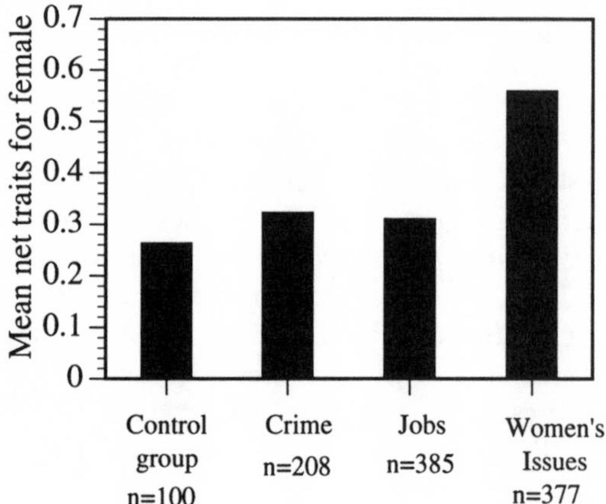

NET LIKES[2]

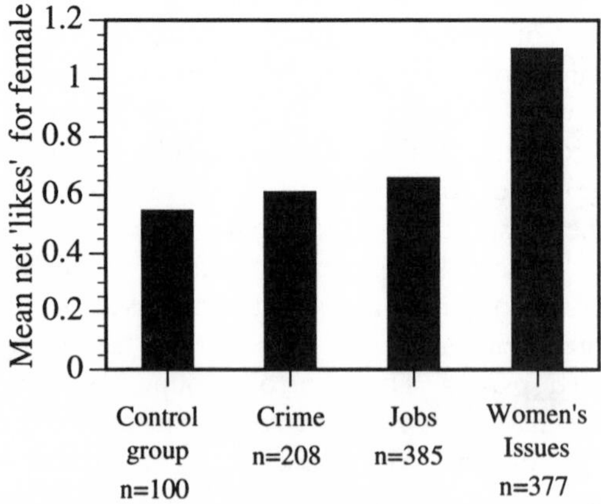

Figure 4–1 The Effects of Campaign Issues on Voter Preferences.

[1]The net traits scale runs from −2 to +2 and is computed by subtracting the mean trait rating of the male candidate from that of the female candidate.

[2]The net likes scale take on values from −2 to +2 depending on the number and tone of open ended comments about both candidates. It is computed by subtracting the net positive score for the male candidate from that of the female candidate.

The remaining panels in Figure 4.1 display the very same pattern of results. The largest positive change in the net trait rating (+.30 trait points) was observed when the campaign focused on women's issues. Similarly, exposure to messages dealing with "women's" issues boosted the net number of positive comments about the female candidates by a margin of .55. In short, female candidates do best when the campaign emphasizes "women's" issues. They are slightly advantaged by campaign messages about unemployment and gain no advantage at all when the issue is crime.

The reliability of the differences noted above was assessed using multiple regression analysis. The three issue categories were converted into dummy variables and included in equations for predicting the three indicators of candidate preference along with a set of control variables. The controls included respondents' party identification, 1988 presidential vote, education, gender, and ethnicity. The results of the regression analyses are presented in Table 4.1.

The results strongly reinforced the differences observed in Figure 4.1. Predictably, the respondents' education, partisanship, and previous vote contributed significantly to the female candidate's support. The gender of the respondent, however, mattered only in the case of voting preference: female candidates enjoyed a 10 percent larger lead among women voters than among men voters. After adjusting for these built-in differences in candidate preference, the only significant campaign effect in all three equations was the presence of campaign messages dealing with women's issues. The controls, however, do not diminish the size of the exposure effects compared to the mean differences presented above. Viewing news or an advertisement about "women's" issues increased the female candidate's lead over the male by an average of 15 percent compared to the baseline group. The effect of "women's" issues exposure lead to a .27 point increase in the net trait ratings. An additional .48 net "likes" was stimulated by "women's" issues content. Exposure to news or advertising on the subject of unemployment did lead to increased support for the female candidates, but the effect was statistically insignificant. Finally, the smallest effect was produced by a focus on crime.

Though the results presented above support the hypothesis that female candidates benefit when the campaign agenda highlights "women's" issues, our evidence is limited because the advertising conditions in which the focus was directed included only Democratic sponsors (Boxer, Feinstein, and presidential candidate Clinton). Participants in the crime and unemployment conditions, on the other hand, were exposed to advertising from either Democratic or Republican candidates. The distinctiveness of the women's issue conditions may simply reflect this partisan imbalance in the source of the campaign advertisement.

The Effects of Women Campaigning on "Women's" Issues

We designed our second test to overcome the potential confounding influence of the source of the advertisement by restricting the analysis to

Table 4.1
The Effects of Issues on Voter Preferences

	Dependent Variables		
	Vote Margin[a]	*Net Traits Score*[b]	*Net Likes Score*[c]
Explanatory variables			
Women's issues[d]	.15**	.27***	.48***
Crime	.01	.06	.03
Jobs	.05	.06	.15
Control variables			
Education[e]	.07***	.11***	.25***
Party identification	.28***	.29***	.57***
Race[f]	.02	.01	.17***
Gender	.10***	.05	.11
Democratic vote in 1988[g]	.25***	.38***	.87***
Constant	−.24**	−.36**	−1.31***
R^2	.20	.28	.18
N =	1060	1060	1060

Note: Entries are unstandardized regression coefficients for U.S. Senate Elections in 1992
** = $p < .05$; *** = $p < .01$

[a]The vote margin variable was coded "−1" for the male or Republican candidate "0" for undecided or not voting and "+1" for the female or Democratic candidate.

[b]The net trait score was the Democratic or female candidate's trait rating minus the trait rating for the male Republican opponent (For example, in a Boxer or Herschensohn condition, the dependent measure equaled the Boxer trait rating—the Herschensohn trait rating). The variable ranges from −4 to +4.

[c]The net likes measure first computed the preponderance of likes over dislikes for each candidate and then subtracted the opponent's score from the sponsor's.

[d]This was scored as a dummy variable for respondents in conditions with ads or news concerning sexual harassment.

[e]A dummy variable consisting of college graduates versus all others.

[f]A dummy variable consisting of black respondents versus all others.

[g]Coded "1" for Democratic vote in 1988 presidential election, all else set equal to zero.

the effects of advertisements aired by women candidates. This second test more precisely measures the effect of female candidate appeals on various issues. Does a woman candidate improve or worsen her prospects when she airs an advertisement on crime, unemployment, or women's issues? These results are presented in Figure 4.2.

The results are virtually identical to those shown earlier in Figure 4.1. When women initiated campaign messages, they fared best with women's issues. The female sponsor's share of the vote increased by 3.5 percent when the advertisement concerned crime, by 4.6 percent when the advertisement concerned unemployment, and 11.5 percent when the subject was women's issues. Women's issues advertisements also lead to a .34

VOTE SHARE

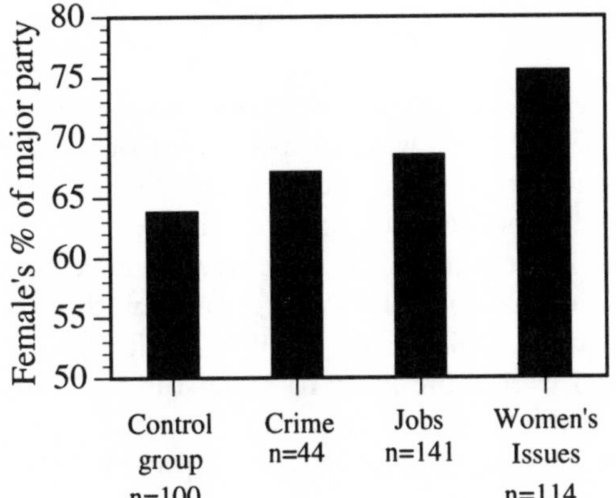

NET TRAITS[1]

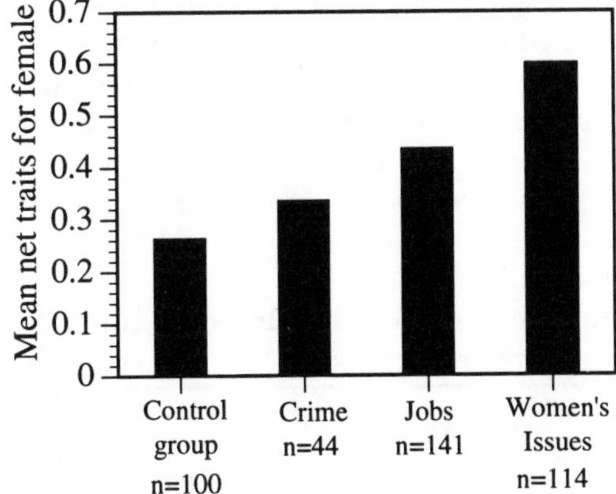

NET LIKES[2]

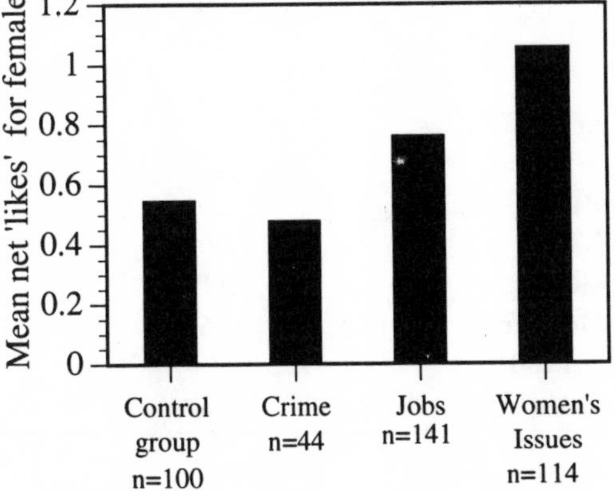

Figure 4–2 The Effects of Female Candidate-Initiated Issues on Voter Preferences.

[1]The net traits scale runs from −2 to +2 and is computed by subtracting the mean trait rating of the male candidate from that of the female candidate.

[2]The net likes scale take on values from −2 to +2 depending on the number and tone of open ended comments about both candidates. It is computed by subtracting the net positive score for the male candidate from that of the female candidate.

point increase in the net trait rating scale, and an increase of .50 net "likes." As one would expect, each of these effects is larger than in the previous test, which included exposure to news about these issues as well as advertisements by other candidates.

The effects of the experimental advertisements were next subjected to multiple controls (Table 4.2). In all three tests, Democrats, those who voted for Dukakis in the 1988 presidential election, and the more educated were more likely to prefer the Democratic Senate candidates. Despite the presence of the control variables, the original pattern of results was unchanged; women's issues provided the greatest benefit to women candidates, crime the least. When Boxer and Feinstein ran advertisements on women's issues their electoral margins increased by 22 percent. Unlike the results from the previous analysis, Boxer and Feinstein also stood to gain significantly by advertising on unemployment—their vote margin increased by 14 percent. The issue with the smallest rate of return for the women was still crime; the crime advertisement proved to be statistically insignificant as a determinant of a female candidate's vote margin.

The net trait and likes variables both yielded similar results. The women candidates' edge on these indicators increased by approximately

Table 4.2
The Effects of Female Candidate-Initiated Issues on Voter Preferences

	Dependent Variables		
	Vote Margin	*Net Traits Score*	*Net Likes Score*
Explanatory variables			
Women's issues	.22***	.29***	.36*
Crime	.08	.07	−.15
Jobs	.14**	.19*	.22
Control variables			
Education	.07**	.15***	.16*
Party identification	.30***	.23***	.48***
Race	.00	.00	.14*
Gender	.11*	.08	.28
Democratic vote in 1988	.26**	.40***	1.03***
Constant	−.15	−.44**	−.89**
R^2	.28	.18	.18
N =	395	395	395

Note: Entries are unstandardized regression coefficients for the 1992 California Senate Elections. All control variables (dummies for race, pid, previous vote, education, gender) are coded identically as in previous tables.

* = p < .1; ** = p < .05; *** = p < .01

one-third (.29 and .36, respectively) of a point when they advertised on women's issues. The advertisement on jobs proved less influential, but its effects on the traits and likes scores were in the expected direction. Finally, the crime advertisement exerted no significant effects on viewers' evaluations of the women candidates.

The results in Table 4.2 also revealed a significant gender gap in support for the female candidates, but only in the case of the vote margin variable. The female candidates' margin was 11 percent higher among women than among men. The gender differences for the other dependent variables, although in the predicted direction, were insignificant. The limited scope of the gender gap suggests that while women voters are relatively "bound" to women candidates, they do not necessarily express more positive evaluations of the candidates than do men.

Of course, the presence of the significant gender gap in the women candidate's vote margin suggests that the gender of the voter is a relevant mediator of campaign advertising when the sponsor of the advertisement is a woman. Quite possibly, the effects of a woman candidate's advertising on particular issues will shift depending on the gender of the respondent. Further research suggests that women responded earlier in the campaign to female candidates, and only later did men begin to catch up (Valentino, 1995).

Overall, the results presented in Figure 4.2 and Table 4.2 corroborate the hypothesis that female candidates do best when their advertising exposes voters to the sponsor's stereotypical strengths. These results are especially telling because they focus exclusively on messages initiated by the women candidates. The issue emphasis in the campaign environment as a whole seems to matter, as demonstrated in our first test, but when voters see female candidates promoting messages which resonate with their preexisting beliefs about the strengths of women, the effects can be even larger.

To this point we have interpreted the differential return for women candidates from advertisements dealing with women's issues, unemployment, and crime as evidence of gender stereotyping. There is, of course, an alternative explanation. Candidates Boxer and Feinstein were female Democrats; their opponents were male Republicans. This built-in confound between gender and party identification can only be overcome in laboratory studies that systematically vary the gender and party affiliation of the candidates. Rather than run additional experiments with hypothetical candidates (for example, Republican "Bob Boxer" versus Democrat "Ruth Herschensohn"), we attempted to disentangle the effects of the sponsoring candidate's party and gender by holding the former constant. Experimental participants were exposed to a range of messages from Democratic candidate Bill Clinton as well as from Democrats Boxer and Feinstein. To the degree the effects of advertisements involving women's issues vary with the gender of the sponsor, we can attribute these differences to the candidate's gender rather than partisanship. This test is also limited since the male Democratic candidate was running for President while the women candidates were running for U.S. Senator. Differences in the effects of particular messages might thus be attributed to differences in viewers' stereotypes about particular offices. However, there is no prima facie reason to expect that presidential candidates would be viewed as less effective on women's issues than senatorial candidates. Furthermore, we believe that the gender-office confound is less problematic than the gender-party confound, and we present the "Democrats alone" analysis in the hope of strengthening our inferences about gender stereotypes.

The results of the Boxer-Feinstein versus Clinton analysis are presented in Table 4.3. The experimental variable compares respondents who were exposed to an advertisement dealing with women's issues with respondents exposed to messages dealing with other issues (unemployment or crime) from the sponsoring candidate in question. News messages about the various target issues were also included in this analysis. The test is made all the more stringent because we excluded respondents who did not view any campaign-relevant information. Does the decision to ad-

Table 4.3
The Effects of Sponsor's Gender and Issue Content on Vote Margin

	Female Sponsor's Margin	*Male Sponsor's Margin*
Explanatory variable		
Women's issues vs. other campaign messages[a]	.11***	.03
Control variables		
Education	.05**	.06
Party identification	.31***	.43***
Gender	.07*	.08
Democratic vote in 1988	.26***	.23***
Constant	−.05	−.016
R^2	.34	.33
N =	576	229

Note: Entries are unstandardized regression coefficients for the 1992 Senatorial and Presidential Democratic Candidates. All control variables are coded identically as in previous tables.

* = $p < .1$; ** = $p < .05$; *** = $p < .01$

[a]Respondents exposed to news or Democratic advertising about sexual harassment were coded 1. All other conditions featuring news or exposure to advertising from Democratic candidates were coded 0. The coefficient measures the change in the intercept when one moves from exposure to any campaign message (including ads on jobs or crime, and news on jobs or crime) to exposure to a message on women's issues. Note that this is an especially stringent test since the null conditions, where respondents received no campaign-relevant information, were excluded from the analysis.

vertise on women's issues rather than other issues have differing payoffs for candidate Clinton than for candidates Boxer and Feinstein?

As shown in the first column of Table 4.3, exposure to a message on women's issues increased the vote margin for female candidates by 11 percent over any other campaign message. However, exposure to a message on women's issues increased Clinton's vote margin by a mere 3 percent vis-à-vis Clinton's other messages. For Clinton, an advertisement dealing with women's issues was no more effective than an advertisement on some other issue. The control variables in Table 4.3 strongly influenced the vote margin for the sponsoring candidate, but their influence could not account for the effect of the women's issues advertisements run by female candidates.

These results suggest that there are inherent differences between male and female candidates in their ability to profit from specific issue appeals. Even when compared to a male Democrat well known for his advocacy of women's issues, female candidates obtained greater returns by campaigning on these issues. While the use of women's issues as a rallying cry significantly improved the women candidates' prospects, it had little impact on Clinton's level of support.

The Effects of Campaign Dialogue

Our analyses of the 1992 election were limited to the effects of one-sided campaign communication. In the studies discussed above, our experimental manipulations took the form of a single advertisement from a single candidate. The one-ad studies were designed to illuminate the effects of particular attributes of campaign messages and the evidence surveyed above suggests that the gender of the sponsoring candidate is an important determinant of the effectiveness of campaign advertisements when one of the competing candidates is a woman. The real world of high profile campaigns, however, is competitive; voters are exposed to a stream of messages from both candidates and the candidates must formulate their advertising strategy, not merely on the effectiveness of their own appeals, but also by considering the actions of the opponent.

Our second study examined the strategic importance of the campaign "dialogue" between a male and a female candidate. In this study voters were exposed to one advertisement from each of the candidates (Pete Wilson and Kathleen Brown) and the issues on which they advertised could be considered to match voters' intuitions concerning "male Republican" or "female Democratic" areas of strength. Our manipulation established three different types of issue agendas. Some participants were exposed to a "male Republican" dialogue in which both Brown and Wilson addressed crime or immigration. Other participants encountered a "female Democratic" dialogue in which both contestants sparred on the issues of unemployment and education. Finally, most of the study participants were

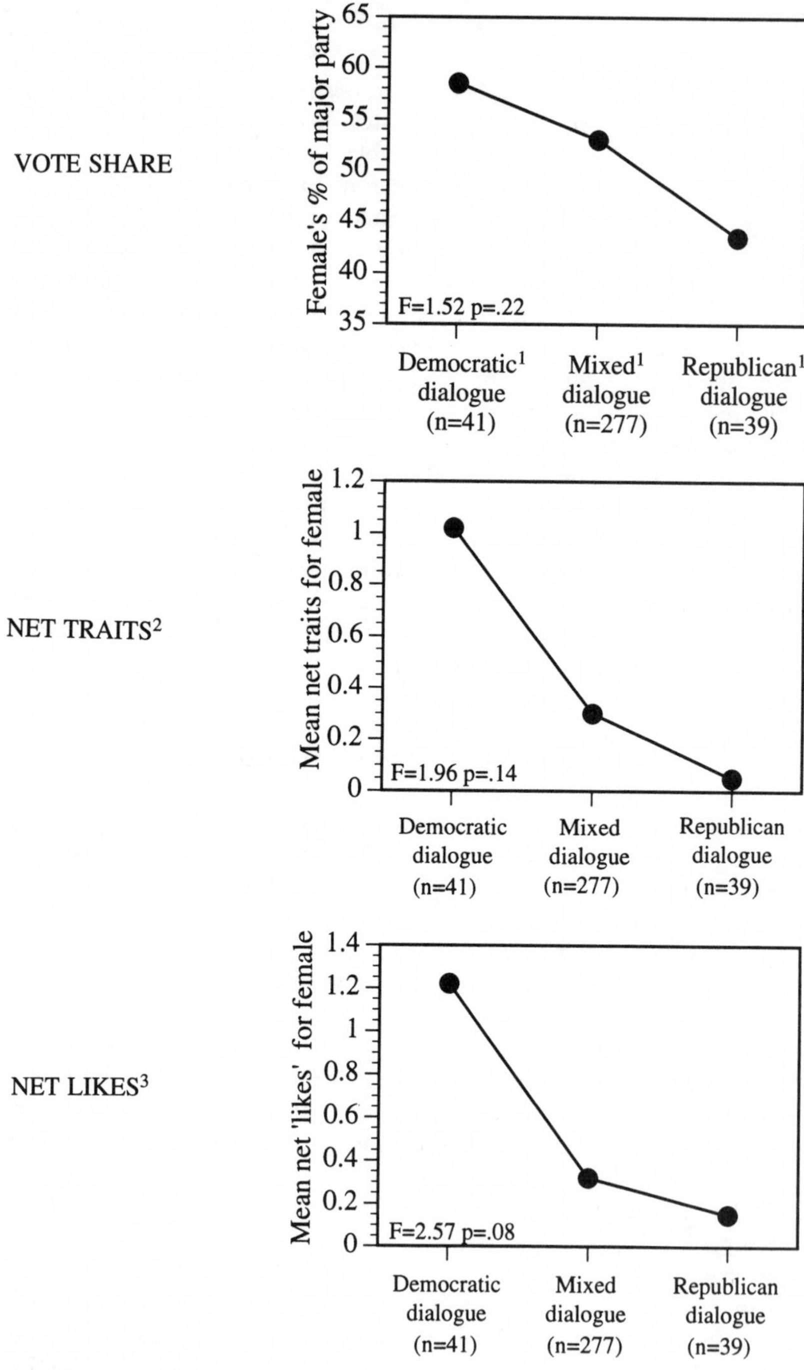

Figure 4–3 The Effects of Homogeneous Versus Mixed Partisan Dialogue on Voter Preferences.

[1]A Democratic dialogue is one in which both the Republican and Democratic advertisements discuss either "jobs" or "education." A Republican dialogue is one in which both candidates discuss crime in their advertisements. Respondents in the 'mixed' dialogue conditions were exposed to a combination of messages about crime and either jobs or education.

→

assigned to conditions featuring a "mixed" dialogue in which each candidate chose to advertise on their respective strengths using issues on which they were likely to enjoy the reputational advantage. Based on the evidence from the 1992 studies, we anticipated that Kathleen Brown would be advantaged when the campaign turned on issues of education or unemployment, while Pete Wilson would benefit when crime or illegal immigration were the central issues.

Figure 4.3 displays the effects of the campaign dialogue manipulation on the candidates' support. Consistent with our expectations, the vote margin indicator fluctuated according to the issue agenda of the campaign. When the content of the campaign centered on education and jobs, Kathleen Brown won handily (with 58.5 percent of the two-party vote). When each candidate advertised on their respective strengths, the race was a standoff (Brown received 52.9 percent of the vote). Finally, when the campaign centered on crime and immigration, Wilson was the clear victor (Brown received only 43.6 percent of the vote). Clearly, the candidates' choice of issues was crucial to the outcome of the election. Had the economy prevailed over crime and immigration, Brown would have been elected. As it turned out, Wilson's campaign was able to overshadow economic concerns with fears of violent crime and swarms of illegal aliens.

This striking pattern was repeated virtually unchanged for the other dependent variables. Brown's advantage on the trait rating and her preponderance of favorable open-ended comments both fell by one full point when the campaign dialogue switched from "female Democratic" to "male Republican" issues. The F statistics shown in the lower left corner of each panel (which are nondirectional tests and therefore quite stringent) reveal that the observed differences in each case of each indicator of electoral support approached statistical significance.

The regression analyses presented in Table 4.4 indicate that, even after controlling for the influence of individual differences among respondents, the effects of campaign dialogue remained significant and large in magnitude. The change in the vote margin produced by shifting the campaign dialogue from "male Republican" to "female Democratic" issues was 11 percent. The effect of changing the subject of the dialogue on the other dependent variables was even more significant, with Brown's trait score advantage improving by .38 points and her edge over Wilson in the net "likes" score increasing by half a point (.48) when the subject of both candidates' advertising was education or unemployment rather than crime or immigration.

---

[2]The net traits scale runs from −2 to +2 and is computed by subtracting the mean trait rating of the male candidate from that of the female candidate.

[3]The net likes scale take on values from −2 to +2 depending on the number and tone of open ended comments about both candidates. It is computed by subtracting the net positive score for the male candidate from that of the female candidate.

Table 4.4
The Effects of Homogeneous Versus Mixed Partisan Dialogue on Voter Preferences

	Dependent Variables		
	Vote Margin	*Net Traits Score*	*Net Likes Score*
Explanatory variables			
Campaign dialogue[a]	.11*	.38*	.48**
Vote on Prop. 187[b]	.34***	1.31***	.82***
Past Democratic vote	.26***	.64***	.48***
Party identification	.34***	.67***	.91***
Gender	.10	−.06	.09
Constant	−.12	.045	.10
R^2	.40	.26	.25
N =	356	356	356

Note: Entries are unstandardized regression coefficients for the 1994 California Gubernatorial Campaign. All control variables are coded identically as in previous tables.

* = $p < .1$; ** = $p < .05$; *** = $p < .01$

[a]This was scored as a trichotomous variable where respondents exposed to consistently "Republican" messages (those who saw both candidates discuss crime or immigration) were coded −1, the null/mixed dialogue group received a score of 0, and respondents exposed to consistently "Democratic" dialogue (e.g. advertising on education or unemployment) were scored as +1. Positive coefficients indicate a shift in support for the Democratic female candidate when the campaign dialogue shifts from Republican to Democratic issues.

[b]Proposition 187 was an initiative on the ballot in California in 1994 which was designed to deny state funded, nonemergency health and education services to illegal immigrants. Respondents who approved of the initiative were coded −1, those who disapproved were coded +1, and all others were coded 0.

Though our 1994 study rests on a more realistic design that is more faithful to the "high volume" characteristic of major campaigns, it suffers from a significant loss of control. The results are only suggestive of gender-based differences in the effectiveness of particular campaign appeals. We cannot determine whether it was the candidates' gender or party identification that made their messages on education/jobs and crime/immigration more or less effective. Taken together with the 1992 studies, the results are consistent with a gender interpretation: female candidates do well to consider their constituents' stereotypes when designing their advertising strategies. In light of these results, Kathleen Brown's decision to respond to the Wilson "soft on crime" attacks during the 1994 race for governor of California may have been a fatally flawed strategy.

Conclusions

We have presented evidence from recent senatorial and gubernatorial campaigns that is consistent with the resonance model of campaigns. Lacking concrete details about a candidate's positions on the issues, voters make inferences based on highly visible and distinctive attributes such as gender. Being a woman or a man conveys information about the candidate's willingness or ability to deal with issues that closely impinge on gender (such as sexual harassment) as well as issues that, on the surface at least, have limited relevance to gender (such as education or unemployment). When these issues become central elements of a campaign, women candidates are advantaged. Our results suggest quite strongly that women candidates should seek out this advantage by emphasizing issues that call for stereotypical female attributes. A woman who calls for educational reform or for more stringent enforcement of gender discrimination laws will be taken more seriously than a woman who calls for the death penalty or more aggressive monitoring of terrorist groups. Seen in this light, the success of so many women candidates in 1992 can be attributed not only to their running in open seat races or their proficient fund raising but also to the national preoccupation at the time with women-related issues such as sexual harassment and the treatment of women by male-dominated institutions.

The 1994 gubernatorial study extends this result to campaigning by a woman candidate *and* her male opponent. We found that Kathleen Brown's prospects were especially promising when she waved the gender flag herself and when she enticed Pete Wilson into a discussion of gender-related issues. An important corollary of the two-advertisement study is that equality of exposure is less influential than the content of the message. Our "dialogue" manipulation proved to be a powerful determinant of electoral choice even though both candidates were equally able to reach voters with their messages. In relatively competitive races, it is the issue agenda of the campaign rather than the volume of each candidate's message that influences voters.

While our evidence strongly suggests that voters interpret identical messages differently depending upon whether the sponsoring candidate is male or female, we are not in a position to offer theories about the specific linkages between the issues under investigation (sexual harassment, education, unemployment, immigration, crime) and particular attributes of male and female candidates. Do women have credibility on certain issues because they are women (that is, they are presumed to have positive contributions to make in a particular subject area) or because they are not men (who are presumed to be uninterested in, or indifferent to, certain issues)? In short, we need to know more about the precise nature of gender-based stereotyping.

It is likely that the use of gender stereotypes depends upon a variety of contextual and individual-difference factors. Campaigns in which a woman faces a man would seem to invite gender-based inferences. But do voters see women candidates through the same lens when a woman runs against another woman? Gender stereotyping is also likely to depend upon the extent to which gender is a salient cue to voters. Female voters may well be more conscious of a candidate's gender and may tend to react on the basis of gender.

In closing, the implications of this research reach beyond the discussion of female candidate message effects. Especially when other substantive information is relatively scarce, as in most subpresidential campaigns, people may use a wide variety of stereotypical cues to guide their choices. Other group characteristics, like race, class, religion, and age, could also serve as significant cues for voters. If people make political evaluations based on "top the head" information, then media emphasis on certain group attributes during a campaign could significantly alter the bases of candidate preference. Since most of us maintain a number of salient group identifications throughout our lives, candidates might have some flexibility in their choice of stereotypes to emphasize during campaigns. When should a female candidate emphasize her gender as opposed to her racial, class, or religious characteristics? Our research suggests that she should pick the characteristics which will resonate best with voters based on the issue environment during that particular campaign season. However, more research is needed to determine how and when certain group identifications become relevant to voters in the crowded information environment of twenty-first-century America.

5

A Gender Gap Among Viewers?

Montague Kern and Marion Just

How do men and women use media messages during the campaign to construct impressions of candidates and arrive at voting decisions? Using focus group methods, this chapter probes the similarities and differences in the way men and women react to particular kinds of televised political messages: news, positive ads, and negative ads. We consider three major issues: do some messages—from particular sources or about certain aspects of the candidate—prove more important to women or men in developing candidate images; in particular, do men and women react to negative ads differently; and do men and women exposed to identical campaign messages bring different issue concerns, attitudes, and values to the process of constructing candidate images?

Gender Differences and Similarities

This chapter works within a "constructionist" approach to communication, which holds that individuals construct meaning from media messages based on their own attitudes, values, and feelings (Gamson 1988; Neuman, Just, and Crigler 1992; Kern and Just 1995). This approach suggests that women and men, watching identical campaign commercials, news programs, and political debates, could come away with very different perceptions of the candidates based on the prior attitudes and values which they bring to the viewing experience.

We would expect male and female viewers to differ because of the well-documented "gender gap" in voting behavior, which was rediscovered in the United States in the early eighties. Significant attitudinal differences between men and women have been documented at the elite and mass level (see in this volume Ladd chapter 6; Kohut and Parker chapter 12; Klein 1984; Francovic 1983; Thomas 1994b). Differences among women and men voters have been found to be particularly strong on "caring" issues such as welfare and education, and on defense issues such as attitudes to nuclear weapons, while controlling for other variables, such as class and economic status. While attitudinal differences between men and women had long been documented, in the eighties the new gender gap had important partisan implications—women leaned more to the Democrats and men to the Republicans—and the gap was more pronounced for some issues than others.

The recognition of an electoral gender gap has had an impact on campaign strategy in the last decade. Today campaign strategists act on the belief that men and women respond to different types of issues and messages. In the Reagan/Bush presidencies, for example, "kinder, gentler" campaign messages were targeted for "caring issues" (education, helping the unemployed, the environment) to confront declining support from women. Simultaneously, references to military buildups and engagements (the old Soviet Union, the Gulf War, Grenada, and Panama) were used to target male voters.

Gender differences in American elections have also been found in candidate strategies. As shown by Kahn and Gordon in chapter 3, men and women running for the U.S. Senate offer different issue agendas to voters, although they present these campaign messages in similar ways. One reason for this difference in issue agendas is that candidates are appealing to sex stereotypes among voters. In chapter 4, Iyengar et al. found that when voters were exposed to identical messages, women candidates were seen as more credible on stereotypically "women's" issues like educational reform or sexual harassment, while men proved more credible among voters on issues like crime and immigration. Iyengar et al. conclude that the gender of the message-sender is an important component of viewer response.

Other work has established differences in women's and men's reactions to campaign messages, especially negative ads. Based on survey data West (1993) found that there were significant gender differences in response to Bush's 1988 ads, particularly the notorious "Revolving Door" commercial on crime. The study concluded that the symbolic appeal of the ad proved to have a far greater agenda-setting impact among women, who were more likely to cite crime as an important issue after watching the commercial, perhaps because the ad played on the symbolism of rape, which struck a chord with women (p.114). Overall, West found that three other ads on peace and crime used in presidential elections had significantly stronger agenda-setting effects on women than men (West 1993, Table 6–5). Other studies based on experimental data have found gender differences in response to negative ads, namely, that women are more likely than men to blame the author, as opposed to the target, of the attack (Garramone, 1984; see also Trent and Sabourin, 1993).

Based on this literature we might therefore expect men and women viewers to respond differently when constructing their images of candidates based on campaign messages on television. In particular, from previous research we might expect to find confirmation of the following hypotheses:

1. Given the long-standing and significant gender gap among voters, women and men will bring different issue concerns, attitudes, and values to the process of forming candidate images.
2. In the light of previous work, we would expect that women will be more likely than men to be influenced by negative attack advertising, in particular that woman will react against the author of attack ads.
3. As a result, we would expect women and men, watching the same campaign messages, to construct different evaluations of candidates.

Methods and Research Design

To explore these issues, male and female focus groups were exposed to the news and advertising broadcasts taken from an actual election campaign. We chose materials from the 1990 United States Senate race in North Carolina, between two male candidates, Jesse Helms, a white, long-time incumbent Senator, and Harvey Gantt, an African American challenger. The surprising closeness of the race in its final weeks, the ferocity of Helms' negative attacks on Gantt, and the issues of affirmative action raised in the campaign attracted national attention. We showed these materials to focus groups who were not involved in the North Carolina race in an effort to understand whether or how Helms' attacks in the last few weeks of the campaign brought about Gantt's defeat. The campaign provides a range of materials which allows us to compare how people use messages in candidate image construction.

This study simulated the patterns of campaign discourse, as groups respond to materials presented to them in a series of exposures corresponding to the sequence of a real campaign. This structure blends some aspects of simulation with the focus group method (Kern and Just 1995). The stimulus materials are divided into segments, representing a two- to three-day span of campaign messages. The focus group discussion after each segment attempts to simulate the social construction of meaning, particularly the development of candidate images. Images have been defined as "perceived attributes" of candidates (Nimmo and Savage 1976) formulated around issues and character (Jamieson 1989; Kern 1989; Kaid and Davidson 1986). Research confirms that voters also form images or impressions of candidates based on how they conduct their campaigns (Kern and Just 1995). These sequenced focus group discussions are an opportunity to compare how men and women build on prior beliefs and values and integrate information gained from exposure to different kinds of campaign messages, in the process of constructing candidate images.

The focus group methodology is not new to social science, although in recent years it has been used more intensively, both in academic and marketing research. The principal advantage of the method is the opportunity to analyze social discourse on some topics in depth. While some focus group researchers have used focus groups as a kind of group depth interview (that is, without any stimuli for discussion), the more common application in the commercial sector is to characterize groups' responses to specific marketing messages. Political advertising has been the chief beneficiary of this methodology (Kern 1989).[1]

While the advantage of discursive public response to persuasive messages is widely appreciated in advertising market research, the use of focus groups in academic research presents a number of analytic problems (Lewin 1947; Merton, Fiske, and Kendall 1956; Krueger 1988; Lederman 1990a, 1990b; Delli Carpini and Williams 1994). Focus groups are not in any sense random samples. The participants are generally recruited to meet target criteria, so that individuals may participate comfortably and relatively equally to the discussions. Because of the lack of external validity of any particular focus group outcome, researchers generally agree that the validity of the focus group method rests on the repetition across groups (two are a minimum) as well as on the elaboration and validation of results from other research methodologies. Our investigation focuses on the similarities and differences between male and female focus group discussions.

The participants in our focus groups were exposed to five segments of televised ads and news coverage, in the same sequence in which they were presented during the last stages of the 1990 Helms–Gantt campaign. We selected men and women who had not elaborated images of the candidates prior to the focus group exposure, in order to illuminate the similarities and differences in the way men and women construct candidate images.

As is typical in the selection of focus groups, the ten participants in each gender group were chosen to be ethnically and socioeconomically homogeneous in order to make them as comfortable as possible in expressing their opinions to a roomful of strangers. Our participants were recruited from lists of registered voters. We selected a target population of white, middle-class ($50,000 family income, education up through second year of college), weak Democrats and independents in southern New Jersey. Our choice represented voters whom we expected could support a black Democratic candidate but might be receptive to Helms' negative messages about affirmative action.

The participants were asked to imagine that they were voters in the 1990 Senate election between Helms and Gantt, and to use the information in the video segments in making up their minds how to vote. By way of introducing the simulation and stimulating discussion around political topics, the participants were asked in Phase One to respond to the general question "Is the country on the right track or the wrong track?" After this introductory segment, subsequent discussion segments (Phases Two through Seven) followed exposure to a brief selection of news and advertising and the neutrally framed question "What's going on here for you?"

Transcripts of the group discussions were analyzed line-by-line for their topics and cognitive and affective elements. The discourse was read by the authors and a graduate assistant. As is common in ethnographic analysis, many lines were multiply coded. Quantitative indicators are used to convey only relative emphasis in the discourse and for comparisons across phases of the discussion or across groups.

The focus groups were offered information in discrete phases, on the theory that the temporal order of messages and their relationship is important in the image formation process. The first video segment introduced the candidates to the focus groups using positive self-referent ads. Our aim was to familiarize the "naive" participants with the candidates in much the same way that voters encounter new candidates, that is, through their initial advertising messages. The subsequent video segments represent two- to three-day periods of new candidate advertising and news coverage, drawn from the final weeks of the Helms–Gantt contest. In the actual campaign, this was the period when opinion dramatically shifted from a dead heat between the two candidates to a Helms victory and when the race's negative advertising drew national media attention.[2]

Our coding of the discourse arises from a constructionist approach to communication, which holds that individuals construct meaning from media messages based on their own attitudes, values, and affects (Gamson 1988; Neuman, Just, and Crigler 1992; Kern and Just 1995). In charting the discourse we specifically noted which remarks arose in response to the media stimuli and which were grounded in the participants. Following the constructionist tradition, our analysis takes account not only of opinions but also of the critical interpretation of information, behavior, issues, and events. The male and female group discussions analyzed here illustrate that individuals interpret information in the light of their own experiences and constructions of political reality.

Advertising and News Stimulus Materials

In the final ten days of the 1990 Helms–Gantt Senate race, Gantt's strategy involved running on "middle-class" issues, such as education and health, and values, such as self-help. He did not raise the issue of affirmative action, nor did he try to protect himself against attacks in this area. Meanwhile, Helms engaged in a series of sharp attacks on Gantt, including an issue-based emotional attack ad which portrayed a white job applicant crumpling a rejection letter for a job purportedly given to a "less qualified" minority applicant. Helms won the election with 53 percent of the vote to 47 percent for Gantt.

The ads which were aired as stimuli represent various styles of political advertising. The materials from the Helms–Gantt campaign contrast candidate strategies centering on emotional attack ads (Helms') with an issue-based approach (Gantt's).[3] For Helms the stimulus included one negative emotional attack ad, two negative emotional character and issue attack ads, two issue-based ads, and one positive character ad; for Gantt there were five issue-based ads and one positive emotional character ad. Because the candidates employed different strategies, we were able to observe the impact of different types of messages on men's and women's construction of candidate images.

The stimulus also included a selection of five news stories about the campaign, four local and one national, which appeared at the same time as the ads were aired.[4] In this case the local news not only followed the incumbent but amplified and legitimized his message. No news stories were developed on journalist reportorial initiative either concerning the issues in the election, or the serious charges which Helms raised against Gantt during this period. In particular, there was no analysis of Gantt's alleged misuse of an affirmative action program while he was mayor of Charlotte. Instead, major news themes replicated campaign themes, especially those which Helms raised in his ads.

Regardless of gender, participants in our focus group simulation were initially favorable to Gantt. This is not surprising, since the participants in the focus groups were Democrats or independents leaning Democratic from the Northeast. A few of the participants had some knowledge of Jesse Helms and their impressions of the conservative Republican Senator tended to be negative. Although the participants in the focus groups were positively disposed to Gantt, they did not find confirmation of their constructs in subsequent ads or news stories to which they were exposed. Just like real voters they had to make continual choices, using their own values and experiences to select information from what they saw to assist them in constructing and reconstructing images of the candidate.

Analysis of Discourse

Self-generated Discourse. In focus groups, most discussion was introduced by participants without reference to information contained in the video stimulus. Such discourse fell into several categories: values, preferences, beliefs, feelings, experiences, and information needs (see Figure 5.1).[5]

The major gender differences were not in the overarching categories, but what the individuals brought to the discussion within these categories. Hence, in terms of experience, for example, women were more likely to cite personal experience with education, while men expressed more neg-

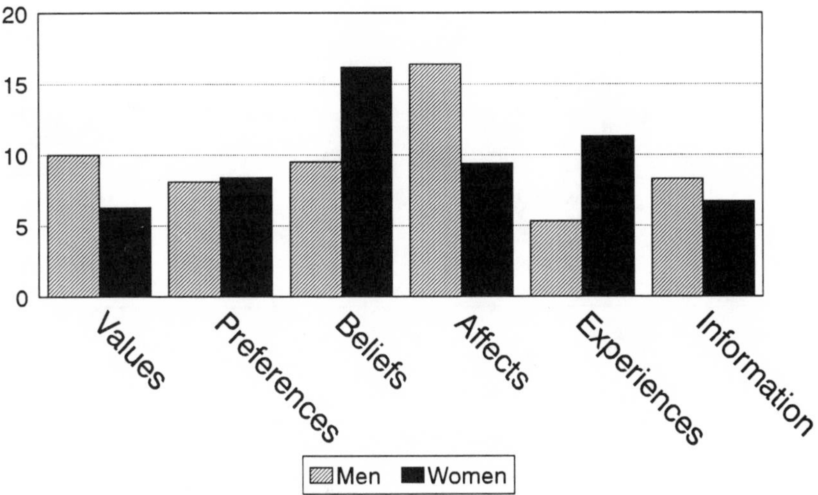

Figure 5–1 Type of Discourse by Gender.

ative experiences toward workplace quotas. There were also differences in the area of values; as expected, the individualistic value of "pulling oneself up by the bootstraps" was more remarked upon by the male group, while in contrast, women expressed greater appreciation for the value of nurturing others. These value differences reflect those which have been found in many other studies of survey data on the gender gap.

Discourse in Response to Media. Almost half the discussion in both male and female focus groups made references to the media stimuli. Positive or negative evaluations of the candidates in response to media stimuli fell into a number of related categories: *character* statements included like and dislike statements about the candidate's personal qualities of empathy and caring, leadership, age, and physical appearance; references to a candidate's record and accomplishments; remarks about the candidate's ties to special interests; and statements about the candidate's credibility. *Campaign* strategy and tactics statements included references to the candidate's campaigning and remarks about the use of negative advertising. Lastly, *issue* statements included those favoring or opposing candidates' stands on the issues such as racial quotas, education, and jobs (see Figure 5.2).

It is clear that character produced the most discussion for both men and women, representing almost a third of the discourse. About half the discussion of character focused on political attributes—such as the candidates' credibility, ability to represent everyone, and associations with special interests. Overall, two-thirds of the character-related assessments were negative, for example, focused on their lack of empathy (the candidate was "out of touch" or "out for himself"). Participants also discussed cam-

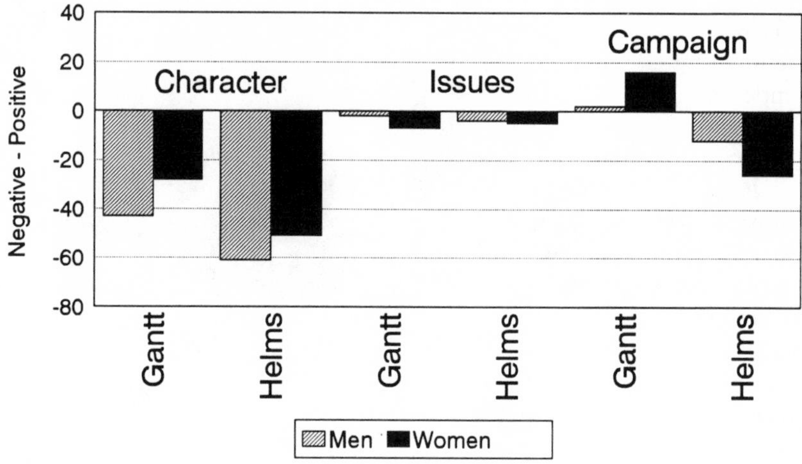

Figure 5–2 Types of Themes by Gender. (Difference Scores for Lines of Discourse)

paign strategy and tactics, representing 7 percent of the discussion. As expected in the second hypothesis, women were found to be more likely than men to evaluate candidates on the basis of campaign tactics, particularly negative advertising. Overall, issue-based candidate evaluations, at 5 percent, were the least significant component of the discourse.

Gender Differences in Response to Stimuli. The media-response component was further analyzed to indicate which messages stimulated discourse, and how men and women responded to media messages from national television news, local television news, ads and news stories, Helms' ads, Gantt's ads, and both candidates' ads. By far the largest amount of discussion came in response to ads (79.1 percent of the total). There were few differences between the men and the women in this category. Men and women were also equally prone to respond to the negative emotional advertising which was the major source of information which entered the discourse. Helms' ads (which followed an emotional attack strategy) generated by far the most discussion for both women and men.

Gender and the Dynamics of Building Candidate Images

The focus group discourse helps us to understand the construction of candidate images through time, albeit much foreshortened. Individuals actively participate in the process—their values, opinions, judgments, feelings, experiences and frames for evaluating candidates come into play—interacting with news and candidate messages. Even though each segment of the discourse was introduced by several minutes of media exposure, our analysis shows that the participants rather than the media generated the majority of the discussion content. Therefore it is not surprising that gender, encompassing different role socialization and life experiences, would differentiate the way groups evaluated media messages.

Feeling Thermometer Scales. The feeling thermometers were measured by written individual evaluations of the candidate, in response to the stimuli, prior to the group discussions. In the feeling thermometers a score of zero is most negative, 50 is neutral, and 100 is most positive. As measured by the feeling thermometer scales, the discourse went through three stages, as men and women brought their values, issue preferences, and experiences to bear on their construction of the challenger's image (see Figure 5.3). At the start Gantt was evaluated slightly more warmly than Helms. In the next stage, from Phases One to Four, support for Helms plummeted sharply among women, who also became more positive about Gantt. Support for Helms slid slightly among men from Phases One to Three, and their support remained stable for Gantt. At Phase Five Helms' negative attack ads ("TV Station Deal/Racial") were introduced. By the concluding stage (Phases Five to Seven) there was a large gender gap in the feeling thermometer for Helms, but the gap closed for Gantt, leaving women and men equally positive toward his candidacy.

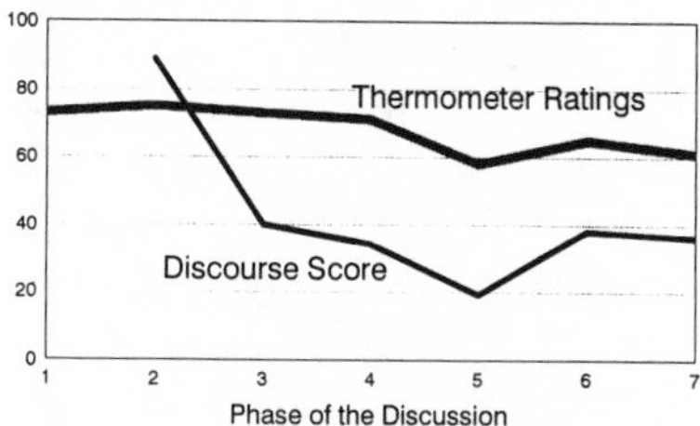

Figure 5–3A Men's Reactions to Gantt.

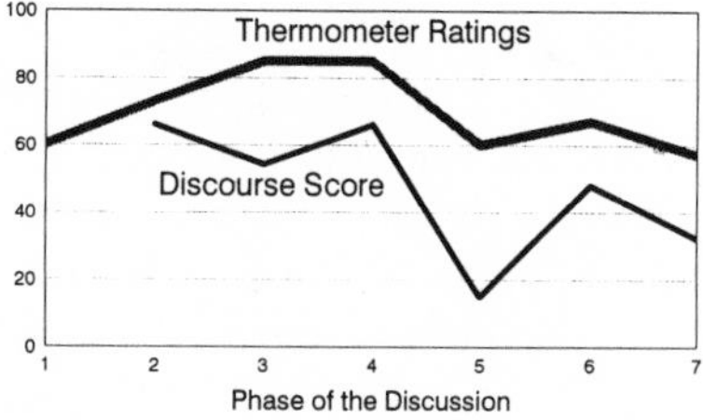

Figure 5–3B Women's Reactions to Gantt.

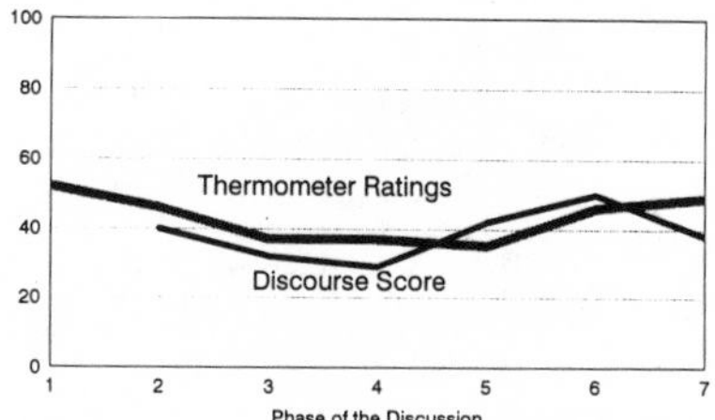

Figure 5–4A Men's Reactions to Helms.

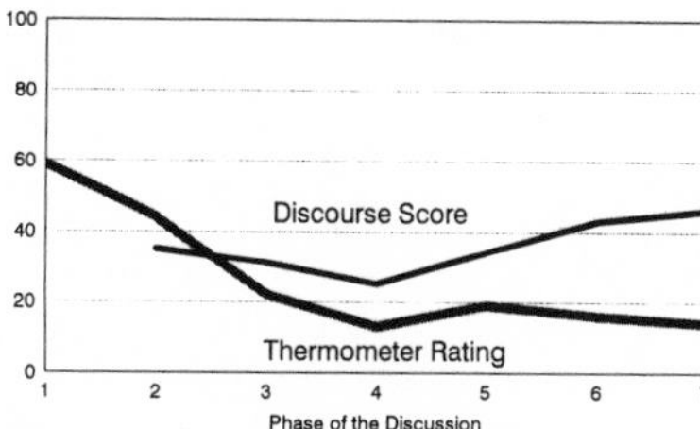

Figure 5–4B Women's Reactions to Helms.

Discourse Analysis. The focus groups then met and the discourse about candidates was coded, as described earlier. Trends lines in these data produced a similar although not identical pattern to that found in the thermometer scores (see Figure 5.4). At the start of the discussion both women and men preferred Gantt to Helms. A gender gap in discussions of Helms emerged in Phases Four to Six, with men becoming more positive than women. The trend line for Gantt fluctuated more sharply than that for Helms. From Phases One to Five, men's support for Gantt declined more strongly in the discussion than in their thermometer ratings, before support recovered slightly by the end. Women became slightly more positive toward Gantt in the early discussions, but in Phases Four to Five women's discourse became sharply more negative, before recovering slightly in later phases. By the end of the discussion phases women and men ended with negative ratings for both candidates, and there were few gender differences in the final ratings. To understand these trends in different phases of the research, and the differences between these measures of support, we need to turn to the stimuli which were being shown to the focus groups and their reactions as reflected in discussions.

Gender and Political Attack Advertising

To understand the overall pattern of change in candidate image construction we need to examine the varied responses to the media messages used during various phases of the campaign. Phase Two demonstrates that the types of ads which stimulated the greatest overall response were those which involve emotional rhetoric. In this phase four different ads were introduced. Two of them offered information which voters used in their construction of candidate images: a Helms emotional attack ad ("Gays/Special Interests") and a Gantt positive emotional issue and character ad ("Bio"). The other two ads, which were informational, were largely ignored.

The dynamics of this phase of the discussion had short- and long-range consequences. The short-range consequence, as previously noted, was voter construction of a positive image of Gantt and a negative image of Helms. The long-range consequence, however, was that *one* of the four ads was an important "sleeper," generating negative discourse and contributing to the ongoing evolution of candidate imagery in a number of subsequent phases. The "sleeper" was Helms' emotional attack ad on Gantt for receiving funds donated by gays ("Gays/Special Interests"). To a lesser degree, however, "Bio," the other positive emotional issue and character ad aired during this period, was also a sleeper—but only for the women, as described below.

Gantt's image during Phase Two was positive, as middle-class participants used their own values to select related bits of information particularly from "Bio," in which his life represents positive values, such as self-help and the importance of getting an education to succeed. Two male participants, who expressed their own concern about education, also used his attack on Helms' record ("SAT Scores Worst") to construct a positive image of Gantt. This image survived several challenges until the topic turned to Helms' negative advertising.

> Ray: He blasted the gay community. . . . and if he's against this one specific group, he's probably against blue collar and everything else.

In the male focus group, however, Helms' emotional attack ad ("Gays/Special Interests") had sown a seed in a climate of distrust of politicians in a submotif of prejudice against gays. The women, however, disliked the ad ("it's dirty"; "why do they have to even talk about it"; "it doesn't matter where they get their money") and constructed a negative impression of Helms based on it.

In Phase Two the emotional attack ad ("Gays/Special Interests") elicited distrust of politicians and a negative evaluation of the candidate who used it. In Phase Three, however, Gantt's image took a dive, particularly among the males, who expanded on their previously expressed negative feelings toward politicians to construct a negative image of Gantt. In doing so they drew on themes from the "Gays/Special Interests" ad, amplified in news stories aired during this phase. Both the charges of gay support and the "secret" (racial) campaign became generalized around the idea that Gantt was linked to special interests. As one man explained the problem: "The fact is . . . you have one single interest putting in so much money. What's this guy going to give back to these people?"

In Phase Four, Gantt attempted to regain control of the agenda, with a return to an issue-based attack ad focusing on Helms' poor record on education and health care in regard to the children of the state. This ran along with Helms' talking head response ad ("Dr. Ellis Paige"). The Helms ad focused the education issue around voter distrust of government and politicians.

In the men's group, information from the Helms ad was used to cast a further seed of doubt about Gantt. By contrast, the women did not connect with this effort to recast education in terms of more abstract, state-federal issues. Instead, they drew on their experiences with schools and continued to support Gantt's critique of the state's poor educational system, for which Jesse Helms, *qua* incumbent (albeit a Senator, not a governor who has more direct responsibility) was held accountable. Information from Gantt's earlier ad, "Bio," clearly a "sleeper," was recalled:

- "He met a payroll."
- "He's an architect."
- "He had to stay within a budget."
- "He has professional credentials."

This information, recalled from memory, was used to construct an increasingly positive image of Gantt, which differed from the increasingly negative image developed by the men. Issue concerns, personal experience, and bits of information recalled from the sleeper ad, "Bio," were used in the ongoing process of candidate image construction.

In Phase Five, with seeds of doubt having been sown in the men's group on education, Gantt's key issue, along with concern about whether Gantt did in fact represent the values of individual initiative and self-help, Helms introduced a scandal message in two versions of an *emotional character and issue attack ad* ("Television Station Deal") accompanied by amplifying news stories. The ads charged that Harvey Gantt, as mayor of Charlotte, used an affirmative action program for personal gain.

In both groups the issue was discussed in terms of moral rights and wrongs. The women concluded that the sale was wrong because "the initial purpose of it [the FCC affirmative action program] was not for that end [one individual's personal gain]." Gantt's defense, that the Helms' charge was "another smear," was presented in ads, and amplified in new stories. Citizens considered it inadequate. As one woman said, "he [Gantt] didn't refute it."

The reservoir of distrust voters have for politicians was then targeted against Gantt, and anti-Gantt sentiment overwhelmed the discourse in both the male and female focus groups. Opposition to quotas as an issue emerged in both groups, as did personal experience with quotas. One female participant defended quotas as a way of undoing past structural injustice to African Americans. Most of the women, however, criticized quotas based on their own and their family's experiences with education:

> *Rose*: Now that bothers me, yes, because I would feel, if we're taking out loans, if I'm working a second job to help my son, working to help him get through Penn State and we have as many children as some of the blacks, you know, I had five children. That makes a person a little bitter.
>
> *Moderator*: What do other people think about what Eilene and Rita are saying. JoAnn, what do you think?
>
> *JoAnn*: It hurts me tremendously. I came from ten in our family and I can remember many times going hungry. . . . And I had to work my way up . . . And I think this country would be better off if everybody did that.

The men concurred, bringing in more work-related experience with quotas. From the discourse, it appears that Helms' racial advertising message connected with individual frames about right and wrong behavior, affects, and personal experiences, as well as character frames for evaluating candidates. Helms' message clearly resonated with the views about racial quotas among the lower-middle-class whites that made up our focus groups.

In Phase Seven the *issue-based emotional attack ad* ("Wringing Hands") was introduced. In it the quota issue was brought home to the individual viewer. A pair of white male hands crumbles a job rejection slip, because a job was given to "a minority" who was "less qualified." In the context of high unemployment rates in New Jersey, this was a potent message for our focus groups. At this point in the simulation, the participants targeted both Gantt and Helms, as they expressed overall negative evaluations of the candidates. Adverse reactions to Gantt linked him with special interests, while issues of credibility surrounded Helms. The voters' overall reaction was to distance themselves from electoral choice.

Conclusions

This analysis of the social formation of candidate images through time permits us to make some tentative judgments about similarities and differences between groups of white middle-class men and women as they construct impressions of political candidates through response to media messages.

The first conclusion is that, as expected by the first hypothesis, women were more responsive than men to negative attack messages, in particular they were more likely to blame the author rather than the object of the attack. This may be because the message of the attack ads conflicted more strongly with the more liberal values of women, while it resonated more sympathetically with the conservative values of men. In general we found that citizens draw heavily on emotional advertising, including negative advertising, in their construction of candidate images.

Second, we can conclude that within the predispositions which individuals bring to the process of constructing candidate impressions there are also differences between men and women. These frequently relate to life experiences. Men are more concerned about the value of self-help, for example, while women are less impressed with the view that individuals "make it on their own." Further, men bring more workplace experience with racial "quotas" into the dialogue. Although equally concerned about quotas, women's political discourse builds more on their experiences with schools and educational institutions. Overall, our findings support the conclusion that experiences and values based on gendered social roles affect image formation.

Lastly, from this analysis it is clear that, regardless of gender, the more affectively laden messages embedded in advertising, reinforced through local and national news coverage, are more likely to figure in the construction of candidate images, particularly as the messages resonate with larger societal values such as self-help or distrust of politicians. The results suggest that the process of candidate image formation is similar for men and women, but that social roles make some issues more salient than others in candidate image construction.

Notes

1. Given the social nature of the focus group, some researchers argue that the individual should not be the sole or even primary unit of analysis. Therefore, we have concentrated this research on the dynamics of group discourse, while tracking individual reactions, logged in paper-and-pencil questionnaires. Our method takes into account the reports of other researchers (Delli Carpini and Williams 1994) that individual participants often do not hold consistent positions over the course of an extended group discussion.

2. While the order of presentation faithfully followed the campaign, some routine news stories from the campaign trail were omitted, and ads that were aired repeatedly in the campaign were shown only once in the focus group exposures. No ads from this period were omitted from the stimulus materials.

3. In this analysis we make a distinction between ads which utilize an emotional rhetoric, and those which do not. All ads which attack an opponent are frequently defined as negative. Within this classification there are, however, strongly emotional negative (harsh reality) ads which utilize grating sounds and affect-laden symbols and connect the opponent with negatively perceived "others" (politicians, marginalized social and ethnic groups, foreigners, etc.) We have termed these *emotional attack ads.* One occurred in this sample, Helms' "Gays/Special Interests," which linked his opponent with homosexual interest groups. There were also negative *emotional character and issue ads*, which are like their counterpart *positive emotional character and issue ads.* In such ads issues are personified through the use of visual and aural effects. Sound and visuals are blended, or "dovetailed," around a story or narrative, exemplifying the values and stated issues (Kern 1989). Such ads offer useful information to voters if the issues are salient and self-explanatory and relate to readily understood individual experiences (Kern 1993; Just et al. 1996).

4. Representative stories were selected following content analysis of a sample of the local and national news stories that were broadcast in the Piedmont Triad during the final weeks of the campaign (Kern 1993). The local stories all dealt with strategy and the "horserace" aspects of the campaign, while the national news story was about "mudslinging" in the Senate races around the country. There was a significant "spin" on the news, which in this case favored the incumbent, Jesse Helms. The incumbent-orientation represents the norm for local campaign coverage (Robinson 1994; Kern 1989).

5. These terms were defined in the coding scheme as follows. *Values* refers to normative standards against which individual behavior is judged. *Preferences* refers to expressions of favor or opposition. *Beliefs* refers to what people think about the world. *Affects* refers to statements carrying emotional values, such as trust, caring, fear. *Experience* refers to discourse arising from the life experience of the voter.

6

Media Framing of the Gender Gap

Everett Carll Ladd

There is a gender gap in American politics, and through survey research we know a lot about it. We know that women and men differ overall in their party identification and voting. We know that gender differences electorally bounce from one election contest to another, but that they have remained relatively constant in magnitude over elections since 1980. Gender differences in voting are paralleled by difference across social and political issues. This chapter brings together the best available survey data showing what the gender gap looks like contemporarily, and how it has been reported by the media.

The gender gap is an important, continuing dimension of American politics. Any researcher plumbing divisions in the body politic needs to keep gender comparisons in his or her analytic arsenal, along with other staples of political assessment: race, religiosity, income, age, education, union membership, and region of the country, among the most prominent. Yet if gender belongs securely in this company, the divide it locates is by no means among the most prominent. Difference between whites and blacks are, obviously, vastly larger. Differences among educational and income groups, among Americans by the levels of their religious participation, between union members and nonunionists, between southerners and residents of other regions, are also typically larger.

So, gender belongs in select company, but the term "gender gap" in a sense gives it more emphasis than it merits. We rarely write of the "education gap" in this context, for example, even though educational groups differ more substantially than do men and women. In the early 1980s, various analysts—some working for interest groups, others in the media and academe—"discovered" the gender gap. An unfortunate degree of hyperbole resulted. The hype detracts from the actual story, which is an important one—its importance in no way diminished by its prosaic character. It is comforting, in fact, that women/men political differences are so straightforward, so much in keeping with what we know about national political life. They fit comfortably into the fabric of our politics.

The hyperbole which surrounds gender-in-politics discussions needs little attention or demonstration here. The sheer volume of reporting on the subject attests to the enthusiasm with which it has been pursued. The newspaper and magazine files of *Lexis/Nexis* contain about thirty-five hundred stories discussing the "gender gap" from January 1992 to November 1995.[1] Just under fifteen hundred stories in this span dissect the "angry white male."

Much of the exaggerated emphasis is obvious. Consider, for example, a 23 April 1995 article by reporter Linda Feldmann in the *Baltimore Sun*. The author began by telling her readers that "the Republicans and the Democrats are already looking ahead to the 1996 presidential election and plotting how to win over a critical constituency: women." Since women are well over half the population and more than half as well of the voting public, both political parties had better pay attention to them. Ignoring more than half the electorate is usually unwise. At the same time, women and men are heterogeneous groups, and thus not readily appealed to on the basis of any one set of characteristics.

Feldmann wrote that "thirteen years after the term 'gender gap' entered the political lexicon—and seventy-five years after women gained the right to vote—the 'women's vote' is as powerful a force as ever." Actually, it is more powerful. Universal suffrage for women did not come until ratification of the Nineteenth Amendment in 1920, and it took some time for women to reach the same voter turnout as men. Moreover, the group structure articulating interests of various groups of women has been elaborated. Still, the "power" is limited by the extent of the differences of interest and outlook between men and women.

There is such an urge in the media to make gender differences brighter and sharper than they in fact are. Feldmann quoted Democratic consultant and pollster Celinda Lake as writing in a recent report that not only was 1994 the year of the "angry white male," it was as well the year of "ambivalent women." "Democrats would have retained control of both the House and Senate if women had been as excited about the Democrats as men were about the Republicans," Lake argued. "Realistically, the Democrats will come back in 1996 only by putting together a message and strategy that excites the base of women and rebuilds support among men" (Feldmann 1995). Undoubtedly there were "angry white men" in 1994—but surely there were as well angry women. We have no idea whether there were more of the one than of the other. Nor do we know if the number of "angry men" increased. Of course the Democrats, who lost control of Congress, would have retained control had they done much better among a group which is half the electorate, assuming they maintained their position in the other half. It is indeed likely that no party will do very well in the future unless it runs strongly among women and men. But appealing to women and men requires a realistic understanding of both the importance and the limits of their differences. The "hype" detracts from a proper recitation of a very interesting story of sociopolitical differences between men and women which are not overwhelmingly large in the aggregate but which are coherent and persisting.

In reviewing the huge collection of gender gap stories that I referred to above, they confirmed my original impression that the coverage has been characterized by exaggeration. Happily, there are exceptions to this. Kellyanne Fitzpatrick, president of the Polling Company, has discussed gender differences in contemporary politics with care and precision. She observes, correctly, that

> polls show that there are no true male or female issues, but issues which affect all Americans and which contain different nuances of varying appeal to each of the sexes. For example, men and women both saw crime as the most important problem facing the country throughout 1994. When probed, men were more likely to be concerned about protecting the Second Amendment and strengthening the death penalty, with women viewing crime as a matter of personal security which necessitates stronger penalties outside of capital punishment. (Fitzpatrick 1995)

Why are such qualifications so infrequent in gender gap assessments? The press tends to oversimplify and exaggerate on almost every complex social development or issue. In other words, the exaggeration in gender gap accounts is simply one case of a general practice. Some observers have inquired as to how, for example, the rush to judgment on "the angry white male" as a campaign story could have occurred in 1994 without any substantial supporting data. From my perspective at the Roper Center, again, I see such leaps without data often occurring.

Let me give one example from an entirely different area. For fifteen years now there has been a plethora of news stories about the "generation gap"—the sixties generation, the 'Boomers', the 'Xers', and so on. We have examined a large body of relevant survey data at the Roper Center and concluded that none of these generations are anywhere to be found. There are age differences, of course, but not generational differences.[2] I received literally hundreds of calls from journalists asking: "If the data on the absence of a generation gap are so persuasive, why do stories on its existence keep appearing?" My answer to them was the same I give here with regard to exaggeration of the gender gap: the press displays an irresistible urge to make everything brighter and sharper than it actually is.

Backdrop—The Gender Gap in Historical Poll Perspective

There is one part of the gender gap story of which we are still uncertain. We do not know whether in overall magnitude it is larger today than its historic norm. Any gender gap in the nineteenth century would have had only limited application in voting, of course, because large majorities of women across the country—there were state exceptions, beginning with the territory of Wyoming in 1871—were denied the suffrage. That does not mean, however, that women were inactive in politics—many were active—nor does it mean that they did not differ from men on important issues. The hypothesis needs to be seriously considered that it is not our own period which is unusual, but rather the New Deal era which is an exception in gender differences. Quite likely, gender differences were unusually submerged from the 1930s into the 1960s.

Serious discussion of gender differences in voting followed the Reagan–Carter election of 1980, as Reagan took office and received consistently lower approval among women than men. In the winter of 1981, the Roper Center produced a substantial survey-data-based review of the gender gap (Ladd and Bowman 1982).

We began our comparisons of the opinions of men and women by examining data from 1948 to 1952. In this period we found that public opinion differences between the sexes were generally very modest. The polling data support the old textbook conclusion that there are no sustained differences in the general social and political outlook of men and women. The biggest differences in this period occurred in expressed levels of political information and interest. On many questions asked between 1948 and 1952, the proportion of women who said they had no opinion on or no interest in political issues was significantly higher than the proportion of men giving such responses. The one large dimension where men's and women's attitudes differed consistently—though not dramatically—involved the use of force. For example, the possibility of war, or foreign policy questions that raised such matters as a "firm stance" against the Russians, found men and women different in overall expressed outlook. The two sexes took what the traditional stereotypes have told us are their "natural" roles.

By the late 1970s, however, a big change was evident in the social and political responses of women and men. They had begun to take on the coloration of other groups in our society whose attitudes on a broad spectrum of issues are different. Differences of social and political outlook between men and women, while not huge, began appearing in a consistent pattern by the mid to late 1970s. It was the new regularity of these patterned differences that was striking.

One of the areas where differences had appeared might be called the "compassion" dimension. Women now say that they place a greater emphasis on the role of government in getting jobs for people who lacked them, in helping blacks, in helping those in need generally, and so on. The "risk" dimension was also one where men's attitudes contrasted with women's. For example, women were more receptive to strong governmental regulation to protect the environment.

Some of the "traditional" issues on which men and women had long differed—such as support for Prohibition or other restrictions on the use of alcohol—were now showing a marked shrinkage of the male–female split. The "wet–dry" issue is especially interesting because at earlier points in U.S. history this was the most dramatic male–female political cleavage. By the late 1970s, however, this issue showed only the slightest trace of its historic capacity to divide the sexes. On "women's issues"—abortion, ERA, vote for women for public office, and so on—there were still no significant men–women differences in the late 1970s and early 1980s.

A striking new split involved confidence in the system. Again and again, women said they were less sure that the country would be strong and prosperous in the future, and were less certain that the society would be able to solve its problems and function successfully. In trying to account for these differences, some possible causes can be ruled out. It was not, for example, that women as a group were less happy or less confident about their personal lives. In fact, insofar as mass survey data can get at such an issue, women showed themselves somewhat more confident personally. Nor was it that women reflected some great personal complaint against the society. And it wasn't that they are more inclined to despair about the capabilities of government—compared to men, they do not see governmental officials as less competent, more dishonest, or whatever. Rather, women were just less hopeful about the performance and prospects of society.

In this review, we erred in not cautioning our readers that the earliest period for which we had survey data might have been aberrational. Our findings did *not* sustain the argument that in the past men and women generally did not differ in sociopolitical outlook. In the early years of polling, the survey questions that were asked showed modest gender differences in many cases—but quite substantial ones in others. It did appear that those where differences were large generally lacked salience in the agenda of the 1940s and 1950s. Arguing as we did that up through the early 1970s, "overall, men and women responded similarly to most questions," was otherwise somewhat misleading. We should have pointed out that even at the time we wrote, in the early 1980s, men and women responded almost identically to many questions. It did appear that the areas in which they differed had become more salient, and probably somewhat more numerous. Furthermore, gender differences in outlook were linked to gender differences in voting in a way they had not been in the preceding three decades. Women were becoming consistently more Democratic than men.

Although we erred in failing to note that American history did not begin with the New Deal, and that the survey picture of the 1930s, 1940s, and 1950s is far less complete than it became in subsequent years, we got some things right. We demonstrated that gender differences were consistently larger in certain areas than in others. Here we noted, in particular, that "use of force" questions—from the death penalty as a punishment for murder, to the use of U.S. military forces abroad—show large gender differences throughout the entire span for which we had survey information. We were also correct in observing that the gender differences that we saw in the late 1970s and early 1980s, while not huge, appeared in a consistent pattern. It was their regularity which was striking.

Misreading the Gender Story: Mythologizing History

Much of the media deserve criticism for the exaggerated, breathless manner with which they have handled the sober story of political differences by gender. At the same time, it needs to be acknowledged that many journalists were reacting to political developments of the late 1970s and on from a perspective given them that was itself wildly exaggerated and crudely stereotypical. Women were not mostly mindless blobs in the 1950s, slavishly following their husband's political choices—but that is the picture which emerged in much of the literature. Little wonder that when journalists began noting real differences in voting and political outlook between women and men at the time of Reagan's election, it seemed to be a powerful departure from the "dark ages" of past gender relations.

If this seems itself exaggerated, consider the following passage from what is perhaps the most famous political science accounting of American politics in the immediate post-Depression era, *The American Voter*—still a much-acclaimed account by the survey research group at the University of Michigan (Campbell et al. 1960). Campbell and his colleagues devote just ten pages of their 500-page volume to discussions of gender differences in electoral politics (pp. 483–93) in a section headed simply, "Sex." The stereotyping achieved in this "classic" account has rarely been equaled and never surpassed.

> What is the significance of these sex differences for the electoral process? We have suggested earlier that a disproportionate amount of the partisan fluidity that is shown by voters from election to election may come from the politically unsophisticated. If this is so, it would follow that the addition of women to the electorate might have as a consequence greater variability in the partisan division of the vote over time. However, in the case of women, there is an added consideration. The wife who votes but otherwise pays little attention to politics tends to leave not only the sifting of information up to her husband but abides by his ultimate decision about the direction of the vote as well. The information that she brings to bear on "her" choice is indeed fragmentary, but it is second hand. Since the partisan decision is anchored not in these fragments but in the fuller political understanding of the husband, it may have greater stability over a period of time than we would otherwise suspect.
>
> We believe this bias arises largely because of female willingness to leave political matters to men. The ultimate behavior of the dependent wife springs from the more sophisticated concepts of her husband. On the other hand, the independent woman may well fill in a set of political concepts more parallel in quality to those employed by men.

> The dependence of a wife's vote upon her husband's partisan predispositions appears to be one reason why the entrance of women into the electorate has tended to make little visible difference in the partisan distribution of the national vote. Issues may arise from time to time to polarize the sexes: the Prohibition issue of the 1920s may have had some such consequence. In the current era, there is no reason to believe that women *as women* are differentially attracted to one of the political parties. (Campbell et al. 1960, 492–93)

This is not, obviously, an empirically based social science account of gender in electoral politics, but rather an elaborate myth. Like any successful myth, it has elements of truth buried within it. The point here is that journalists must be forgiven for considering the gender-related developments which they began seeing in the late 1970s as quite extraordinary, if so authoritative a source as *The American Voter* told them that previously women had blindly followed their husbands and had almost no impact on American politics. The ahistoricism of the passage quoted above is quite extraordinary. Prohibition was not, for example, some casual issue, but a dominating one for many decades. The two major parties divided sharply on it. Women assumed positions of great influence and leadership in the Prohibition movement, as through the Women's Christian Temperance Union (WCTU). What is more, the temperance issue did not stand alone; it was part of a cluster of "moral issues" that have often loomed large politically.

Gender and Voting: The Story the Polls Tell

Tables 6.1 and 6.2 summarize what we have learned from surveys about gender differences electorally. In presidential voting, the gaps recorded in 1980 again look relatively large, although the biggest one ever found came in 1936. The average gender gap in recent presidential elections is only a couple of points higher than in the earlier contests. What is interesting and important is that the Democratic presidential candidate now always does better among women than among men (see Table 6.1). Similarly, as Table 6.2 shows, women now regularly give Democratic congressional candidates more backing than men do. Often, though not always, younger women and men differ more than do their elders, and college and postgraduate women and men more than those of only high school training.

The gender gap in the 1994 congressional balloting was larger than in any preceding off-year congressional contest. It does not seem, though, that this indicates a general sharpening of gender differences, but rather the nationalizing of House of Representatives races that made the 1994 race so unusual in so many regards. The *Contract with America* was a concerted effort to get voters in disparate House races across the country to think in terms of national party differences (Ladd 1995). If they in

Table 6.1
The Gender Gap in Presidential Vote 1936–92

Election	*% Women*	*% Men*
1992		
Dem. (Clinton)	45	41
Rep. (Bush)	37	38
Other (Perot)	17	21
1988		
Dem. (Dukakis)	49	42
Rep. (Bush)	51	58
1984		
Dem. (Mondale)	42	38
Rep. (Reagan)	58	62
1980		
Dem. (Carter)	46	38
Rep. (Reagan)	47	55
Other (Anderson)	7	7
1976		
Dem. (Carter)	48	53
Rep. (Ford)	51	45
1972		
Dem. (McGovern)	38	37
Rep. (Nixon)	62	63
1968		
Dem. (Humphrey)	45	41
Rep. (Nixon)	43	43
Other (Wallace)	12	16
1964		
Dem. (Johnson)	62	60
Rep. (Goldwater)	38	40
1960		
Dem. (Kennedy)	49	52
Rep. (Nixon)	51	48
1956		
Dem. (Stevenson)	39	45
Rep. (Eisenhower)	61	55

Table 6.1
Continued

Election	*% Women*	*% Men*
1952		
Dem. (Stevenson)	42	47
Rep. (Eisenhower)	58	53
1948		
Dem. (Truman)	56	56
Rep. (Dewey)	44	44
1944		
Dem. (FDR)	51	53
Rep. (Dewey)	49	48
1940		
Dem. (FDR)	51	52
Rep. (Wilkie)	49	48
1936		
Dem. (FDR)	52	67
Rep. (Landon)	48	33

Source: 1936–1976—Postelection surveys taken by the Gallup Organization in each year; **1980–1988**—Exit polls taken by CBS News/New York Times in November of each year; **1990–1992**—Exit polls taken by Voter Research and Surveys (VRS) in November of each year.

fact did, gender differences in assessment of the national parties would loom larger in the vote results. It's also probably the case that the specific tone and issue mix of the 1994 contest heightened electoral differences between men and women somewhat. We have seen such a heightening in various key state races over the last fifteen years.

The gender gap is not uniform. It increases and decreases in magnitude, within a certain limited range, depending upon the mix of candidates and issue appeals. Contests in which the Democratic candidate is a women and the Republican candidate a man often, though not always, yield a big gender gap. As Tom W. Smith and Lance A. Selfa have shown, gender differences are typically smaller when the reverse applies—when it is the Republican candidate who is a woman and the Democrat a man (Smith and Selfa 1992). In 1994 the pattern Smith and Selfa had found again obtained. The largest gender gap in a race featuring a Republican woman and a Democratic man was the Maryland governor's contest, in which *women backed the male Democrat far more highly than men did.* The gender gap is not a product of the candidate's gender but of his or her party and issue stands.

Table 6.2
The Gender Gap in Congressional Voting by Social Groups, 1994 (Percentage voting Republican)

	% Women	*% Men*
Everyone	46	57
By Age		
18–29	42	57
30–44	48	58
45–59	47	58
60+	46	55
By Education		
Less than HS	43	38
HS grad	49	55
Some college	51	65
College grad	47	63
Post grad	33	50
By Race/Ethnicity		
White	53	63
Black	5	13
Hispanic	40	4
By Income		
Less than $15,000	32	42
$15,000–29,999	45	52
$30,000–49,000	49	59
$50,000–75,000	46	61
$75,000–100,000	52	64
$100,000+	59	65
By Party ID		
Democrat	9	13
Republican	91	92
Independent	52	63
By Ideology		
Liberal	12	26
Moderate	41	44
Conservative	76	83

Table 6.2
Continued

	% Women	*% Men*
By Denomination		
Protestant	56	64
Catholic	44	60
Other Christian	42	59
Jewish	25	19
None	22	47
By Union Membership		
Union household	34	43

Source: VNS Exit Poll, November 1994.

Women are more Democratic than men in partisan identification. As in voting, the differences are not usually large, but they are persistent and relatively consistent. There is, of course, the normal bounce from one survey to another. In 1995 the late June *CBS/NYT* poll put the gender gap in party identification at five percentage points (women 37 percent Democratic, men 32 percent). The June *Los Angeles Times* survey put it at four points. On the other hand, two June and July Gallup surveys had the gap considerably larger at ten and fourteen percentage points respectively. The latter is at the outer edge of the observed range.

The gender gap in party identification and voting carries over into assessment of Presidents once elected. Clinton consistently gets higher marks from women than from men; both Reagan and Bush received higher approval from men. Gender differences were the weakest in the case of Jimmy Carter among the last four Presidents, the most *consistently* high for Ronald Reagan, and yet in certain periods reached their all-time (for polling) highest during Bush's presidency. Thus, women are more Democratic than men and hence more inclined to approve of a Democratic President, whom they had voted for by a higher margin than men. Finally, in presidential ratings as in the other areas of political choice, we see considerable fluctuation in the levels of gender differences. For example, of two Gallup polls taken in June 1995, one showed the gender gap in Clinton approval at ten points, while the other showed it nonexistent.

Gender and the Issues

As I indicated above, for as long as we have survey data, men and women have differed significantly in their responses to a variety of issues, foreign and domestic, where the use of force is involved (see Table 6.3). This has

Table 6.3
The Gender Gap on "Use of Force" Issues Over Time

Question	*Women*	*Men*
Do you favor or oppose the death penalty for persons convicted of murder? **Source:** Survey by the Gallup Organization, 1937		
% Favor death penalty	57	69
Suppose the German army gets rid of Hitler, gives up all the countries Germany has conquered, and offers to make peace. If that happens, should we make peace, or should we continue the war until the Germany army is completely defeated? **Source:** Survey by Gallup, October 1943.		
% Should continue the war until the Germany army is completely defeated	64	76
What do you think we should do now in Korea—Keep trying to work out a way to stop the fighting in Korea, stop fooling around and do whatever is necessary to knock the Communists out of Korea once and for all even at the risk of starting WW III, or pull out of Korea right away and let them handle their own problems with the Communists? **Source:** Survey by the Roper Organization, October 1952.		
% Whatever is necessary to knock the Communists out	33	45
People are called "hawks" if they want to step up our military effort in Vietnam. They are called "doves" if they want to reduce our military effort in Vietnam. How do you describe yourself—as a "hawk" or as a "dove"? **Source:** Survey by Gallup, April 1968.		
% Describe self as a "hawk"	32	50
There has been some discussion about the circumstances that might justify using US troops in other parts of the world. I'd like to ask your opinion about some situations. First, would you favor or oppose the use of US troops if . . . ? **Source:** Survey by Gallup, October/November 1990.		

Table 6.3
Continued

Question	*Women*	*Men*
% favor the use of US troops if . . .		
Soviet troops invaded Western Europe	50	66
Iraq invaded Saudi Arabia	47	57
The government in Mexico was threatened by a civil war or revolution	42	55
Arab forces invaded Israel	41	46
Do you approve or disapprove of the U.S. having gone to war with Iraq? **Source:** Survey by ABC News/*Washington Post*, January 1991.		
% Approve	68	84
Should American bombers attack all military targets in Iraq including those in heavily populated areas where civilians may be killed, or should American bombers attack only those military targets that are not in heavily populated areas? **Source:** CBS/NYT, January 1991.		
% American bombers should attack all military targets	37	61
Do you think there should or should not be a law that would ban the possession of handguns, except by the police and other authorized persons? **Source:** Survey by Gallup, December 1993.		
% Should be a law to band possession of handguns	48	28
. . . [A]n American teenager who lives in the Asian nation of Singapore recently confessed to carrying out out multiple acts of vandalism in that country over several days . . . [caning described in some detail]. Some people think the youth deserves caning because he admitted carrying out multiple acts of vandalism . . . and because this is Singapore law. Others think the punishment of caning is inhumane. . . . Do you approve or disapprove . . . ? **Source:** Survey by the *Los Angeles Times*, April 1994.		
% Approve	39	61

been true for sixty years now on the death penalty, and holds for many issues of foreign intervention. During the Persian Gulf war men were substantially more supportive of the military undertaking than were women. Available data suggest no overall trend in this issue domain. Some questions show somewhat larger gender differences than others, but it is hard to see any broad trend. There does seem to be some movement on specific issues. For example, gender differences on the death penalty are smaller today than in earlier periods. The historical record suggests, however, that it is not on use of force but rather on "moral issues" that women's and men's differences of outlook have been their largest and most consequential. From slavery on, women have been deeply engaged by various moral questions and, it appears, have often differed in their aggregate responses from these men.[3]

Much of the discussion of men's and women's differences on these issues historically is soft and anecdotal, but in a few cases the empirical record is impressive. One involves support for Prohibition. Here we are indebted to the State of Illinois and to a constitutional peculiarity in that state—not unique to it, we should note—whereby for a time women could vote for certain offices but not for others. The Illinois State Supreme Court had ruled that the provision in the state constitution barring women's suffrage applied only to the so-called constitutional offices—such as Governor and Lieutenant Governor. The legislature could provide if it chose, the high court ruled, for women to vote for other offices—such as school boards—and on ballot questions. The legislature did so provide, and for several decades prior to the introduction of full suffrage Illinois women voted in some contests but not others. This constitutional peculiarity required that the state print separate ballots for women and men, and tally the results separately. Thus, we have data on women's greater support for an early introduction of Prohibition—from a ballot question in 1919.

The differences across the state on Prohibition (Goldstein 1984) compare favorably in magnitude to what we see today on "big gap" issues. It is rare for a contemporary ballot question to yield bigger differences. What conclusion would we reach if instead of the few issues which can be examined with solid empirical data as a result of this unusual fillip in a state's law, we had systematic information on scores of different issues—including those involving "compassion" and war and peace? What, too, if we had systematic data on women's relative support for political reform in the early twentieth century, especially Progressivism? Nothing I have been able to find in the record challenges the hypothesis that the differences prevailing in earlier eras might compare favorably in magnitude to those of our own.

It is plausible, though in no sense established, that the politics of the Depression era—which reduced the salience of moral questions and elevated a variety of economic-recovery concerns—for a time limited the overall salience of men's and women's political differences.

The one area where current gender differences do appear to be far more imposing than anything parallel we know of in the past involves the debate over the role of government. When broad questions of government's responsibilities are raised in public opinion polls or on state ballot questions, women typically declare themselves more supportive of governmental intervention than men.[4] Developments involving increased incidence of economic need in single parent, female-headed households may well account for the appearance of this new dimension of the gender gap.

The issue of affirmative action, now being debated so heatedly, captures many of the features which we see across the policy spectrum. Women and men *do* differ on *certain dimensions* of affirmative action. But the differences are hardly uniform across all the dimensions. On some, women and men differ hardly at all.[5] When the issue is posed directly as a matter of group interests—men's and women's—the latter show significantly greater support for the programs. On the other hand, when the issue is posed less in terms of group interests and rather more generally—as whether or not legislation providing for affirmative action is now necessary—the differences are typically smaller. And, when asked to assess their own personal experiences involving job discrimination, women and men differ little. Large majorities of both groups say they have not experienced discrimination in hiring or promotions.

Conclusions

The gender gap is at once clear and recurring, and limited. Women as an aggregate group are consistently more Democratic than men, and consistently take different stands on a variety of policy questions. The latter differences are typically moderate in magnitude, less than that routinely obtained for educational and income groups, for example. Moreover, the magnitude of gender differences varies with subtle features of the setting. Some campaigns and some issues widen the gap, while others diminish it. Within a given policy area, as we have seen for affirmative action, some dimensions of the issue yield considerably larger gender differences than do others of equal importance.

The point here is, again, that the gender gap is normal in the context of American politics. Whatever the precise mix of their origins—from objective economic interests, to values introduced through "nurture," to others having roots in biology and psychology—women and men sometimes differ in sociopolitical outlook. They probably have differed thus through much of American history. They appear to differ on policy questions in other countries as well (Norris 1988).

The differences we see separating large and heterogeneous groups in the United States are typically quite stable. This is true even of differences among income strata, for example, from the Depression to the present.

The greater economic deprivation of the Depression era and the policy responses of the Democratic administrations of the day heightened class splits—but only modestly. In the same way, it is likely that the level and character of gender differences we see currently have deep historic roots—and that they will persist. Together with other group differences in social and political outlook, the gender gap helps shape the highly complex environment in which parties and candidates must contend for support.

Notes

1. The first reference in the *Lexis/Nexis* system comes in a *Washington Post* article of 29 March 1982.

2. We have reported these data in a number of publications. For the most complete review of the data, see Ladd, Everett Carll. January/February 1994. "Twentysomethings: Generation Myths Revisited." *The Public Perspective* 14–18. *Reader's Digest* asked us to explore the subject even more thoroughly by conducting a specially designed survey, to probe for differences relating to *generational experience* rather than simply to *place in the normal age cycle.* Again, the putative generations were nowhere to be found (Ladd, Everett Carll. January 1995. "Exposing the Myth of the Generation Gap." *Reader's Digest* 49–54).

3. See, for example, Breckinridge, Sophonisba P. 1972. *Women in the Twentieth Century: A Study of Their Political, Social and Economic Activities.* New York: Arno Press; Ware, Susan. 1981. *Beyond Suffrage: Women in the New Deal.* Cambridge, MA: Harvard University Press; and Goldstein, Joel H. 1984. *The Effects of the Adoption of Women Suffrage: Sex Differences in Voting Behavior—Illinois, 1914–21.* New York: Praeger Publishers; Rice, Stuart A. and Malcolm M. Willey. "American Women's Ineffective Use of the Vote." *Current History Magazine* July 1924.

4. These women–men differences on government intervention questions are well shown in the election-day surveys taken by *Voter News Service* (VNS) in November 1994.

5. Ladd, Everett Carll. June/July 1995. "Affirmative Action, Welfare, and the Individual." *The Public Perspective* 24–42.

Part III

CHANGING IMAGES OF WOMEN IN POWER

7

Media Coverage of Women in the 103rd Congress

Susan J. Carroll and Ronnee Schreiber

In recent years scholars have devoted considerable attention to understanding the obstacles that women in politics confront, the factors that restrict women's access to public office, and the impact that women public officials have on public policy (Thomas 1994; Burrell 1994; Dodson and Carroll 1991; Darcy et al. 1994; Witt et al. 1994). However, relatively little systematic research has focused on the relationship between women politicians and the media.

We now know more than we did several years ago about how the news media report on women candidates for major statewide offices and how gender affects the coverage of political campaigns (Kahn and Goldenberg 1991; Kahn 1992, 1993, 1994a, 1994b). Nevertheless, research analyzing how the media treat women who are elected to office is sorely lacking. This chapter begins to address this need by examining the quantity and the content of newspaper coverage of women who served in the 103rd Congress.

Much Speculation and a Little Research

Political women and observers of women public officials and candidates frequently point to perceived biases in treatment by the press. Political women argue that the media treat them less seriously than they treat men, focus too seldom on issues and too often on their appearances and their family lives, and relegate stories about women and politics to the style pages. For example, after describing how a television reporter opened a story on U.S. Senate candidate Josie Heath with footage of Heath on the floor of her kitchen wiping up broken eggs, Linda Witt, Karen Paget, and Glenna Matthews asked, "Why is it that . . . women's hairstyles and family relationships, their femininity or cheerleader smiles, their kitchens or whether they can scrub egg yolk off vinyl—are grist for the media mill, while similar attributes of comparable men are not?" (Witt et al. 1994, 182).

Celinda Lake, a political consultant who has worked with the campaigns of numerous women candidates, voiced a similar complaint in a report prepared for EMILY's List:

> The press, candidates feel, also covers personality, attire, and campaign organization more than issues. Women, on a number of counts, are especially sensitive and vulnerable to such coverage. . . . analyses of press conferences have shown that reporters systematically focus more attention on the appearance, personal life, abortion stance of female than male candidates. . . . For example, virtually every press article during her 1986 campaign reported on Barbara Mikulski's stature and attire. Who knows Rostenkowski's weight and suit color? (Greenberg-Lake, 55)

Pat Schroeder, Congresswoman from Colorado, was so upset by how she and other women members of the Congressional Caucus for Women's Issues were treated by the *Washington Post* that she included comments about the newspaper in a 24 February 1993 floor statement regarding the Violence Against Women Act. She explained:

> We are also sending a letter to the *Washington Post.* As we met yesterday with Hillary Clinton, they put it on the style section. That is one of the problems with dealing with the very serious issues the caucus is dealing with. When we talk about women's health, women's economic status, and violence against women, it gets put on the style section by this city's major paper, and they talk about what we wear. It is time we move those issues to the front page. It is time that they are taken seriously. And it is time that women lawmakers are given the same play in the paper with their issues that the others are by that newspaper. (*Congressional Record* 24 February 1993)

Kim Kahn's research on the campaigns of women running for statewide offices suggests that some of the complaints about differential treatment by the press may be well founded. She has found that women candidates for the U.S. Senate consistently receive less campaign coverage than their male counterparts and that the coverage they receive is more likely to be negative, emphasizing that they are unlikely to win (Kahn 1994a). She has also found that reporters tend to emphasize the same issues that male candidates do while largely ignoring alternative issues emphasized by female candidates (Kahn 1993).The observations of women politicians and the findings of Kahn's research led us to anticipate that we would find clear biases in the coverage of women in the 103rd Congress.

The Effects of "The Year of the Woman"

Women candidates received unprecedented attention during the 1992 elections. Although other elections had been referred to as "The Year of the Woman" because they, like 1992, represented some major "first" for women candidates, never had the media or the public paid so much attention to women who were running for office (Cook et al. 1994).

The major breakthrough for women in the 1992 elections was at the congressional level, where gains in previous elections had been incremental at best. In 1992, twenty-four new women were elected to the U.S. House of Representatives, increasing the number of women members of the House from twenty-nine to forty-seven. Four new women were elected to the U.S. Senate (while one won reelection), increasing the number of women Senators to six in a legislative body where no more than three women had ever served simultaneously. The number of women in the U.S. Senate increased to seven with the election of Kay Bailey Hutchison in a special election in June 1993.

The excitement surrounding women's campaigns in 1992 seemed to follow the new women members into the 103rd Congress. Many of the new Congresswomen and Senators had run and were elected to office on platforms advocating change, and both supporters and skeptics watched to see what they would do. This climate of enhanced public interest regarding women and politics led us to expect to find a large number of press stories focusing on women in the 103rd Congress.

Description of the Study

The research presented in this chapter is part of a larger project, conducted by the Center for the American Woman and Politics (CAWP) and funded by the Charles H. Revson Foundation, focusing on the impact of women members of Congress during the 103rd Congress. The primary data base for the overall project consists of more than 250 in-depth interviews conducted in 1993 through 1995 with women members of Congress and with staffers and lobbyists who worked on seven major policy issues that were considered during the 103rd Congress (health care reform, abortion, women's health, the crime bill, NAFTA, internal congressional reform, and campaign finance reform). Although we draw upon the knowledge we have gained about the actions of women members of Congress both through these interviews and through our examination of paper and on-line documents focusing on the 103rd Congress, this chapter relies primarily on information drawn from the *Lexis/Nexis* data base.

Most of the analysis presented in this chapter is based on a data set consisting of 291 distinct articles on women in the 103rd Congress published in twenty-seven major newspapers throughout the United States in the months between January 1993 and October 1994.[1] Because the women serving in the 103rd Congress came from various parts of the country, we wanted a broad geographical spread in the newspapers we examined. Consequently, we relied on the "major papers" classification in *Lexis/Nexis*, omitting international newspapers and domestic newspapers where only abstracts of articles were included.[2]

We searched all major papers using the following four sets of key words: "women in Congress," "Congresswomen," "women in the House of Representatives," and "women in the Senate." After excluding inappropriate articles (for example, those that used "Congressmen and Congresswomen" as a gender inclusive reference to members of Congress generally, and those that discussed women in state senates), we conducted a content analysis of the remaining 291 articles.[3] Of these 291 articles, 201 were articles where the central focus of the article or a major focus was on women members of Congress; the other 90 gave only brief mention or superficial attention to women in Congress. For some parts of the analysis in this chapter, we use all 291 articles; for other parts we use the more restricted group of 201 articles where women in Congress were a major focus.

In addition to the findings of our content analysis of this data set, we also present findings from another search of the "major papers" component of the *Lexis/Nexis* data base. For this search we used the names of all twenty-four of the women members of the U.S. House who were first elected in 1992—the "Year of the Woman" class. For comparison we also searched for the names of the fifty-one male members of the House from the same states as the women who were first elected in 1992.[4] From these searches we were able to obtain information about the frequency with which members of the "Year of the Woman" class received coverage in the print press.

Quantity and Placement of Coverage

The number and placement of newspaper articles on women in Congress indicate the seriousness with which the media consider this group and may send a potentially powerful message to readers. If women in Congress are covered frequently and on the front pages, this may signal that women are significant and important political players; if they are covered infrequently and relegated to the style section, readers may well get the impression that the presence of women in Congress is unimportant and that their contributions are marginal. In this section we consider four factors related to newspaper coverage of women in the 103rd Congress: how much attention they received, when they received it, where the articles were located, and who wrote them.

How Much Are Women in Congress Covered?

All the hoopla surrounding the "Year of the Woman" and the 1992 elections would lead to the expectation that women in the 103rd Congress would have been the subject of considerable press attention. One also might expect that women in Congress would have received more coverage in the months immediately following the historic elections and that over time press interest in women in Congress would have declined as the novelty of having record numbers of women enter Congress wore off.

The total amount of general coverage of women in the 103rd Congress was not particularly impressive even though articles were found across a range of major newspapers. During the twenty-two months between January 1993 and October 1994, 328 articles (including 37 that were reprinted from one of the other major papers) were published in twenty-seven major papers; that is an average of just 12 articles per paper for the twenty-two-month period or slightly more than 1 article per paper for every two months of the 103rd Congress. When only articles with a significant focus on women in Congress are considered, the total number of articles decreases to 230, making the average 9 articles per paper over the twenty-two-month period. As one might expect, some papers published more articles on women in Congress than others; the papers with the most coverage were the *Chicago Tribune*, which had 24 articles with significant content on women in Congress during the twenty-two-month period, the *New York Times* which had 21 articles, and the *Washington Post*, which had 20 articles.

Because the number of general articles on women in the 103rd Congress seemed smaller than one might expect following "The Year of the Woman," we decided to examine the coverage which individual women members received. In order to have a baseline of men for comparison, we compared the coverage received by all twenty-four women in the "Year of the Woman" class with that received by the fifty-one men in their first term who were from the same states as the women. The first-term women members seem to have had an advantage over the first-term men in newspaper coverage (Table 7.1). On average, newly elected women received more mentions by name in major papers than their male counterparts, especially in 1993 following the highly visible 1992 elections.

Table 7.1
References to New Members of the U.S. House

Year	*Women*	*Men*
1993	127	82
1994	112	106
1993–94	239	188

Note: Average number of mentions of the names of new members of the U.S. House of Representatives in major papers.
Source: *Nexis/Lexis* search.

Table 7.2
Trends in Coverage of Women in the 103rd Congress

	Average Number of	
Time Period	*General Articles on Women in Congress Per Month*	*References to New Women Members Per Month*
January–June 1993	18.7	216.0
July–December 1993	17.2	290.5
January–June 1994	13.5	253.0
July–October 1994	8.5	290.3

Note: Search in major newspapers.
Source: *Lexis/Nexis.*

When Are Women in Congress Covered?

Interesting patterns emerge when both the general coverage of women in Congress and the coverage of first-term women and men are examined over time. The number of general articles on women in Congress was highest during the first six months of 1993 and then declined over the course of the term (Table 7.2). There were twice as many articles per month during the first six months of the 103rd Congress as there were during the final months of the term. This pattern is consistent with the expectation that the interest in women in Congress following the "Year of the Woman" would decrease over time.

However, when we examine press coverage of the individual members of the "Year of the Woman" class, no similar decrease in attention over time is evident (see Table 7.2). Instead, newly elected women members were actually mentioned in major newspapers less often during their first six months in office than they were during any other part of the term. The increase after six months in the frequency with which first-term Congresswomen were mentioned in major newspapers may parallel their increased involvement in legislative activities or increased attention to their own personal press operations. After all, during the first six months in office, new members spent most of their time learning their way around the Capitol.

Overall, the patterns in press coverage suggest that interest in general stories about women in Congress declined as the "Year of the Woman" faded into memory. However, this decline was partially compensated by increased attention after the first six months to the activities of individual Congresswomen.

Where Are Women in Congress Covered?

Political women and observers of women public officials often perceive a bias in the placement of articles concerning women elected officials. They argue that one of the ways the media treat women less seriously than they treat men is by relegating stories about women and politics to the style or women's sections of newspapers instead of placing them in the front section of the paper where they belong. Such positioning suggests that the activities of women in Congress are not serious news, and the placement of stories in the style section may create the impression that women's legislative behavior is less important than what they wear or feed their families.

A notable proportion of articles—14 percent of all articles on women in Congress ($N = 291$) and 10 percent of those articles with significant content on women in Congress ($N = 201$)—were published in the style sections of major newspapers. Nevertheless, the majority of the stories—54 percent of all articles and 60 percent of those with significant content on women in Congress—made their way into the front or national news section, suggesting that women in Congress more often than not are being taken seriously as national news and policy makers.

Although most papers seem to publish most of their articles about women in Congress in the front section of the paper, Congresswoman Schroeder's complaint, described earlier in this chapter, about the *Washington Post* relegating stories about women in Congress to the style page appears quite justified. One-quarter of all articles published in the *Washington Post* that had a significant focus on women in Congress were found in the style section; that is more than twice the average for all major papers. The *Post* more often than most major papers seems to be sending out the message that the interests and activities of women in Congress are not important enough to be considered hard news. Representative Schroeder and other women in Congress may have good reason to be concerned since the *Washington Post* is a major source of political information for members of Congress as well as for other political elites and opinion makers.

Who Covers Women in Congress?

While women have been traditionally underrepresented as journalists and editors (see Kay Mills in this volume), their numbers in the profession have been increasing. Mills argues that as this has happened, "women reporters have helped bring women candidates into the mainstream" and "have also had an impact in shaping political coverage and thus the climate in which women decide to run for office." Because of the changing gender composition of the newsroom, one might expect to find more women than men writing stories about women in Congress.

Our data support this hypothesis. Of articles with a significant focus on women in Congress ($N = 201$), 46 percent were written by women and 33 percent were written by men.[5] Perhaps women more often volunteer to write these stories or perhaps they are more frequently assigned to them because of their gender.

Nevertheless, when men write stories on women in Congress, they are more likely to have their stories appear on the front pages. Of the articles on women in Congress written by men, 61 percent were published in the front or news section of the paper; of the articles on women in Congress written by women, only 47 percent were published in the front section of the paper. In contrast, 20 percent of women journalists' stories ended up on the style page compared with only 8 percent of the stories by male journalists.

Biases and Themes in Press Coverage

In addition to the amount and placement of coverage, the content of the coverage which women in Congress receive also is important. In this section we examine both possible biases and major themes in newspaper articles on women in Congress.

Biases in the Content of Press Coverage

One of the most persistent complaints voiced by women politicians is that the media focus on the negative—on the problems that women in politics confront rather than on their accomplishments. For example, in a personal interview Tillie Fowler, a Republican Congresswoman from Florida, made the following observation about reporters:

> All they wanted sometimes . . . was "How have you been mistreated by the men? How have they acted chauvinistic toward you?" And my response would be . . . "They've been great to me. I haven't had any problems with them." They didn't want that. They only wanted the negatives. (Fowler, June 1995)

We examined press stories to see if they emphasized two of the most common problem areas for women politicians—juggling the demands of family and career and the sexism and exclusion they encounter within political institutions. We found that 15 percent of newspaper stories with significant content on women in Congress ($N = 201$) mentioned themes relating to sexism or exclusion and a much smaller proportion, 4 percent, discussed the problems of managing both families and political careers.

Perhaps the most frequently quoted example of sexism was a comment made by Representative Henry Hyde on the television show *Firing Line* in 1993. Hyde observed that "there are some who say there are so many women now on the floor of Congress, it looks like a mall" (*New York Times*, 16 September 1993). Stories about patronizing language from male colleagues and examples of women members being mistaken for staffers or other nonmembers were common.

One of the best examples of stories with the theme of juggling family and career was a lengthy article that made the front page of the *New*

York Times with the headline, "Even Women at Top Still Have Floors to Do" (*New York Times*, 31 May 1993). Among other fascinating facts about women in Congress, one learns from the article that Senator Dianne Feinstein picks up bath towels her husband refuses to hang up and that people are surprised to find that Congresswoman Lucille Roybal-Allard would be interested in a recipe.

Women in politics also accuse the media of emphasizing the superficial and the trivial. To test for this type of bias, we examined articles to see whether they discussed women's appearance or their attire, and we looked for articles assessing the bathroom situation on Capitol Hill.

An occasional article did comment on women's attire. One example was an article in the style section of the *Washington Post* (20 January 1993), which observed of the twenty-eight Congresswomen and five women Senators who attended an EMILY's List luncheon in their honor: ". . . the lineup of women on the stage of the ballroom . . . was eerily reminiscent of the Miss America pageant. But all of them were wearing suits." However, for the most part, reporters for the major papers seem to have gotten the message that it is inappropriate to discuss the appearance and clothing of Congresswomen. Only 3 percent of articles with significant content on women in Congress made explicit reference to how women members looked or dressed, and few of these references were particularly offensive.

The topic of congressional bathrooms was slightly more popular. Although only a few articles (4 percent of those with a significant focus on women in Congress) mentioned the restroom situation, bathrooms were important enough to be the focus of a major article written by a reporter for the *Orlando Sentinel* (11 May 1993), which was reprinted in the *Sacramento Bee* (30 May 1993) and the *Houston Chronicle* (29 May 1993). The headline for the original article in the Orlando paper, "No Plumbing Parity on Capitol Hill: All Bathrooms Are Not Created Equal in the House and the Senate," was rather timid compared to the headlines in the Sacramento paper, "In the Capitol, Congressmen Get the Royal Flush," and the Houston paper, "Skip to the Loo: Despite No Plumbing Parity, Congresswomen Can Complaints." The article described the inequities between the nearby "commodious restroom complete with enormous windows, a shoeshine stand, outsized gilt mirror, ceiling fans, a television and a water fountain" plus six toilets and four urinals available for male members and the distant "small, windowless ladies room equipped with three sinks, three toilets and a vanity table" available for female members. The article then raised the question of whether a new Congresswomen's bathroom should be constructed closer to the House floor similar to the recently constructed new restroom for women in the Senate. The Congresswomen and Senators interviewed for the story seemed irritated to be queried about bathrooms. When asked whether the construction of a women's restroom was a sign of progress, Senator Barbara Mikulski replied, "To ask me that question is really demeaning and patronizing." Senator Nancy Kassebaum quipped, "I still don't know where it is. I haven't needed it."

In addition to articles on bathrooms and occasional references to Congresswomen's appearance, there were several other examples of coverage that could be considered frivolous or trivial. For example, four articles focused on women members playing congressional baseball or basketball. The rumor that first-term women members of Congress rated the derrieres of male members over dinner also was reported in the press. Finally, one press report observed that as a result of the increased number of women serving in the Senate, kissing has joined back slapping as a congratulatory gesture.

Women in Congress as Agents of Change

The themes that were emphasized in coverage of women in the 1992 elections—Anita Hill, the "Year of the Woman," and sexual harassment—continued to be popular themes in coverage of the women who won election to Congress. Twenty percent of the articles with significant content on women in Congress ($N = 201$) explicitly mentioned Anita Hill, and almost as many made explicit reference to "The Year of the Woman" (17 percent) or to sexual harassment (19 percent). To the extent that Anita Hill and the "Year of the Woman" had by 1993 become symbols of change, in invoking these symbols journalists may well have been reinforcing the view of women in Congress as agents of change in the minds of their readers.

The idea that women in Congress are agents of change was addressed less symbolically and more directly in much of the press coverage. In fact, of the 201 articles with significant content on women in Congress, 16 percent mentioned that women in Congress have different perspectives than their male colleagues or that they make a substantive difference in public policy.

Another theme echoed in many of the articles was the theme of women members of Congress working together on issues where they had common interests. Articles recounted, for example, how women in the House worked together to try to defeat the Hyde Amendment to restrict Medicaid funding of abortions, how women in the Senate banded together to try to have Frank Kelso retired as a two-star rather than a four-star admiral because of the harassment of women by Navy pilots that took place at the Tailhook conference; how a delegation of women members traveled to Mexico on a fact-finding trip during the NAFTA debate; and how the women members sent jointly signed letters about common concerns to people ranging from Fidel Castro to Barbra Streisand to Bill Clinton. Several articles also focused on the cooperative effort of several first-term women in the House who as a group attended a series of reelection, fund-raising dinners in each other's districts. More than one-quarter of the articles, 29 percent, with a significant focus on women in Congress

($N = 201$) explicitly talked about women in Congress working together in some way. While some of these as well as other articles mentioned divisions and differences among Congresswomen (6 percent), the theme of working together was much more prevalent.

On which specific issues were women most often portrayed as working together? Table 7.3 presents the number of articles with significant content on women in Congress which focused on each of the legislative policy areas that are part of the larger CAWP study of women in the 103rd Congress. The two issues that received by far the most press attention were abortion and women's health, perhaps not coincidentally two of the major issues that were a priority for the Congressional Caucus for Women's Issues in the 103rd Congress. There was some overlap with a few articles mentioning both women's health and abortion; nevertheless, 41 percent of all articles with significant focus on women in Congress ($N = 201$) discussed women's health, abortion, or both.

Health care reform ranks a distant third to abortion and women's health as a topic covered in newspaper articles focusing on women in Congress (see Table 7.3). However, Congresswomen's involvement in health care reform, as reported in these articles, often had to do with provisions of proposed legislation dealing with abortion or women's health. Thus, of the twenty-four articles that discuss Congresswomen's involvement in health care reform, only six do not mention abortion or women's health.

Violence against women is the fourth most frequently mentioned issue in Table 7.3. Women in Congress were actively supportive of the Violence Against Women Act (VAWA), which was incorporated into the Omnibus Crime Bill. However, there was little discussion and no controversy within Congress over the Violence Against Women Act; in fact, VAWA passed on the floor of the House with a unanimous vote (Carroll

Table 7.3
Coverage of Selected Policy Areas

Policy Area	*Number of Articles*	*% of Articles*
Abortion	52	25.9
Women's health	43	21.4
Health care reform	24	11.9
Violence against women	15	7.5
Crime	11	5.5
Congressional reform	6	3.0
NAFTA	6	3.0
Campaign finance reform	5	2.5

Note: Mentions of selected policy areas and legislative initiatives in articles with significant content on women in Congress appearing in major newspapers, 1993–1994. $N = 201$
Source: *Lexis/Nexis* search.

1995). Consequently, it is not surprising that there was little coverage of VAWA in newspaper reports about women in Congress.

Relatively little coverage is given in the articles on women in Congress to the seemingly nongendered issues of crime, NAFTA, congressional reform, and campaign finance reform (see Table 7.3). Women members were actively involved in working on all these issues, but their impact was more as individuals and less as a collective force than in the areas of abortion and women's health.

For a final look at the content of newspaper coverage, Table 7.4 presents a list of the ten topics that emerged most frequently as the central focus of articles on women in Congress. While more than one subject may have been mentioned in an article, only the single most central theme or topic was coded for each article. The single largest category of articles presented in-depth profiles of one or more women members of Congress. Election coverage was the topic that was second on the list, followed closely by articles where the central focus was on the difference made by women in Congress; one of every ten articles had as its central focus a discussion of the ways that women in Congress were bringing different perspectives to bear on their work in Congress or were having a distinctive impact on policy or the institution. Four of the next five items on this list of most frequently mentioned central topics are policy areas where women played an active role—Admiral Kelso's retirement decision (which at its core was about sexual harassment), women's health, abortion, and health care reform. Also making this list of frequently mentioned central foci of articles about women in Congress are discussions of the numbers of women in Congress, the problems women in Congress confront, and fundraising for women's campaigns.

Table 7.4
Subject of Coverage of Women in Congress

	Number of Articles	*% of Articles*
In-depth portrait	23	11.4
Elections	22	10.9
Difference women in Congress make	20	10.0
Admiral Kelso retirement	17	8.5
Women's health	17	8.5
Abortion	13	6.4
Representation (numbers) of women in Congress	9	4.5
Health care reform	7	3.5
Problems Congresswomen confront	7	3.5
Fund raising for women's campaigns	7	3.5

Note: Most frequently mentioned subject of articles with significant content on women in Congress appearing in major papers, 1993–94. $N = 201$
Source: *Lexis/Nexis* search.

Coverage of Individual Women Members

We selected articles for our content analysis that made reference to Congresswomen collectively or to more than one woman member; we did not search for every article mentioning an individual Congresswoman. Nevertheless, an examination of the coverage which individual women received in more general articles on women in Congress is quite illuminating (Table 7.5).

Almost without exception, as one might expect, individual Senators were mentioned more frequently than individual members of the House. The two clear exceptions are Nancy Kassebaum, the Senator who received the least coverage, and Pat Schroeder, the most senior Congresswoman who received more coverage than any of the Senators and far more coverage than any other woman member of the House.

There are a number of possible reasons for the large amount of coverage Schroeder received. First, as the most senior Democratic woman in

Table 7.5
Women Members of Congress with Most Coverage

	Number of Mentions
Senators	
Dianne Feinstein (D-92)	50
Carol Moseley-Braun (D-92)	45
Barbara Boxer (D-92)	44
Barbara Mikulski (D-86)	37
Patty Murray (D-92)	37
Kay Bailey Hutchison (R-93)	31
Nancy Kassebaum (R-78)	16
Representatives	
Pat Schroeder (D-72)	54
Nita Lowey (D-88)	17
Maria Cantwell (D-92)	16
Olympia Snowe (R-78)	14
Cynthia McKinney (D-92)	14
Marjorie Margolies-Mezvinsky (D-92)	14
Anna Eshoo (D-92)	13
Barbara Kennelly (D-82)	12
Maxine Waters (D-90)	12
Karen English (D-92)	12
Lynn Woolsey (D-92)	12
Eva Clayton (D-92)	11
Lynn Schenk (D-92)	11
Leslie Byrne (D-92)	10

a Democratic-controlled House and as the Democratic cochair of the Congressional Caucus for Women's Issues, she was an obvious spokesperson for efforts organized by the caucus or, in fact, any efforts where women worked together. As Timothy Cook has noted, most members of Congress would rather get local than national press coverage, since they have to be reelected by people who read the local paper, not the *Washington Post* or the *New York Times* (Cook 1989, 82–83). However, members may be very oriented toward getting national press coverage if they have officeholding ambitions beyond Congress or want to advance a particular policy agenda (Cook 1989). Despite retiring from Congress in 1996, Schroeder may well harbor other political ambitions; after all, she explored running for President in 1988. She also has been a major proponent of women's health and women's rights more generally and has played a critical role in helping to set the congressional agenda in these areas. Finally, Schroeder is extremely quotable, which as Cook points out, is an asset in attracting media attention (Cook 1989, 54); she has a good sense of humor and usually manages to come up with clever one-liners.

Two other findings from Table 7.5 are particularly striking. The first is that Republican women are mentioned far less often than Democratic women members. The two Republican Senators received fewer mentions than any of the Democratic Senators, although Kay Bailey Hutchison may have fared better had she entered office before June 1993. Only one Republican woman member of the House received more than ten mentions—Olympia Snowe, who in the 103rd Congress was the Republican cochair of the Congressional Caucus for Women's Issues and who during much of the term was preparing to run or running for a U.S. Senate seat. In large part, this partisan difference in coverage undoubtedly reflects the fact that the Democrats were the party in power; the distribution probably would appear quite different in the 104th Congress where the Republicans control both houses.

The other finding—the prominence of first-term women—is even more striking and offers some of the strongest evidence in this chapter of the effect of the "Year of the Woman" in influencing media coverage. On the Senate side, three of the first-term Democratic women were cited more frequently than the senior Democratic woman Senator, Barbara Mikulski, and the fourth newly elected Democratic woman Senator received an equal number of citations. On the House side, nine of the fourteen women who received ten or more individual mentions in major newspaper coverage were in their first term. Clearly, the "Year of the Woman" class received an extraordinary amount of press attention relative to their more senior women colleagues.

Discussion and Conclusions

Three sets of conclusions emerge from this analysis. First, the "Year of the Woman" and the high level of interest surrounding the 1992 elections did seem to influence coverage of women in the 103rd Congress. Both the "Year of the Woman" and Anita Hill were frequently mentioned in articles about women in Congress. The women who were elected to Congress for the first time during 1992 clearly received more media attention than one would normally expect first-term members of Congress to receive. Not only did they receive more media attention than their first-term male colleagues but also many of them were more often mentioned in general articles about women in Congress than were most of the more senior women in Congress. As time passed and the saliency of the "Year of the Woman" waned, general press coverage of women in Congress declined. However, this decline was partially compensated by an increase in attention to individual first-term members following their first six months in office.

The second conclusion to emerge from this study is that some fairly clear messages about women in Congress are conveyed in newspaper coverage. For the most part the impression that the reader receives is a positive one. Women in Congress are portrayed as agents of change who are making a difference despite having to struggle against sexism and to juggle family lives and careers. However, the reporting on women in Congress definitely leaves the impression that women members are most concerned with and active around issues of women's health, abortion, and to a lesser extent sexual harassment. It is on these issues that they are portrayed as agents of change who are making a difference.

This leads to the third conclusion. We found some limited support for some of the accusations of bias and trivialization that sometimes have been voiced against the media by political women and their supporters. There were some articles about bathrooms, occasionally a reporter would mention a woman's appearance or attire, and some articles about women in Congress were relegated to the style pages. However, the major problem we found with coverage of women in Congress could be better characterized as one of *omission* rather than one of *commission*. The major problem is not so much with the coverage that exists but rather with what does not exist. Half the picture has been reported reasonably well, but the other half is missing.

What is missing from general press coverage on women in Congress is any sense that women are important players on legislation other than women's health, abortion, and a handful of other related concerns. There is barely a mention anywhere of women's involvement in foreign affairs, international trade, the appropriations process, or regulatory reform, for example.

In reporting on women, reporters seem to focus on what women do collectively or the problems they share as women, and since women in Congress banded together to work on women's health, to support pro-choice legislation, and to oppose Kelso's retirement as a four-star admiral, those are the efforts that received coverage in the press. Women in Congress are the primary proponents for legislation such as women's health and abortion, and press coverage accurately conveys this. However, Congresswomen also are active on a wide range of other types of legislation, but one would never know this from reading general press coverage on women in Congress.

It certainly is possible for the press to focus on women as a category—to write a story on women—and yet to examine what women in Congress do individually to influence legislation. But stories focusing on the broader and multifaceted contributions of women, as individuals as well as collectively, are not written. The lack of such stories means that press coverage of women in Congress presents a narrow portrayal of what women in Congress can and did accomplish and reinforces, rather than challenges, the perception that women in Congress only do "women's stuff."

For example, we know from our larger research project on women in the 103rd Congress that individual women made substantial contributions to the Crime Bill and were key players in the health care reform debates.[6] On the Crime Bill, Dianne Feinstein was the architect and chief sponsor of the assault weapons ban in the Senate. Senator Carol Moseley-Braun offered a package of amendments to the Crime Bill dealing with juveniles and crime, the most controversial of which permits juveniles age thirteen and older to be tried as adults when they commit certain violent federal crimes. Senator Kay Bailey Hutchison sponsored an amendment to the bill which prohibits inmates from obtaining Pell grants to pay for their college educations, and Senator Barbara Boxer sponsored a successful amendment barring states from releasing personal information provided on motor vehicle records. On the House side, Congresswoman Susan Molinari was responsible for a provision that allows evidence of a defendant's prior sex offenses to be admitted in federal sex crime trials, and Congresswoman Jennifer Dunn was instrumental in adding a provision that requires registration of sex offenders and allows police to notify communities of their presence.

Women members of Congress also made substantial contributions to the debate over health care reform. Not only did the women in Congress create a political environment in which women's health and reproductive health provisions could not be ignored, but also individual women lobbied for other "nongendered" issues to be included in health care reform legislation. For example, because of their placement on the House Ways and Means Committee, a committee with jurisdiction over health care legislation, Congresswomen Barbara Kennelly and Nancy Johnson were especially engaged in the debates over health care reform. Nancy Johnson offered at least eighteen amendments that passed. These included provisions to lessen the financial impact of insurance costs on employers and to cap malpractice awards. Barbara Kennelly introduced an amendment to prevent cost shifting in insurance which passed by voice vote. Other women were also involved. Patsy Mink sought to have Hawaii exempted from any health care reform package, and Lynn Woolsey offered amendments to cover the cost of medical foods for specific diseases and to train physicians in wellness, health promotion, alternative therapies, and self-care.

In the newspaper articles focusing on women in Congress which we examined for this chapter, contributions such as these that women, acting as individuals, made to the Crime Bill and health care reform are invisible. Future research might well explore the reasons why editors and journalists fail to investigate what women as a category do individually as well as collectively to influence legislation such as the Crime Bill and health care reform. Why are there no stories which examine how the contours of the Crime Bill, the debate over health care reform, or the provisions and fate of any major piece of legislation might have been different without the individual, as well as the collective, contributions of women members of Congress?

The question of why general articles on women and Congress limit their policy-related focus to collective efforts on behalf of women's issues is certainly one important question for future research. However, because the research presented in this chapter represents one of the first attempts to assess media coverage of women serving in public office, it suggests several other questions for future research as well. One important question is whether women members of Congress are covered differently in newspapers located in the districts of specific members than they are in the major newspapers examined for this analysis. Although we found that coverage of women in Congress in major papers conveys the impression that women in Congress are active mostly around women's issues, papers which serve a member's specific constituency may convey a very different message about the contributions of the woman member or women in Congress more generally. Because many of these papers tend to be less professional than the major papers, they may be more likely than the major papers to exhibit biases such as treating women less seriously than men, focusing on their appearances and family lives, and relegating stories about women in politics to the style pages. In addition to examining whether coverage of women in Congress shows different patterns in district-based newspapers, future research might also examine whether patterns in the coverage of women in Congress vary across media like television, radio, and magazines. Also important is the question of whether women serving in state and local offices are covered in ways similar to the patterns we found for women serving in Congress. Finally, a careful, systematic comparison of the press coverage received by women and men serving in Congress or other offices would be very useful. Certainly, more research is needed if we are to enhance our limited understanding of how the media portray women public officials and how media coverage influences public perceptions of women in politics and their political careers.

Notes

1. We used October 1994 as the final month for our search because the reporting in November and December focuses largely on election coverage and women who were elected to the 104th Congress.

2. The major newspapers which had at least one article on women in Congress and are included in our data set are: *New York Times*, *Washington Post*, *USA Today*, *Chicago Tribune*, *Los Angeles Times*, *Cleveland Plain Dealer*, *Atlanta Journal* and *Constitution*, *St. Louis Post-Dispatch*, *Phoenix Gazette*, *Sacramento Bee*, *Newsday*, *Orlando Sentinel*, *Arizona Republic*, *Boston Globe*, *San Francisco Chronicle*, *Seattle Times*, *Chicago Sun Times*, *Hartford Courant*, *San Diego Union-Tribune*, *Baltimore Sun*, *Houston Chronicle*, *Dallas Morning News*, *Minneapolis Star Tribune*, *Rocky Mountain News*, *St. Petersburg Times*, *Pittsburgh Post-Gazette*, and *Fort Lauderdale Sentinel.*

3. Several of these articles were published in more than one major newspaper. We chose to treat reprinted articles as a single case for purposes of this data set, but we did record all major newspapers where the article was published.

4. For these searches we counted every entry in the "major papers" category including international papers and newspaper abstracts.

5. 1.5 percent of articles were coauthored by members of both sexes; 2.0 percent were written by authors with gender-ambiguous names; and 16.9 percent were compiled from wire services or were without an author for some other reason.

6. For more information on the impact of women members of Congress on health care reform, the Crime Bill, and other legislation, see Dodson et al. 1995; Dodson 1995; Carroll 1995.

8

Women Leaders Worldwide: A Splash of Color in the Photo Op

Pippa Norris

Historically women have always been underrepresented in the highest offices of state. Margaret Thatcher, Indira Gandhi, and Golda Meir swept the world stage but they remain the exception: only twenty-three women have ever been elected heads of state or government (see Table 8.1). In 1994, membership in the exclusive club of Presidents and Prime Ministers included 180 men, and 9 women (United Nations 1995a). Worldwide women are 9 percent of parliamentarians, and 5.6 percent of cabinet ministers (United Nations 1994). The familiar gender imbalance in government office, evident at every level, is most dramatic at the apex of power. In Jean Blondel's study of world leaders, less than .005 percent were women (1987, 116–17).

Studies have examined many plausible explanations for this situation including the supply of candidates, the demands of gatekeepers, and the structure of opportunities in the political system (Norris and Lovenduski 1995). Most work has focused on women in local, state, and national legislative office, the first stages of political careers (see, for example, Darcy et al. 1994; Burrell 1994; Carroll 1994), although a growing literature is starting to explore women as national leaders (Genovese 1993; Beckman and D'Amico 1994; D'Amico and Beckman 1995).

One factor which may prove an obstacle for women at every level, but which has yet to receive systematic attention, is the role of the media. The feminist literature has long expressed concern that women newsmakers are not mirrored by the media in a way that accurately reflects their roles and responsibilities. Many believe media coverage may influence women's participation in public life by reinforcing sex-role stereo-

Table 8.1
Women Elected Heads of State or Government

	Leader	*Country*	*Office*	*First Elected*
1	Siramavo Bandaranaike	Sri Lanka	PM	1960
2	Indira Gandhi	India	PM	1966
3	Golda Meir	Israel	PM	1969
4	Isabel Peron	Argentina	President	1974
5	Margaret Thatcher	UK	PM	1979
6	Maria de Lourdes Pintasilgo	Portugal	PM	1979
7	Lidia Geiler	Bolivia	President	1979
8	Vigdis Finnbogadottir	Iceland	President	1980
9	Eugenia Charles	Dominica	PM	1980
10	Milka Planinc	Yugoslavia	President	1982
11	Corazon Aquino	Philippines	President	1986
12	Gro Harlem Brundtland	Norway	PM	1986
13	Benazir Bhutto	Pakistan	PM	1988
14	Ertha Pascal-Trouillot	Haiti	President	1990
15	Violeta Chamorro	Nicaragua	President	1990
16	Mary Robinson	Ireland	President	1990
17	Khaleda Ziaur Rahman	Bangladesh	PM	1991
18	Edith Cresson	France	PM	1991
19	Tamsu Ciller	Turkey	PM	1993
20	Kim Campbell	Canada	PM	1993
21	Hanna Suchocka	Poland	PM	1993
22	Agathe Uwilingiyimana	Rwanda	PM	1994
23	Chandrika Bandaranaike Kumaratunga	Sri Lanka	President	1994

Source: *The World's Women: Trend and Statistics* (United Nations 1994).

types throughout society, shaping the aspirations of women and men, and influencing the attitudes of key gatekeepers like campaign donors, party activists, and voters.

The aim of this chapter is to explore whether the news media depict world leaders through a gender-relevant or gender-neutral perspective. The core questions are threefold: are there significant differences in the *news visibility* of women and men leaders; are women leaders portrayed in *sex-stereotyped* ways in terms of issues concerns and personal traits; and is the portrayal of women leaders in the news seen through a *gendered frame*?

Expectations about the Visibility of Women Leaders

Based on the previous studies we would clearly expect female leaders to be less visible in the news than their male counterparts. Research has documented the way that women were underrepresented in the U.S. news in the 1970s, especially as public officials, although this pattern has changed slightly in recent years. Early studies noted that women tended to be either invisible or a silent presence in news programs, in the United States and European countries (see Gunter 1995) The first systematic report in 1977, by the *U.S. Commission on Civil Rights*, studied American network news from March 1974 to February 1975. The study found that of all "newsmakers" (people identified by the anchor, reporter, or appearing in the news) 13 percent were female. Of these, most were covered as the wives of leaders, or as experts in areas which were considered "women's topics" such as abortion or birth control. Few women were government officials or public figures in their own right. Moreover, the commission found no news stories focused on women's achievements or accomplishments (U.S. Commission on Civil Rights 1977, 49–54).

The follow-up study for the U.S. Commission on Civil Rights identified even fewer women as newsmakers (7 percent) in 1979. In total the follow-up study analyzed 330 stories, and found these included as newsmakers two female government officials, one woman expert, and three wives of public figures. The remaining eighteen women newsmakers were covered as helpless victims of crime or natural disasters (*U.S. Commission on Civil Rights* 1979, 24–25). Studies during the 1970s found a similar picture of little news about women public officials in other countries (see Gunter 1995). By depicting women in news only as wives, mothers, or sex objects, Gaye Tuchman argued that they experienced a "symbolic annihilation" (1978a).

More recent research has found greater coverage of women in the news, although women remain far from parity. *Women, Men and Media* (1994) has monitored the front pages of twenty American major and minor newspapers, and network television news in a series of annual studies from 1989 to 1995. The research has found women's visibility as sources or subjects has grown during this period. The number of women referenced on newspaper front pages almost doubled from 1989 to 1995, from 11 percent to 19 percent. During the same period, the proportion of front-page photos of women expanded from 24 percent to 39 percent. On network television news, the study found one-quarter of those interviewed as sources were women (see also Rakov and Kranich 1991).

Yet although women have generally become more visible in the news, *Women, Men and Media* concluded that few women newsmakers were political or opinion leaders. The survey found little coverage of national public figures like Senator Carol Moseley-Braun, Representative Patricia Schroeder, Attorney General Janet Reno, or even Hillary Rodham Clinton. In 1994, of the eighty-nine members of Congress interviewed on the sample of network news stories, only five were female (*Women, Men and Media 1994*).

Similarly Johnson and Christ (1989) analyzed coverage of newsmakers in *Time* magazine. The study found only 14 percent of the covers of

Time showed images of women. Of these most of the women were entertainers (37 percent), and only 12 percent were political leaders, activists, or government officials. Douglas (1991) examined the ten analysts who appeared most frequently on the *CBS*, *ABC*, and *NBC* nightly news, and found that all were men, and some appeared as many as fifty-eight times in a single year. Looking more directly at press coverage of campaigns, Kahn (1991) studied candidates for the U.S. Senate in elections from 1982 to 1986. The study found that all-male Senate races received more press coverage than races which included female candidates. Greater reporting of male politicians has also been found in other countries. Thoveron (1987) carried out a cross-national study of television news broadcasts in the ten member states of the European Union. The research found that women were 16 percent of those interviewed on the news, but only 9 percent of the politicians interviewed.

How the evidence is to be interpreted depends upon the appropriate benchmark against which news coverage can be judged. On the basis of the study of American news coverage, Betty Friedan, echoing Tuchman, concluded that little had changed since the 1970s:

> We are still largely invisible in the media, still subject to symbolic annihilation, despite our increasing numbers in politics and in the workplace. (Women, Men and Media 1994)

Yet when this evidence was presented to editors, the common defense was to argue that the media functions as a "mirror of society": few women leaders are featured on the front pages because there are few women in power. In interpreting the evidence we therefore need to consider how much media attention women and men politicians receive compared against an appropriate benchmark for their position in power. On a simple basis, if women are 9 percent of the political personalities interviewed in European news, but 20 percent of Europe's national politicians, then framing effects can be demonstrated. But it is difficult to establish an appropriate benchmark to judge coverage of government leaders.

The consensus from the available studies strongly suggests women are less visible on the front pages. Yet despite this evidence there remain plausible reasons to believe that as government leaders on the world stage, the amount of coverage may be either gender-neutral, or women might attract more front-page attention than men.

Coverage of women Presidents and Prime Ministers might be different from routine reporting of politicians at lower levels, because news about government leaders is institutionalized. The White House press covers the President, whether male or (if ever) female. Coverage is automatically built into news organizations. Moreover, news about world leaders may be largely country-related and event-driven; these leaders are referred to if their countries are regarded as newsworthy, in stories about international conflict, economic trade, or development, which affect international interests. Studies of international news flows, stimulated by the debate about the New World Information Order, have found well-established patterns of which countries receive most attention in American and British media (Norris 1996d). As such, the amount of attention given to each leader may be a by-product of events in their country, rather than their gender.

Moreover, because women world leaders remain exceptional, they may be regarded as more newsworthy. News concerns events which are unexpected and novel, within the limits of what is familiar (McQuail 1992a, 207). Journalists may regard press briefings about Corazon Aquino, Golda Meir, or Benazir Bhutto as more interesting front-page material for their readers than similar stories about Fidel Ramos, Yitzhak Rabin, and Nawaz Sharif. In photos of Group of Seven leadership summits, Kim Campbell and Margaret Thatcher may have stood out as a splash of color against the gray suits.

Expectations about Sex Stereotyping of Women Leaders

Visibility represents one issue. Even more important, when women politicians are covered, the common critique is that a gendered lens in the media presents women leaders in terms of sex-role stereotypes. In this book, as discussed in the introduction, *stereotyping* means describing individuals positively or negatively on the basis of characteristics seen as common to their group. For politicians these characteristics can be in terms of their personal traits or their issue concerns. In the latter case, a woman politician may be seen as more knowledgeable about child care, for example, while a man might be perceived as stronger on national security issues, irrespective of their personal experience, interests, or expertise. In just the same way, regardless of their own position, an African American member of Congress may be seen as a liberal who favors welfare spending, while we may assume that a white Republican member from Alabama prefers conservative tax cuts. Stereotypes are widespread, since we all have some views about groups but we lack perfect information about individuals. Such stereotypes may prove an advantage or a liability for leaders, depending upon the context. As shown by chapters by Kahn and Gordon, and Iyengar et al., in their image-building and communication strategies in campaigns politicians may try to emphasize, or distance themselves from, traditional stereotypes. Reporting which relies upon group stereotypes may present an inaccurate portrayal of individual leaders, since it ascribes characteristics to them which may not be true.

Previous research based on survey and experimental evidence has repeatedly found that the public relies on gender stereotypes to cue their expectations and evaluations of women and men candidates (Huddy and Terkildsen 1993a, 1993b; Kahn 1994; Sapiro 1982; Sigelman and Sigelman 1984; Leeper 1991; Burrell 1994; Norris and Lovenduski 1995). These studies suggest a distinction can be drawn between stereotypes based on *issue competency* and those concerning *personal traits.* When asked about public policy issues, many people assume that male leaders can deal more effectively with problems of international affairs, the economy, and foreign policy, while women are seen as stronger on domestic and "compassion" issues like health, family welfare, and education. In terms of personal characteristics, the public believes that men are more likely to prove strong, ambitious, and tough leaders, while women politicians are commonly seen as more caring, approachable, sensitive, and honest (Norris and Lovenduski 1995). These stereotypes are not unexpected, since they represent simple extrapolations from women's private, domestic roles to public issues and problems (Sapiro 1983, 146). Images of women which were pervasive in the 1950s may continue to shape coverage of women's roles today, in a cultural time-lag, despite the transformation in women's lives. This process may be particularly evident in coverage of women leaders, since those who have become Presidents or Prime Ministers challenge some of our most deep-rooted beliefs about the appropriate division of sex roles.

Given the evidence that sex stereotypes are widespread in society, we might expect such stereotypes to be reflected in media coverage. Biographical and personal accounts commonly suggest that descriptions of women leaders focus on gender-based evaluations of dress and demeanor, rather than the substance of decisions and actions (Witt, Paget, and Matthews 1994). Previous research by Kim Kahn (1991, 1994) looked at newspaper coverage for U.S. Senate and gubernatorial candidates in the 1980s. She found that journalists differentiate between male and female candidates, particularly in Senate races. As challengers, women were presented by the press as less viable than men. Moreover, policy coverage was gendered: "male" issues such as foreign policy, defense, economics, and agriculture received far more coverage in campaigns than "female" issues like social policy, the environment, and minority rights. In addition, the press discussed "female" issues more frequently when covering women candidates, and reported "male" issues more extensively with men candidates. Women candidates were also more likely to be described in terms of the personal traits associated with traditional "female" stereotypes. Whether this proved an electoral advantage or disadvantage for women running for office depended upon the broader context of the campaign.

As discussed earlier, studies of women leaders have concluded that women leaders are extremely diverse, and few fit conventional "feminine" stereotypes (Genovese 1993). There is little in common between leaders such as Gro Harlem Brundtland, Mary Robinson, Margaret Thatcher, and Kim Campbell, beyond their sex. D'Amico and Beckman (1995, 26) suggests that ideas about gender difference appear to have little use when generalizing about the policy agenda, or decision-making style, of women national leaders. Moreover, women leaders span the ideological spectrum from feminist to antifeminist, and from pacifists to those who have overseen programs of military expansion and nuclear weapons development. Given their records in office, there was little conventionally "feminine" about Prime Ministers Golda Meir, Indira Gandhi, or Margaret Thatcher. If women leaders are described in a common way in the news, despite these differences, this suggests the media are viewing women through sex stereotyped lenses.

Expectations about Gendered News Frames

Lastly, since the 1970s critics have commonly suggested that one reason for the paucity of women in public life is that the news media usually use a gendered frame when covering women leaders. By a "news frame," as discussed in the book's introduction, we mean the "peg" which is used to structure stories of women leaders. As argued earlier, news frames guide the selection, presentation, and evaluation of information, for journalists and readers, by slotting new events, issues, or actors into familiar categories. The other chapters in this book demonstrate the extent of gender framing in the news in different regards, and although there is biographical and anecdotal evidence, previous studies have not looked systematically at how women leaders have been framed.

Research Design

To analyze these issues, this chapter compares coverage of twenty world leaders, chosen as powerful elected Prime Ministers or Presidents, with a significant impact on world politics, although drawn from divergent political systems and national cultures. The ten women leaders include Margaret Thatcher (UK), Corazon Aquino (Philippines), Benazir Bhutto (Pakistan), Gro Harlem Brundtland (Norway), Tansu Ciller (Turkey), Edith Cresson (France), Violeta Chamorro (Nicaragua), Kim Campbell (Canada), Indira Gandhi (India), and Mary Robinson (Ireland).[1]

What should be stressed is the great diversity of these women, and their political systems, as other studies have emphasized (Genovese 1993; D'Amico and Beckman 1995). This strengthens the research design, because if there are similar patterns in media coverage, this is not because the women themselves share much in common. This list includes leaders of countries where women are well established in public life (Norway), while others have few female parliamentarians (France). Some nations have a well-entrenched women's movement (Canada), while others have many religious fundamentalists hostile to women's independence (Turkey, Pakistan). It includes large and small countries, developed and developing economies, as well as established and emerging democracies. Pathways to power varied substantially: some were appointed to leadership through patronage (Ciller, Cresson), some followed the "family mantle route"

(Aquino, Bhutto, Chamorro), while others fought strongly contested independent elections (Robinson, Campbell). Some had lengthy careers in power (Thatcher, Gandhi), while others were relatively short-lived (Campbell, Cresson). Some were self-identified feminists (Robinson, Brundtland), while others rejected this label (Thatcher). In 1995 half of these leaders remain in office, while the remainder retired during the 1990s (with the exception of Indira Gandhi who was assassinated in 1984). As the comparison is limited to only ten women we need considerable caution in generalizing about minor differences in the results. Nevertheless this small group does represent almost half of the universe of women who have ever been elected as government leaders.

The analysis uses a paired sample design. The media coverage these women received is compared with their closest male counterpart (see Table 8.2). Women holding office today are contrasted with their immediate predecessor (among Norwegian Prime Ministers, for example, Gro Harlem Brundtland is contrasted with Jan Syse). Those women who retired are compared with their immediate successor (Margaret Thatcher, for example, is contrasted with John Major).

Eight sources were selected from the *Lexis/Nexis* data base to include English-language media with extensive coverage of international news, and with data for the whole period of the analysis.[2] This included three newspapers, the *New York Times*, the *Washington Post*, and the *Financial Times*. The two largest wire services are included, namely, *Associated Press* and *Reuters*. *The Economist* and *Newsweek* were selected as representing leading weekly news magazines. Lastly, given its unique breadth of in-

Table 8.2
Leadership Coverage in International News Media

	Women Leaders	*Total Stories*	*Stories Per Day*	*Men Leaders*	*Total Stories*	*Stories Per Day*
Canada	Campbell	706	5.35	Chretien	1,673	2.72
France	Cresson	1,404	4.40	Beregovoy	2,171	6.03
India	I. Gandhi	11,229	6.42	R. Gandhi	11,384	6.14
Ireland	Robinson	506	.30	Hillary	9	.00
Nicaragua	Chamorro	679	.36	Ortega	11,444	2.91
Norway	Brundtland	1,332	.78	Syse	78	.21
Pakistan	Bhutto	5,465	8.65	Sharif	2,274	2.54
Philippines	Aquino	2,146	.36	Ramos	4,224	5.72
Turkey	Ciller	1,565	2.07	Demirel	3,427	3.82
UK	Thatcher	51,141	12.12	Major	21,082	12.50
Mean		76,173	3.81		57,766	4.43

Note: Search for stories in Reuters, Associated Press, *New York Times*, *Washington Post*, *Financial Times*, BBC World Service, *The Economist*, *Newsweek*.

ternational reporting, the *BBC World Service* was included. Over 100,000 stories from these sources were counted in this comparison.

All these sources are Anglo-American in origin, which would be an important bias if we were attempting to compare cross-national coverage of different leaders. This factor, however, should not affect the paired comparison of women and men leaders *within* each country. Moreover when measuring the amount of coverage each leader received, there were strong intercorrelations between these different sources. Leaders who were frequently reported in, say, *The Economist*, were also likely to be widely covered in the *New York Times* and the *BBC World Service.* When the data were tested for reliability, the amount of coverage in each source was found to form a consistent measure (Cronbach Alpha = .92). To measure the amount of coverage the study used a simple count of stories across all sources.

To measure the more subtle forms of sex stereotyping and gender framing the study adopted a more focused, qualitative, and interpretative approach. We start by sketching out the main themes which emerge from newspaper stories in the *New York Times*, the *Washington Post*, and the *Financial Times.* Framing effects can be expected to be particularly strong in the appointment period, when readers are presented with detailed biographical portrayals of leaders when they first become President or Prime Minister. To understand how women leaders are covered we concentrate on articles about them during the first week of their appointment. This coverage (which can be seen as analogous to reporting of the early primaries in American elections) may be particularly important since it helps shape initial perceptions of a leader's character, experience, and background for readers with little prior background information. In this period, commentary often relies quite heavily on conventional interpretive frames. These frames may change as journalists can judge leaders on their records in office. Later coverage is usually characterized by more routine reporting about specific events, activities, or policy initiatives by leaders, while the record, character, and achievements of a leader are again reassessed when they leave office. But the initial frames provide an important indication of what is expected about women in politics. The nuances of sex stereotypes and framing can best be understood through a detailed qualitative deconstruction of what is, and is not, said about their portrayal, rather than through a more formal content analysis.

Are Women Leaders Less Visible in the News?

To examine the amount of coverage the content analysis counted the total number of stories mentioning each leader's name in each source.[3] In total 133,939 stories were identified from the search. It should be noted that the story could include just a passing reference to the leader, ("Kim Campbell attended the G-7 meeting, along with President Clinton and John Major") or it could involve an extended treatment of their policies and character. This is a crude measure, which makes no attempt to gauge the length of each story. Nevertheless a story count is probably a more reliable measure to use across different sources, since there are systematic variations in the length of stories from newspapers, magazines, and the wire services. For a consistent comparison between pairs, we needed to control for how long each leader was in power. The total number of stories about each leader was divided by the number of days each held office. This standardized the average number of daily stories per leader.

The first results of this analysis, in Table 8.2, show the total amount of coverage each leader received, and the standardized measure. Most importantly the study found, contrary to some initial expectations, that women leaders were covered in slightly fewer stories (3.8 stories per day) than men (4.4 stories per day). When subjected to T-tests for paired samples this difference proved statistically significant (t-value = 3.1, p = .006). Expressed simply, this means that each male leader is covered in about 1,600 stories per year, compared with 1,400 stories about each female leader, a modest but still significant gender gap.

Why, then, is there a perception among some observers that women leaders receive headline treatment? If we turn to the total number of stories about these leaders, it is apparent that these perceptions may be heavily influenced by coverage of Margaret Thatcher, and to a lesser extent of Benazir Bhutto and Indira Gandhi, each of whom were widely reported in the press. In total 51,100 stories mentioned Mrs. Thatcher in the sample, more than twice as many as any other leader. This overwhelming coverage partly reflects the British origin of many of the sources, and also the fact that she enjoyed a long tenure at No.10. If we turn to the standardized measure, it reveals that, contrary to expectations, the gray John Major receives more daily news coverage than the remarkable Mrs. Thatcher. In the pairs, the women leaders who proved more newsworthy included Benazir Bhutto, Indira Gandhi, Kim Campbell, Gro Harlem Brundtland, and Mary Robinson. In the others, the male leaders who received more coverage included Pierre Beregovoy, Daniel Ortega, Fidel Ramos, Suleyman Demirel, and John Major.

Based on these results we can conclude that, contrary to some impressions, among world leaders men usually receive slightly more press attention than women. The number of leaders in this study is limited, however, so we should be cautious about drawing broader generalizations from these results, and the difference in coverage is fairly modest. Nevertheless, based on analyzing over 100,000 stories in different sources, the gender gap in reporting proved statistically significant. The lower visibility of women politicians, found as candidates for office, is also evident even at the top.

Do Stories of Women Leaders Focus on Sex Stereotypes?

Sex Stereotyping in Personal Appearance. There is considerable variation in the portrayal of women leaders when first appointed President or Prime Minister. Nevertheless several themes emerge as common in these stories. The focus rarely reflected the simple and crude sex-role stereotypes found among the public, in terms of describing either personal characteristics or issue concerns. If one looked very hard, one can very occasionally come across clear examples of gratuitous remarks about personal appearance or simple sexism. Kim Campbell was described as "the glamorous former Justice Minister, who was once photographed bare-shouldered behind her legal robes" (Clyde Farnsworth, *New York Times* 13 June 1993, 3). It was reported that Turkish newspapers labeled Tansu Ciller as the "lady with a smile of steel" (John Murray Brown, *New York Times* 3 July 1993, 3). Assiduous readers of the newspaper of record learned that "Mrs. Brundtland is the mother of four children. Three of her children, Jorgen, 13 years old, Ivar, 15, and Kaga, 17 live at home. Knut, 19, is currently working on an offshore oil rig" (*New York Times* 4 February 1981). Moreover it was revealed that President Benazir Bhutto was "known as Pinkie to her friends" (*New York Times* 2 December 1988). Meanwhile Britain's Prime Minister was described as "the less experienced, stridently aggressive Thatcher, who lectured Britain like a stern schoolmistress" (Leonard Downie, *Washington Post* 7 May 1979). President Chamorro was seen as having "aristocratic bearing, silver hair and motherly warmth. 'She is like a mother figure,' said an international official" (Mark A. Uhlig, *New York Times* 27 February 1990). In one vicious commentary, headlined "A man-eater with no teeth," Cresson was depicted as "all blather and no policy," and what seemed even worse, an hour late for lunch (Ian Davidson, *Financial Times* 20 May 1991). But, it must be stressed, these sorts of remarks are highly exceptional and do not reflect the vast bulk of the coverage.

Personal Traits of Leaders. If we compare descriptions of the personal traits of leaders, there are few references to the traditional stereotypes seeing women leaders as conciliatory, compassionate, and sensitive while men are regarded as strong, ambitious, and tough. As politicians, most of the women are seen as ambitious, effective, and often more confrontational than their rivals. Cresson was described as "left-wing and interventionist, nationalist and combative" with a "combative style and left-wing political instincts . . . Where Mr. Rocard has built his political technique on consultation and compromise, Mrs. Cresson—never one to mince her words—tends to decide rapidly, intuitively and forcibly" (*Financial Times* 16 May 1991). The *New York Times* (16 May 1991) closed its story by describing how Cresson lost an earlier contest for a parliamentary seat, "but her vigorous campaign earned her the sobriquet 'la battante'—'the fighter.' " Bhutto was described as "a strong, Western-educated politician of skill and experience in her own right" (*New York Times* 2 December 1988). Campbell was portrayed as "relaxed and comfortable, radiating energy and alertness . . . an energetic, self-confident woman with a strongly intellectual bent" (*New York Times* 14 June 1993). Mary Robinson was widely admired for fighting an independent and outspoken campaign, which flouted the conventions of Irish politics (*Financial Times* 10 November 1990). Coverage of Mrs. Thatcher framed her in predictable ways, stressing her particular brand of conviction politics, outspoken philosophy, determination, and lack of compromise (*Washington Post* 4 May 1979). Brundtland's image was seen as "energetic and managerial" (*Washington Post* 4 February 1981). She was "an excellent administrator and organizer" (*New York Times* 4 February 1981). Ciller was seen as outspoken " 'She is not a person who's frightened of breaking eggs to make the omelet and she has very strong determination,' one Western diploma said" (*New York Times* 3 July 1993). Only Aquino and Chamorro, who came to power via the widow's route, were depicted in terms of more conventional feminine characteristics.

Sex Stereotyping in Issue Coverage. Comparing the issue focus of stories, again these showed great divergence, reflecting the considerable differences between candidates, rather than boxing women into "compassion" issues. For Mary Robinson feminist causes were seen as the heart of her campaign. "Mrs. Robinson has stood on hustings in towns and villages arguing the case for divorce laws. She has said contraception should be freely available. She has talked of the women who are still forced to travel to Britain for abortions. She has taken issue with the Roman Catholic church and with the courts" (*Financial Times* 10 November 1990). "She has accused the 'patriarchal, male-dominated presence of the Catholic Church' of subjugating women in Ireland" (*Washington Post* 10 November 1990). Brundtland was also seen as supporting women's rights, including abortion, as well as being an ardent environmentalist (*Washington Post* 4 February 1981). In contrast, the dominant issues for Cresson were protectionist European trade policies, industrial competition, and unemployment. For Ciller they were seen as inflation, the Kurdish rebellion, radical trade reform, and foreign policy concerns about the Balkans, northern Iraq, and the Caucasus. Bhutto stressed economic growth, privatization, and international affairs, as did Mrs. Thatcher. Campbell emphasized the problems of the government's deficit, unemployment, and constitutional issues of Quebec separatism.

In short, none of these women was seen to campaign for the leadership on traditional "compassion" issues, nor was this seen as their area of greatest strength and competency. Women's rights were stressed by some, but only Mary Robinson was defined first and foremost by these issues. We can conclude that journalistic reporting of the characteristics and concerns of these individual leaders was far more subtle and complex than simple sex-role stereotypes would suggest. The information in these stories provided readers with a rounded picture of complex and idiosyncratic personalities, with particular strengths and weaknesses, who were not reduced to a single female type.

Are News Frames of Women Leaders Commonly Gendered?

Nevertheless, the evidence suggests that coverage reflected a more subtle conventional wisdom about how women are seen as politicians. Rather than sex-role stereotypes, the stories showed certain gendered news frames with common themes which proved pervasive and recurrent in early coverage of these diverse women. The framing conventions tell us something significant about what is expected from women leaders. The most common frames revolved around the breakthrough this appointment signified for all women, the woman leader as outsider, and the woman leader as agent of change.

Women Leadership Breakthroughs. Most strikingly, in story after story, the headline and lead almost invariably focuses on the "first women" breakthrough, with a positive slant for the woman who won against the odds. This familiar framing device is common in many other stories, whether about the first female army general, astronaut, or Nobel Prize–winning scientist. These leaders each came to power with widely differing political philosophies, careers, and policy goals, yet the uniformity of the opening lines by different journalists covering different leaders for different papers over a twenty-year period is quite remarkable.

> Kim Campbell has written herself into history books with a Tory leadership triumph that makes her the first woman to serve as Canada's Prime Minister and one of only 20 women to head a national government this century. (Clyde Farnsworth, *New York Times* 15 June 1993, A1)
>
> SLAIN PREMIER'S DAUGHTER TRIUMPHS:
> Pakistan People's Party leader Benazir Bhutto was named prime minister tonight, making the 35-year-old daughter of the late prime minister Zulfiqar Ali Bhutto one of the youngest leaders of a major country and the only woman to head a modern Islamic state. (Richard M. Weintraub, *Washington Post* 2 December 1988, A29).
> Bruntland, 42, currently Labour Party vice chairman and the foreign relations committee chairman in the Norwegian parliament, will be the first woman prime minister in Scandinavia. She will be the second currently in power in Europe, following Britain's Margaret Thatcher. (*Washington Post* 4 February 1981).
>
> LADY BEARS A FAMOUS NAME INTO A POSITION OF POWER:
> Latin America knows few female heroes [*sic*] are scarcely any women as national leaders. With her victory yesterday in Nicaragua's presidential elections, Mrs. Violeta Barrios de Chamorro has already made her mark: she will be the first female president in Central America. (Robert Graham, *Financial Times* 27 February 1990, 6)
>
> TURKEY'S FIRST WOMAN PM MUST REFORGE PARTY IMAGE: CILLER OFFERS CHANGE FROM GREY-SUITED POLITICAL MAINSTREAM.

> Mrs. Tansu Ciller, a former economy minister, is to be predominantly Moslem Turkey's first woman prime minister after being elected leader of the largest party in parliament yesterday. (John Murray Brown, *Financial Times* 14 June 1993)

> SOCIALIST FEMINIST WINS IRISH PRESIDENCY:
> Ireland has elected its first woman president, Mary Robinson, a feminist and socialist reformer whose long-shot victory over the candidate of Prime Minister Charles Haughey's entrenched political machine marked one of the biggest political upsets in Irish history. (Glenn Frankel, *Washington Post* 10 November 1990, A20)

Women Leaders as Outsiders. The second framing theme which emerges from the stories is a common stress on the lack of the conventional qualifications and prior political experience of many of these women leaders. The broader experiences they do bring to office are commonly undervalued. This confirms observations by Jeane Kirkpatrick (1995), who suggested that women experience a process of dequalification when acting in what is perceived as a man's world of diplomacy and international security. This process consists of undermining or underestimating a woman leader's capabilities and experiences, and seeing the appropriate qualification for the job in terms of the (masculine) characteristics of the past officeholders.

Hence we learned that "Brundtland is a physician in Norway's public health service, whose only Cabinet experience was an environmental minister" (*Washington Post* 4 February 1981), although she grew up in a family imbued with politics; she was even placed in a party children's group when seven, and was active in Labour politics at high school and college. She worked in municipal and national health services, took a master's degree in public health at Harvard and qualified as a doctor, as well as entering parliament and becoming vice chair of the Norwegian Labour Party. Qualified, she seems to be. In a long political career Edith Cresson had held ministerial posts in agriculture, external trade, and European affairs. Readers of the *Financial Times* could learn that although seen as an outsider to Irish politics, Mary Robinson had been Trinity College's youngest ever Professor of Law, an experienced barrister, a member of the Irish Senate for twenty years, who had twice fought for seats in the Dial (*Financial Times* 10 November 1990). Margaret Thatcher had held only one ministerial post (Education Secretary), while Ciller rose to the top after only a few years in parliament, after an academic career teaching economics, and ministerial office. Campbell's lack of experience was often stressed. After an academic and legal career she had spent only five years in federal government, holding office as junior minister for Indian affairs, minister of justice, and minister of defense in rapid succession.

The greatest emphasis on the lack of experience focused on Chamorro, Bhutto, and Aquino, who all rose via the family inheritance route. In the words of one observer of Aquino's campaign, quoted in the

New York Times: " 'It's astonishing,' says a member of her husband's family, 'She was just a housewife. Her strength has astonished us all' " (26 February 1986, 1). Prior to the election, "She was known as a political wife, serving coffee while her husband talked endlessly of politics with visitors" (*Washington Post* 26 February 1986). Mrs. Chamorro was also depicted by the *Financial Times* as little more than the loyal wife of Pedro Joaquin Chamorro, who was assassinated in 1978: Under the headline: "LADY BEARS A FAMOUS NAME INTO A POSITION OF POWER," the opening lines noted, "She will be the first female president in Central America. However she owes this to what she stands for, rather than to her own career" (27 February 1990, 6). Yet later we learn that she served nine months in the prerevolutionary government in exile, then in the first postrevolutionary junta. After that she ran the newspaper *La Prensa*, the main focus of anti-Sandinista opposition, often shut down by the authorities. Throughout the media coverage, she seems to have been judged as a cipher to her husband, "a name," rather than as an independent actor.

Women Leaders as Agents of Change. The third theme common to coverage is that women are widely portrayed by journalists as agents of change, who will clean up corruption in politics. In part this frame reflects campaign themes by some of the women. Any change in leadership is likely to attract this angle, but with the entry of women this becomes one of the dominant motifs. Commenting on Ciller's appointment, the *New York Times* (3 July 1993) saw this as symbolizing a change of the old guard:

> Paradoxically for the 67-year-old Mr. Demirel, though, the election of the 47-year-old Mrs. Ciller sends the rather less comforting message that people have tired of a generation of old-guard politicians, like himself, who have traversed the stage of public life . . . for more than three decades.

For Mary Robinson, too, her campaign was seen as "a breath of fresh political air," a break with the "ossified political system," a "defeat for Fianna Fail and its style of politics, perceived by many to be outdated and based on patronage and favoritism" (*Financial Times* 6 November 1990). Chamorro's victory represented change of a different sort: the end of the Sandinistas, the war in Nicaragua, and a new period of alliance with the United States. Aquino's accession to power also meant the end to the corruption of the Marcos regime, and the restoration of democracy, while Thatcherism heralded a decade-long revolution of a different kind.

Conclusions

This study remains a limited analysis of only certain types of media, certain leaders, and a certain period of early coverage. Far more work is required before we can see whether the findings in this study are replicated in other contexts. Nevertheless, three main conclusions can be drawn from the stories which we have reviewed. First, the results confirm that women leaders are less visible in the news, as previous studies have found, although the difference in the amount of coverage is not that great. Given the limited number of cases we have examined, further research is required to see whether this pattern is confirmed with other leaders. Second, the study found little evidence that journalists employ simple sex stereotypes when covering the emergence of new women world leaders. The diversity of the women's personalities and policy concerns emerge clearly from the reporting. Women leaders were not described in ways which emphasized "feminine" characteristics, nor were they seen to focus on "women's" issues. The extensive amount of available information about women world leaders, and their diverse backgrounds, personalities, and interests, probably discourage the use of any simple stereotypes among good journalists.

Nevertheless, certain common themes which are apparent in the coverage suggest that when women leaders first rose to power the news media employed common gendered frames for their stories. These frames usually emphasized the breakthrough the appointment represented for all women, women leaders as outsiders, and women leaders as agents of change.

The headlines stressed how the rise of the first woman President or Prime Minister symbolized an important and positive breakthrough for all women. This "first woman" news frame is a common device in all fields of achievement, from astronauts to generals. In emerging democracies like Turkey and Pakistan this development is framed as part of the modernization process, where countries are demonstrating their willingness to reject traditional ideas of the past and to embrace Western ideas of equality for women.

The second common journalistic frame is to see women leaders as "the outsider," politicians who fail to follow the conventional path to power, whether because of their prior political careers, their political styles, or their policy interests. One of the most influential journalistic biographies of Margaret Thatcher portrayed her as the classic outsider, not "one of us" when she first came to power, by virtue of her sex, class, style, and radical ideas (Young 1989). This touches on a theme common in the media portrayal of many women leaders. Their rise to power is often seen as unexpected, and the prior experience of women leaders is often downplayed or undervalued, set against conventional qualifications.

Lastly, as Carroll and Schreiber found in coverage of women in Congress in the previous chapter, women leaders were widely portrayed as agents of change, symbolizing a break with politics as usual. To some extent this theme is common among new male leaders as well, but it is particularly characteristic when women first rise to power. This framing device may prove positive for women leaders, if their country is going through a period when people want a change from the past, such as the end to the old politics of corruption and graft. Nevertheless, this frame may create false expectations for what the new leader can achieve and, therefore, in the long term may set women leaders on a pedestal from which they can only fall.

This study provides only a preliminary analysis, a first cut at this issue, and the approach could be replicated in a number of different contexts. Further research is required to establish whether this pattern of gender framing continues throughout the lifetime careers of leaders; whether coverage varies in terms of popular (tabloid) and "quality" media; whether the pattern has changed in recent decades; whether a more systematic analysis of the language and descriptors would find a similar pattern; and lastly whether coverage has significant effects on the opportunities for women's political participation. There is a large research agenda here which is only starting to be examined systematically. Nevertheless, this preliminary interpretation suggests that the media are innocent of some of the simpler accusations of sex stereotyping, but gendered framing remains common. As long as women remain such a minority among world leaders, we can expect this pattern to recur, because the fact that a woman breaks through is still seen as relevant to the definition of headline news.

Notes

1. Certain leaders like Siramavo Bandaranaike, Golda Meir, and Isabel Peron had to be excluded because data were not available on a consistent basis for their periods in office in the 1960s and 1970s. Others like Eugenia Charles (Dominica) and Lidia Geiler (Bolivia) were excluded as there were too few stories about any leaders in their countries in the selected media for a reliable analysis.

2. Unfortunately most of the available television and newspaper sources are only available in *Lexis/Nexis* from 1990 onward. Sources needed to be available on a consistent basis over time to compare leaders in different periods of office.

3. The search was checked using alternative nomenclature, then the most conventional identifier was used to maximize references for each leader. That is, stories usually referred to "President Aquino" not Corazon or Cory Aquino, to "Mrs. Thatcher" not Margaret Thatcher or Prime Minister Thatcher (a peculiar Americanism), and to "Kim Campbell." It should be noted, however, that these alternative nomenclatures may produce some variations in key-word searches. Fortunately all the names were sufficiently distinctive (with the possible exception of "Kim Campbell") to avoid confusing the identity of different people with the same names.

9

The First Lady, Political Power, and the Media: Who Elected Her Anyway?

Betty Houchin Winfield

"Buy one, get one free," promised Bill Clinton during the 1992 presidential campaign. With Hillary Rodham Clinton campaigning for her husband, no one, yet everyone, elected her, too. She was a visible player in the highest echelons of political power during that campaign and afterward as first lady. She was working toward the same political and policy goals as an equal partner. That partnership was news.

After November 3 1992, Hillary Rodham Clinton found herself in a role influenced by years of tradition. As first lady, like her predecessors, she faced public expectations about this position. For more than two hundred years, the American media have both judged and relayed societal expectations about what is acceptable or not acceptable behavior for a first lady.

The aim of this chapter is to focus on press coverage historically to understand how the role of the American first lady has been framed by the media, and how this framing has changed over time. By "framing," as discussed in the introduction, we mean the persistent patterns of selection, emphasis, and interpretation which shape news. Frames structure how journalists cover women and men in public life, and function as the story "pegs" around which the narrative flows. The conventions which are adopted by the press tell us much about expectations for women's roles in public life.

The framing conventions for the first lady tend to fall into four main categories. The earliest frame depicts the first lady primarily in an "escort" role: the wife is mentioned by virtue of accompanying her spouse, not because of any independent function. The next most frequent frame adopted by the early press covered first ladies in their "protocol" role: leading fashionable society at social, ceremonial, and diplomatic events. In the twentieth century the press came to place increasing emphasis on the first ladies' "noblesse oblige" role: charitable and good works concerned with orphanages, the homeless, or the poor, which represents a natural extension of women's volunteer work in the community. Lastly, the press has also covered the first ladies' "policy" role: helping to formulate, develop, and influence public policy issues. The question is whether the media still expect at least the first three roles, despite immense changes over time in the lives of women, and whether the press continues to be critical of the first ladies who adopt a policy role. Answers to this question tell us a great deal about the ambiguities in coverage of Hillary Rodham Clinton, as well as ambiguities toward women in positions of power in America.

This chapter uses historical records of newspaper coverage to focus upon two major periods. The first section examines the earliest first ladies, when the position was established, including Martha Washington, Abigail Adams, Dolley Madison, first lady-to-be Rachel Jackson, and Sarah Polk. Coverage during the era of the partisan press legitimized the first lady position and defined the early role.

The second section focuses on preinaugural expectations of three first ladies during the twentieth century who subsequently received extensive coverage: namely, Eleanor Roosevelt, Jacqueline Kennedy, and Hillary Rodham Clinton.[1] The sources used include the prominent newspapers and magazines of the eras. The conclusion considers the implications of the analysis for understanding the changing role of the first lady over time.

The Early "Escort" and "Protocol" Roles

Martha Washington

In the early period, when newspapers mentioned the first lady at all, they usually referred to her in connection to her spouse, such as "Lady Washington," or "The President of the United States, and his Lady." The *Pennsylvania Gazette*, for example, reported, "Mrs. Adams, the Lady of the President of the United States, arrived in this city yesterday evening on her way to Manchester" (28 February 1801). The fact that the first lady was covered at all was notable, because she was usually the only woman mentioned in the news columns. Sometimes first ladies were not even noticed. Martha Washington attended the second inauguration, but the newspapers did not mention her presence (Thane 1960, 306). Even when Martha Washington filled in for the President on several occasions, the newspapers ignored her. When President Washington had been ill and could not attend church or a public memorial service held for the late General Nathanael Greene, diaries noted her presence with the Congress, government officials, and the Society of Cincinnatus; yet, no contemporary coverage mentioned that she had stood in for the President (Caroli 1987, 8; Anthony 1990, 43).

Early press coverage of Martha Washington rarely mentioned her social function, but this role gradually evolved over time. The European-based protocol of the President receiving guests and dining with Cabinet officials and congressional members was already in place when Martha Washington arrived in New York City. The President's New Year's Day receptions, open to all, where Martha Washington presided, had no contemporary press report of her. When she went to the President's birthday balls, akin to European ceremonies for kings, the newspapers covered the events but ignored her. Yet the social function of the first lady gradually expanded. Martha Washington began a type of "open house" for receiving visitors as a separate function from the President's receptions. The federalist *Gazette of the United States* alerted the citizens: "Mrs. Washington, we are informed, will be home every Friday, at 8 o'clock p.m., to see company" (20 July 1789).

Abigail Adams

The news coverage of first ladies was often linked to the President's popularity. George Washington was so beloved by so many people that this may have extended to his wife. The second President, John Adams, on the other hand, was viciously attacked in the partisan press for deceiving the public about the "almost war" with the French and for enforcing the hated Alien and Sedition Acts. The *Aurora and General Advertiser* criticized Abigail Adams for admiring the British elites too much, as when she "shed tears of sensibility and delight upon the occasion of the song 'The President's March,' at the Fox Theater" (*Aurora* 27 April 1798).

With Abigail Adams the first lady's political influence became a consideration. Such a concern was mentioned in official letters, but not covered by the press until her obituaries in 1818 and 1819. As a close reader of newspapers and magazines, Abigail Adams referred to the administration as "ours" and "we" in hundreds of letters (Caroli 1987, 11). She commented upon the editors, such as Benjamin Franklin Bache, Ben's grandson, and wrote her sister, "We are now wonderfully popular except with Bache and Co., who in his paper calls the President old, querulous, bald, blind, crippled, toothless Adams" (to Mary Cranch, 28 April 1798). Abigail Adams also responded to press criticism by arranging for letters-to-the-editor retorts. Her brother-in-law copied her letter and sent it in under a pen name to appear as "A Correspondent." She wrote her sister, "I saw the Centennial last Saturday and though I knew my own letter but, did not know whether it was an extract from one to you, or to Mr. Smith, to whom I freely scribe" (to Mary Cranch, 28 February 1798). Years later, in her own name, she also directly answered critical accounts about the elitism of her receptions in the news magazine of the era, *Niles Weekly Register.*

Under Abigail Adams the first lady developed a stronger role in influencing public policy. Yet this influence was known and mentioned in officials' letters, but not covered in the partisan newspapers. Secretary of State Thomas Pickering wrote that the President "was under the sovereignty of his wife" (*Diary of William Bentley*, vol. IV, 1914, 556). Congressman Albert Gallatin, who later became Jefferson's Secretary of the Treasury, called her "Mrs. President of the United States, but of a faction" (Adams 1879, 185). Years later, Abigail Adams' reputation for power caused her grandson to attempt to correct the record. Charles Francis Adams wrote in his introductory "Memoir" to the Adams letters, "A great many persons, in the lifetime of parties, ascribed to Mrs. Adams a degree of influence over the public conduct of her husband, far greater than there was any founding for in truth. . . . that her opinion, even upon public affairs, had at all times, great weight with her husband, is unquestionable true, . . . there is no evidence that they either originated or materially altered any part of the course he had laid out for himself" (Adams 1840, iv). Her political partnership was unusual, but not enough of an issue to be challenged in newspapers.

Dolley Madison

By 1809 the White House social endeavors reached an apex with Dolley Madison as first lady. She oversaw a magnificent inaugural ball unlike any function before and was a noticeably gracious hostess. Younger than Abigail Adams or Martha Washington, her youthful beauty and more energetic style were recorded in diaries (M. Smith 1905, 58). So, too, were her latest European fashions, daring, low-cut bodice dresses, her makeup of rouge, and her vivacious nature.

No matter how unusual this first lady, the major capital newspaper, the *National Intelligencer*, initially ignored Dolley Madison's presence. In referring to that inaugural ball, the *Intelligencer* said, "In the Evening there was a grand Inauguration Ball, at Long's Hotel, the most brilliant and crowded ever known in Washington . . ." (*National Intelligencer* 6 March 1809). Margaret Bayard Smith, the wife of the publisher of the *Intelligencer*, wrote in her diary that Dolley Madison "looked extremely beautiful," and was "like a queen" (M. Smith 1905, 61–62).

Rumors and gossip about the first lady were also not printed. Even the viciously antifederalist press ignored the Washington rumors about Dolley Madison's virtue. The wife of the publisher of the *National Intelligencer* wrote, "I really admire Mrs. M. Ah, why does she not in all things act with the same propriety? She would be much beloved if she added all the virtues to all the graces" (M. Smith 1905, 58). Only later would such rumors be reported in newspapers, as with Rachel Jackson.

Dolley Madison's social talents and grand balls were too newsworthy to be invisible for long. The staid *National Intelligencer* acknowledged,

"In the evening there was a ball in compliment to Mrs. Madison, and the whole day and evening were spent with the greatest harmony and sociability" (31 March 1812). This first lady was an asset to the social and cultural aspects of the presidency. Yet as newsworthy as Dolley Madison's social events were, the press ignored her most unusual actions, such as the fact that she was a director of the Washington Orphans' Asylum.[2] The press did not report her courageous flight from the British with George Washington's portrait, important papers, and other White House valuables, as the capital was being sacked.[3]

While recognizing the first lady's social role, the press appeared to expect that she would walk a tightrope between the "republicanism" of a democracy and the sophistication of the European courts. Her receptions must be "republican" in nature, open to all, or else she would risk being accused of "elitism" by being too exclusive. Nor were dinners to be too lavish, or too frequent. The public first took notice, albeit in diaries. There were complaints during Washington's second term about Martha's drawing room levees as "aping royalty," or "awkward imitations of royalty," yet the aim was not necessarily at her, but at her husband. By mentioning the first lady's connections with the ritual, diplomatic, and ceremonial aspects of the White House, the press not only defined her hostessing functions but set the perimeters of her entertaining.

Rachel Jackson

The earliest first ladies were not a part of the election campaigns or even an issue in the partisan press. By 1828 the worthiness of a candidate's wife became a campaign issue. The presidential race between John Quincy Adams and Andrew Jackson was, as Robert V. Remini wrote, probably the "dirtiest, coarsest, most vulgar election in American history" ("Election of 1828" 1971, 426). Rachel Jackson's corpulent appearance, modest clothing, and use of a long clay pipe had already been unsettling. Yet these were minor indiscretions beside the charges of bigamy and adultery based on the timing of her divorce from Lewis Roberts and her marriage to Andrew Jackson. Newspaper editorials rehashed her divorce in the *National Banner* and the *Nashville Whig*, and pamphlets such as *The Friends of Reform and Corruption* campaigned against her "lack of virtue." The editor of the *Cincinnati Gazette* used the inflammatory words of "bigamist" and "adulterer" (Remini 1971, 427). The public charges greatly hurt the Jacksons; she, mortally so, for she died from a heart attack after the election. The first lady had become a symbol of morality and a representative of the country's social virtues.

Sarah Polk

Few other nineteenth-century first ladies were as politically involved as Abigail Adams. Almost a half-century later, Sarah Polk might be the notable exception. She openly held a position as James Polk's secretary, adviser, political counselor, muse, and emotional resource (Caroli 1987, 62). Childless and her husband's assistant when she did get to the White House, Sarah Polk handled the President's paperwork and served as his secretary. The Vice President felt misplaced (Nelson 1892, 94–96, 114). There were questions about her influence and even domination over her husband (Sellers 1957, 143).

The Changing Role of Contemporary First Ladies

By the end of the nineteenth century national magazines began giving considerable attention to the wives of candidates (Caroli 1987, 108). Railroads offered the wives the opportunity to travel across the continent to be seen with their husbands by the voters. Feature stories were now part of the newspaper content and found in magazines. By 1901 *Cosmopolitan* magazine wrote that the first lady was "an ideal American woman—the spouse, helpmate, comrade, or the first citizen of a greatest free nation . . ." (February 1901, 408). After the passage of the Nineteenth Amendment for suffrage (1920), hopes as well as many questions remained about the roles of women, including their equality, educational ambition, and career aspirations. Into this milieu stepped the first ladies-to-be Eleanor Roosevelt, then Jacqueline Kennedy and Hillary Clinton.

A first lady's career was a major issue by 1932. In fact, all three women emphasized here had careers; two were journalists, Eleanor Roosevelt had a column and a radio series, and Jacqueline Kennedy had worked as a roving reporter/photographer at the *Washington Times-Herald*[4]; and Hillary Clinton had been named by the *National Law Journal* as one of the top 100 attorneys in the country, the only Arkansan and one of four women nationwide. In the twentieth century, press coverage denoted boundaries for acceptable behavior for these first ladies and shaped expectations before the inaugurations of 1933, 1961, and 1993. The most significant change was the addition of the "noblesse oblige" role and the even more controversial "policy" role for the first lady.

Eleanor Roosevelt

Eleanor Roosevelt's role as an independent partner was noted in the press before 1932. In 1928 the *New York Post* referred to her prominence in a headline, "Roosevelt's Wife is his Colonel House," and *Good Housekeeping* singled her out in August 1930 as "the ideal modern wife." Eleanor Roosevelt emphasized, "Partnership. Companionship. It is a major requirement for modern marriage." She stressed individual independence and her own niche as an ideal wife. This was unusual.

The press chronicled not only her career but her boundless energy and many interests. When questions emerged about whether she could devote the necessary time and attention to her new duties, and suggestions were made that she might disassociate herself from her various organizations, she said, "The writers mean well, I suppose, but it is difficult to sever so many pleasant connections" (*New York Times* 27 January 1933). The *New York Times* enumerated her activities and energy, "During the dinner she chatted animatedly, as if a trip from New York by plane and train, a dinner, a lecture and two receptions in one day were not much of a strain" (22 January 1933).

Eleanor Roosevelt's independence went much further than Abigail Adams and Sarah Polk. Before the 1933 inauguration, the *New York Times* warned her about her outspokenness; in particular, her offer to be a national sounding board about the Depression. She had asked people to write to her about Depression-related problems. The *Times* editorialized, "it is not indelicate or impolite to express the hope that she will refrain from such utterances in the future. The very best helpers of a President are those who do all they can for him, but keep still about it" (28 January 1933). Eleanor Roosevelt did not keep still about it. In fact, this *New York Times* editorial echoed a similar article in 1929 before the talented Lou Henry Hoover became first lady. "The gifted wife of a distinguished husband has a difficult role if she is to keep individuality intact without overshadowing his. This is an achievement we demand of our President's wives, even in this day of universal suffrage and of theoretical equality of the sexes" (*New York Times* 3 March 1929). Whereas Lou Henry Hoover mostly kept quiet about her talents, Eleanor Roosevelt did not. She did keep her individuality intact; whether she overshadowed "him" is still open for historical interpretation. And, the press noticed.

Her statements about keeping a career while first lady were unprecedented and shocking. In December 1932, the *New York Times* featured her, "Mrs. Roosevelt in the Classroom," with a subtitle warning of her independence, "the Wife of the President-elect Explains her Theory of Education and Says that Her Duties as Mistress of the White House will Not Interrupt the Profession She So Thoroughly Enjoys" (4 December 1932, *Magazine*, 1). The *Times* in one sense defended her decision, "Mrs. Roosevelt will not only create a new tradition of the first practicing professional woman to be mistress of the White House, she will stand as a symbol of the vast increase in the numbers of women in the professions." During that Depression era when many people accused married women of taking jobs, Mrs. Roosevelt often defended careers for women and retorted, "The principle of denying work to any one who wants to work, married or single, is an obnoxious one" (ibid.).

While she had said that she planned to continue her teaching and association with the Todhunter School, she was waylaid. She moved more into journalism. Right after the 1932 election she signed a contract with the National Broadcasting Company to talk on a general topic once each week on Friday evenings. To meet the potential criticism about the misuse of her new position, she said she planned to donate her earnings to unemployment relief (*New York Times* 3 December 1932, 4). She even wrote a Sunday copyrighted feature for the *Times* on serving humanity through politics (4 December 1932, Sec. 2,1). At the same time, the *Times* covered her NBC remarks when she referred to marriage as "no longer the only aim and object in life" (17 November 1932, 1-A).

At the same time, Eleanor Roosevelt often reiterated the expectations of the first lady, well in place by the time of that 1932 campaign. As for the first lady's "escort" and "social" roles, she never violated that expectation, "You must live up to the standards just as any other first ladies would do" (NBC Mrs. Roosevelt's Radio Talk, 2 May 1940). On another occasion, she wrote in her 1935 column, "there is no question but what the public official has more to gain from the right kind of wife than has a man in almost any other walk of life. She can make friends for him and oh, how she can make enemies for him" (5 April 1935). She made friends for him as well as enemies. Moreover, she made sure that the media covered the first lady's role in those social and cultural aspects of the White House.

Eleanor Roosevelt's partnership was complementary; two different careers, gone in separate ways. She had distinct policy differences with her husband. There is no one program that has her imprint on it, unlike Lady Bird Johnson's highway beautification legislation, or Betty Ford's attempt to have Congress pass an equal rights amendment, or Rosalynn Carter's Mental Health System's Act. Eleanor Roosevelt's power was indirect: she might have influenced the appointments of Frances Perkins and other women in the administration (Beasley 1987, 103), and she may have caused changes in the National Recovery Administration codes to give women the same minimum wage as men. Yet questions about her exact influence over policy have remained unresolved. In areas where she worked so hard for change, such as civil rights, she admitted her husband's reluctance, his hesitation "annoyed me very much" (Hoff-Wilson and Lightman 1984, 99).

Speculations about her power came up again and again during the 1936 and 1940 campaigns. Eleanor Roosevelt did the unprecedented by speaking to the Democratic National Convention in 1940 and appealing to the delegates for party unity over the nomination of Henry Wallace. In his meetings, the President would often refer to her, "My missus tells me . . ." (Beasley 1987, 104). She was controversial. Such controversy was news. She was lampooned in film and theater. Impersonators imitated her voice and manner; her image was even alluded to in a *Popeye* cartoon (Anthony 1990, 476). Even her first name indicated an individuality, although one still politically connected to him. The 1940 campaign buttons highlighted her: "We Don't Want Eleanor Either."

The mass media may have discussed her participation, yet the news stories and editorials did not dwell on her political influence, perhaps because she was so open about her views and said that she and the President did disagree. The country may have accepted her autonomy because of his infirmity and the necessity for her to be his "eyes and ears." The media of the era repeated those first lady constraints about outspokenness, a career, financial independence, and attempts to influence policy, yet they covered her unusualness.

Jacqueline Kennedy

By the time of the 1960 election, Jacqueline Kennedy was portrayed in the media, not as another Eleanor Roosevelt, but rather as another Dolley Madison. The messages were about her youthful and fashionable looks as assets. In 1959 *Life* magazine introduced her as "John Kennedy's Lovely Lady" and even said "the U.S. is going to see more and more of one of the prettiest women to decorate a flag-draped speakers' platform." In contrast to many predecessors, Mrs. Kennedy's coverage pointed out her unusualness, her "striking appearance and ultra-smart clothing make her one of America's ten most photographed women but they fit no known image of a prospective first-lady-to-be." (24 August 1959, 76).

Jacqueline Kennedy's youth and education also appeared to be a possible issue. *U.S. News & World Report* questioned, " 'Jackie' Kennedy: First Lady at Thirty?" (25 July 1960, 60). *Newsweek* defended her as a, "Stunning Egghead" and focused on her education, her grades, her fluency in languages, and her age, "at thirty the youngest and prettiest wife of a presidential candidate since Dolley Madison" (22 February 1960, 29).

Rather than focus on her previous career, the coverage emphasized her "escort" and "social" role, her help to Jack Kennedy's career, and her partnership in his efforts to win the presidency. Jackie Kennedy campaigned for him on her own, unlike so many previous candidates' wives. By doing so, she took what had become the accepted, if not the expected, route leading to the White House (Caroli 1987, 219). The news articles emphasize over and over this type of partnership, her supportive role, despite her pregnancy and lessened travel.

Her "social" role was politically helpful. *Life* magazine quoted an unnamed Congressman, "She is the ultimate political weapon." *U.S. News & World Report* profiled the candidates' wives before the primaries and pointed to Jackie's role, "she makes no big speeches because, 'They'd rather hear Jack.' " (15 February 1960, 54). When asked about her political opinions, unlike an independent Eleanor Roosevelt and later Hillary Clinton, Jackie Kennedy responded, "Because I'm his wife. My opinions are his. But I think he can explain them better than I can" (*Newsweek* 22 February 1960, 32). Her political views were to be as silent as Martha Washington's.

More than all previous candidates' wives, Jackie Kennedy used every kind of media to boost her husband and canvass voters for him. She, according to *Life*, "is making broadcasts in the three foreign languages she speaks fluently." She was credited with her weekly newspaper column, "Campaign Wife," which was distributed by the national committee, her "Helpmate" newspaperwomen teas, her efforts with the "Calling for

Kennedy Week," and a series of films called, "Coffee with Mrs. Kennedy," with different casts for different states (10 October 1960, 150). The press was not critical of these publicity efforts. The coverage focused on looks and fashion style. The news magazines noted, "One of her chief interests is high fashion. She is regarded as a pacesetter in choosing and wearing new clothing styles" (*U.S. News & World Report* 8 August 1960, 67). By the end of the campaign, Jackie's expensive taste in clothing was an issue. When asked if she spent $30,000 a year on clothes, she made a spirited retort, "I couldn't spend that much if I wore sable underwear" (*Newsweek* 17 October 1960, 33).

Right after the election, she held her only press conference and after saying, "I have every confidence my husband will be magnificent and give himself completely," she emphasized, "I assume, I won't fail him in any way" (*New York Times* 11 November 1960, 22). She would be a different type of political wife, as *Newsweek* emphasized, "this, then is Jackie Kennedy—by no stretch of the imagination the conventional political wife" (17 October 1960, 34). *U.S. News & World Report* said, "One of her intimate friends once described her as an 'incredibly independent little spirit who is somebody in her own right' " (8 August 1960, 67). On the eve of the 1961 inauguration, Jacqueline Kennedy enthralled the nation as a beautiful young first lady with a high fashion style, much in the manner of Dolley Madison. Her partnership was as a supportive escort, without a political agenda of her own. Her newsworthiness was such that after the election, she hired the first of the first ladies' press secretaries and remained a style pacesetter with her own television documentary to highlight her work on restoring the White House.

Hillary Rodham Clinton

During the 1992 presidential campaign, Hillary Clinton was targeted for being "incredibly independent" and "an egghead" in a different way. As mentioned, she was a "three-fer": wife, mother, and successful corporate lawyer. Yet, she challenged the conventions about the first ladies' function by adding an overt policy role. In fact, she became "everybody's favorite target for all that was dangerous about being independent, smart, impatient, articulate, outspoken, ambitious," so explained the *Washington Post* on the eve of the election (30 October 1992). The *Post* elaborated, "By any standard, Hillary Clinton has been a handful for America to deal with." She could hurt his campaign as an issue herself. In that last week, the *Post* reassured the reader, "The polls indicate she is no longer a liability to Bill Clinton" (30 October 1992, B-4).

Between autonomy and sublimation, between legitimate ambition and career subjugation, the ambivalent message is the confusing paradox of independence and dependence, of attempting to have it both ways. In 1992 all three wives of the baby-boomer party candidates (Hillary Clinton, Marilyn Quayle, and Tipper Gore) agreed to curtail professional careers not because of the birth of their children but because of their husbands' political careers. While she said during a 1988 campaign interview, "I'm not just a little housewife that's been sitting at home," Marilyn Quayle said to the 1992 Republican GOP convention, "Our marriage is a partnership, and for me it was a reasonable decision, it wasn't caving in" (*Washington Post* 1 November 1992, 13).

The American press raised as an issue the type of partnership in 1992. Rather than the question of whether Hillary Clinton was worthy of the first lady position, as had been mentioned with Rachel Jackson, the issue focused on whether she was overqualified, even a candidate herself, a would-be "copresident." She appeared to be running openly. The concern was not just about her overt partnership, but about her potential political power. She was called everything from "the Winnie Mandela of American politics" to "the overbearing yuppie wife from hell" (*Washington Post Magazine* 1 November 1992, 12).

Hillary Clinton dared to tell the *New York Times* in February 1992, and unlike any previous first ladies-to-be, she was involved in the campaign because of the issues and the "policy impact she hoped to have." Bill Clinton reinforced the image. He told a CNN interviewer that he might appoint her to a Cabinet post, "I wouldn't rule that out. She'd be the best I could find" (*Post* 1 November, 1992, 14). This was not just a statement at fundraisers of "Buy one, get one free"; this meant a major difference in political partnerships. The headlines would quote her, "If you vote for him, you get me" (*Detroit News* 22 March 1992, 1-B).

As the *Detroit News* pointed out, other presidential candidates' wives had been campaign confidantes, such as Eleanor Roosevelt, and may have even had an agenda, yet Hillary Clinton already had a successful policy record. The real question, defined by the Clintons, was: did Americans want a "two-for-one" presidency? The subtext meant that she would have a great deal of political influence and that she would overtly have political power. The mass media condemned her for breaking such norms. The *Los Angeles Times* wrote, "We just don't seem to be ready for an unabashed First Partner" (24 July 1992, E-3). For the media, this candidate's wife was stepping outside the acceptable boundaries for first ladies.

"Hillary-bashing" was one of the great subthemes of the campaign coverage, the subtext was about the role of women at the end of the twentieth century. She was breaking the acceptable boundaries of a presidential candidate's wife. Hillary Clinton was the equal partner, the wronged wife, who stood by her husband through the awkward questions on *60 Minutes* about Gennifer Flowers. And she answered back. As she noted, the first person to attack her that campaign year was Richard Nixon. "He," she said, "never forgets anything," including the fact that she had been a staff attorney for the House Judiciary Committee in 1974.

Hillary Clinton and the 1992 campaign coverage represented the competing choices for women at the end of the century: successful careers and self-fulfillment and the gender-based roles of mothers and wives. She became a campaign issue as the GOP tried to make her an emblem of all that was wrong with family values, working mothers, and modern women in general. In response, she was the unabashed political partner. She articulated issues; she made headlines; she was a key campaign adviser; she spoke with authority; and she did not retreat into a shell.

The news magazines' covers and articles emphasized the challenge to the conventional expectations: "The Hillary Factor, Is She Helping or Hurting Her Husband?" (*Time* 2 November 1992) and "Are We Ready for a First Lady as First Partner?" (*Glamour* September 1992). The *Chicago Tribune* predicted that she would not "be your mother's first lady" (26 March 1992, 29A). For the media, there was an expectation gap among the generations. For older women, it was not "ladylike" that she had been involved in her husband's business of politics (*Los Angeles Times* 24 July 1992, E-3).

Clinton proudly talked about his wife's individuality as an asset, "far more organized, more in control, more intelligent and more eloquent" than he (*Chicago Tribune* 26 March 1992, 29A). The *Los Angeles Times* warned, "To many, this is worrisome" and predicted in July that "she is . . . sure to be a major influence on her husband should he win the election" (24 July 1992, E-1). In fact, just before the election, the press quoted Richard Nixon's warning, "If the wife comes through as being too strong and too intelligent, it makes the husband look like a wimp" (*Washington Post* 1 November 1992, 13). Such condemnation set an agenda.

After the Clintons won, James S. Rosebush, chief-of-staff for Nancy Reagan, cautioned the new first lady in a *New York Times* "Op-Ed" piece, reminiscent of those warnings for Eleanor Roosevelt and Lou Henry Hoover, "to tread lightly." He said that some dimensions of the job never change: taking care of the President's health, intellectual, and spiritual well-being; being her husband's most trusted adviser; being an official representative of the American people as a public spouse; working for the American people. He then suggested to Mrs. Clinton "Be yourself" and "Address yourself to issues on which you feel deeply." (11 November 1992, A25).

The first lady's political role remained an issue. In the *Times*, Kitty Kelley asked, "What is so threatening about an intelligent professional woman as the wife of the President?" (28 November 1992, 19). The dilemma was what role this first lady would play. Anna Quindlen asked, "Now that we have a First Woman as educated, intelligent, superachieving and policy-savvy as her husband, what do we do with her?" (8 November 1992). In December Ted Koppel, among the reporters on the networks who tried to examine this new first lady, had a *Nightline* program on the "First Lady's Proper Role" after she took part in the President-elect's Little Rock economic conference and participated openly in discussions over Cabinet and agency appointments.

The issue of political power was heightened by her actions in three other postelection areas. Hillary Clinton surprised everyone when she announced that she wanted to be called by her full name, "Hillary Rodham Clinton," that she would have an office in the West Wing (significantly in close proximity to the apex of power), and that she would supervise the drafting of a proposal for a health-care system. Her appointment as head of the Task Force on National Health Reform was the most powerful official post ever assigned to a first lady. President Clinton justified her policy role, "she's better at organizing and leading people from a complex beginning to a certain end than anybody I've ever worked with in my life" (*New York Times* 26 January 1993, A1). Unlike Eleanor Roosevelt, she did not reassure the country that she would fulfill the social, ritual, and cultural aspects of the presidency.

The *New York Times* editorialized about Hillary Clinton's partnership, "The argument that she was not elected is only half-true, since she was clearly as much a running mate as Al Gore. Did anyone doubt that she would play a policy role? Need anyone really mind?" (27 January 1993, A22). Many did.[5] And now, four years later, people and the American media still do. With Hillary Rodham Clinton, the press coverage denoted violations to the accepted boundaries of her "policy" role, echoing accusations about Abigail Adams and subsequent first ladies.

Conclusions

In the past two centuries, the first lady has become a collective image, undefined when the country was founded, but framed by the media. The partisan press began legitimizing the position of first lady by mentioning Martha Washington at a time when women were rarely referred to in the partisan press, had no political power, and were appendages to their husbands. Press coverage emphasized the first lady's role as "escort" to her spouse.

From the beginning, the press mentioned the first lady's "social" role with levees which were separate from the President's receptions. The partisan press acknowledged Dolley Madison's social skills in presiding over dinners and White House functions. Above all, the coverage indicated that the country wanted the first lady to be dignified, virtuous, a moral leader, "a lady," as the election of 1828 demonstrated. In the campaign coverage, the boundaries of acceptable behavior were violated by Rachel Jackson's past, which became a campaign issue. By emphasizing the first lady's connections with the ritual, social, and ceremonial functions of the presidency, the nation's early press defined the first lady's duties, with implications for social norms about the role of women in public life. The trend-setting role of the first lady in fashionable society can be found in the emphasis on the youth, beauty, and fashion of Dolley Madison and Jacqueline Kennedy.

Yet at the same time if the press mirrors the social values of the time, then political influence for women was outside the acceptable social conventions. Press references were made to Abigail Adams' political influence in her obituaries; the *New York Times* expressed caution to Eleanor Roosevelt as well as Lou Henry Hoover, and gave warnings to Hillary Rodham Clinton. The media have always reinforced unwritten rules about female independence. At the end of this century, the first lady's position continues to reflect the anachronistic concept of an official consort to the President, a confining role. In this regard, Hillary Rodham Clinton is still expected to be Martha Washington. Before the inauguration Hillary Clinton recognized the ambiguities of the position, saying, "Right now, I'm confused about what the rules are" (*Detroit News* 22 March 1992, 4-B). Today, the first lady as well as the press are confused about the rules of acceptable behavior for this position.

Notes

The author wishes to thank Janice Hume, Ph.D. student at the University of Missouri, for her research assistance.

1. The *New York Times* coverage of the twentieth century first ladies during their first complete year came to 320 articles on Eleanor Roosevelt (1934), 348 on Jacqueline Kennedy (1962), and 212 on Hillary Clinton (1994) (Winfield 1988, 335, fn 12).

2. Not even the *National Intelligencer*, which supported and boosted the asylum, mentioned her connection (10 October 1815).

3. Dolley Madison wrote herself about the incident in a letter to her sister and later pamphlets repeated Mrs. Madison's letter (Clark 1914). The story was repeated in biographies.

4. Eleanor Roosevelt had been an editor of the Bernarr MacFadden publication *Babes, Just Babes* before she was first lady. During her twelve White House years, she wrote hundreds of articles for general magazines, such as *Reader's Digest*, *McCall's*, *Collier's*, and *The Nation*, and women's magazines, such as *Good Housekeeping*, *Women's Home Companion*, and *Ladies' Home Journal.* In 1936 she began her advice column, "If You Ask Me," and her diary column, "My Day." She also had a radio series for Pond soap and Shelby shoes in the 1930s. Jacqueline Kennedy had been the "Inquiring Camera Girl" for the *Washington Times-Herald* before she married.

5. By February 1993 *Newsweek*'s cover story was headlined, "Hillary's Role. How Much Clout? Exclusive: The First Lady Speaks Out on the Issues."

Part IV

FRAMING THE WOMEN'S MOVEMENT, FEMINISM, AND PUBLIC POLICY

10

Feminists and Feminism in the News

Leonie Huddy

An emerging consensus among political theorists suggests that feminism represents not one but many political ideologies. As testament to this consensus, recent books on feminist ideology employ similar distinctions between liberal, socialist, radical, and less frequently cultural, postmodern, existential, and Freudian feminism (Tong 1989; Donovan, 1990; Echols 1989). Despite "feminism's" varied meanings, it enjoys widespread popularity as a term to describe the beliefs and adherents of the women's movement. "Feminist," unqualified by modifiers which might connote its different shades of political meaning, appears in everyday conversation, is used widely by the authors of popular articles about the women's movement, and elicits sensible responses from most men and women when asked questions about feminists in public opinion polls.

Real diversity and disagreement over the theoretical meaning of feminist, coupled with widespread usage of "feminist" and "feminism" as words to describe the women's movement, raises the central question of how most people learn the meaning of these terms. It is unlikely that the majority of women and men derive their understanding from college classes in feminist theory. For most people, the media are the most obvious source of information. Movement leaders felt that the media were instrumental in teaching the public about the women's movement in the late 1960s. Moreover, many activists felt that coverage of the movement in the mainstream press at that time was distorted and unflattering (Douglas 1994, 165). There is similar concern among feminists in the 1990s about a possible backlash against feminists in which they are portrayed in the media as "overly aggressive, man-hating" and "deliberately unattractive" (Douglas 1994, 7; Faludi 1991). A closer examination of the ways in which the media have defined, described, and used the terms "feminist" and "feminism" will help to explain what most people are likely to have learned from the press about these political terms.

It is unreasonable to expect, however, that journalists will have provided clear and simple definitions of feminist and feminism for their readers. As Gans (1995) observes in his analysis of the etiology of the label "underclass," journalists are unlikely to look up or cite the definition of political terms for their readership or audience. Moreover, he suggests that the way journalists "use terms or labels can be (or have to be) gleaned from linguistic context" (Gans 1995, 38). Thus to understand the meaning of feminist and feminism as they have been presented in the news media, I delve into media coverage to examine the implied associations between these terms and specific people, organizations, ideas, and policies. Through an analysis of the direct and indirect meaning given to feminist and feminism, I hope to better explain public perceptions of these complex terms, which have multiple and diverse meanings.

The Media and Social Movements

Varied meanings of feminism coupled with the widespread use of "feminist" as an everyday term raises a series of questions about how the media have portrayed feminists. In particular, what is the image that journalists have conveyed of feminists since the inception of the modern women's movement? How accurately have they portrayed the diversity within feminism and the varied goals of the women's movement? To what extent has this portrayal kept pace over time with changes in the women's movement? And if there is evidence of media bias, why and how does it occur? To formulate testable hypotheses that will help answer these questions, I draw on an emerging literature that concerns the relationship between social movements and the media.

In a review of the recent and growing sociological literature on the link between social movements and the media, Gamson and Wolfsfeld (1993) describe the relationship as one of interdependence. In their view, social movements need the press to mobilize their constituents, establish their credibility through external validation, and enlarge the scope of the dispute by bringing in third party mediators. The media need social movements, in turn, to provide the elements of interesting news: "drama, conflict, and action; colorful copy, and photo opportunities" (p. 116). This view is echoed by Gitlin (1980) in his account of media coverage of the student protest movement of the late 1960s, and by Costain et al. in the next chapter.

As Gamson and Wolfsfeld point out, however, this is not a marriage of equals. Social movements need the media more than the media need them. This inequality may contribute to systematic distortions in the popular portrayal of a movement's message, caused either by the actions of social movements themselves or by internal pressures at work within news organizations. As Gamson and colleagues (Gamson and Wolfsfeld 1993;

Gamson et al. 1992) have suggested, social movements often alter their message to gain news coverage of their cause. Gamson and Wolfsfeld (1993) detail three factors that they believe ensure social movement access to the media: (1) greater professionalism, resources, coordination, and strategic planning; (2) a division of labor between official representatives and activists; and (3) narrow demands that do not challenge the system. These three factors taken together can modify and moderate a movement's message, especially a movement dedicated to radical change, to fit with journalistic demands.

At the same time, the economics of news creation impels the media to cover social movements in ways that can minimize or distort their message. First, the media's need to emphasize a movement's entertainment and dramatic value can result in the choice of flamboyant movement leaders and actions that may not represent the movement as a whole (Gamson and Wolfsfeld 1993). Second, to keep news stories interesting but simple, the media often present a social movement as counterbalanced by a single opposition that is often implicitly presented as if it were of equal power and size. This is consistent with a journalistic preference for conflict in which an issue is reduced to two competing sides (Gamson and Modigliani 1987) or a campaign issue is highlighted on which two political candidates disagree (Patterson 1980). As Gitlin (1980) points out, however, this can seriously distort media coverage of a social movement. As an example, he cites coverage of antiwar protest activities in the 1960s in which the numbers of anti- and pro-war demonstrators were presented as roughly equal when in fact antiwar protesters vastly outnumbered their opposition (Gitlin 1980, 47–48).

Third, the need for journalistic efficiency can lead to the establishment of a pool of preferred movement leaders who regularly supply journalists with quotes and background information about the movement (Gans 1979; Sigal 1973). This may result in the movement being presented as less diverse than it really is. Fourth, as noted by Gitlin (p.35) "[News] Deadlines increase the pressure to keep the story simple." In Gitlin's view, this often leads to an emphasis on specific events to provide a suitable news "peg" or "frame" and, thus, minimizes coverage of other issues, demands, or ideology supported by movement activists that might serve to complicate the news story.

Taken together, these factors do not necessarily lead to adverse media coverage of social movements. There are several well-documented instances in which media coverage of a movement has been decidedly sympathetic (Gamson 1988; Hallin 1987; C. Ryan 1991). Nonetheless, the media's emphasis on a movement's flamboyant actions, the need to present the movement balanced by an opposition, the reliance on a handful of movement leaders, and the need to simplify the story and to focus on events at the expense of a broad ideological agenda can seriously distort the ways in which a social movement's objectives are presented to the public.

Hypotheses Concerning Media Use of "Feminist" and "Feminism"

Based on the foregoing analysis, there are four basic hypotheses about the ways in which the media have used the terms "feminist" and "feminism" when covering the second wave women's movement. This research focuses on the extent to which organizations, events, or individuals associated with the women's movement are depicted as linked to a social movement through their designation as feminist or portrayal as supportive of feminism.[1]

The first hypothesis is based on expectations that journalists need to keep a story simple by presenting a social movement in connection with a specific event and not troubling to explain a movement's broad ideology. Accordingly, this hypothesis predicts that *the terms feminist and feminism will often be presented simplistically and in association with support for a single issue.* Only rarely will the terms feminist and feminism be presented in connection to a broader ideology or a larger set of issues. This suggests that at any given point in time, the media will provide a limited view of feminists' goals and issue agendas.

The second hypothesis states that *the media have tended to minimize the diversity among feminists by reserving the label feminist for a few prominent women "superstars" but rarely using it for the many other individuals who call themselves feminist, including ordinary women and men.* This expectation is derived, in part, from the media's preference for colorful and flamboyant movement leaders and the media's tendency to rely on a few select spokespersons to represent a social movement. News coverage of the Equal Rights Amendment (ERA) during the mid to late 1970s contributed further to the view that ordinary women were not feminists. The media's interest in presenting two conflicting sides of an issue resulted in feminists being pitted against housewives, mothers, and ordinary women in coverage of the ERA. These stories implied that feminists were a minority and conveyed the message, quoted directly from Phyllis Schlafly, that "The women's lib movement is not relevant to most women" (quoted in Douglas 1994, 233).

The third and fourth hypotheses are based on a consideration of the attributes of a movement that ensure it greater access to the media: increased professionalism, a division of labor between activists and spokepersons, and the pursuit of narrow demands. A consideration of these concerns leads to the third hypothesis, which states that *the media will have more commonly associated feminism with well-organized, professional groups than with small, local groups that often have a radical focus.*

Feminist organizations can be divided into those that pursue influence within the mainstream and those that are more comfortable working outside or on the periphery of the political system (Freeman 1975; Echols 1989; Gelb 1995; B. Ryan 1992). Examples of larger, centrally organized groups include the National Organization for Women (NOW) and the National Women's Political Caucus (NWPC); both groups are based in Washington, DC, employ full-time lobbyists, and actively work with elected representatives. As a consequence, they are more likely to gain media access than smaller decentralized groups such as a local rape crisis center or small consciousness-raising groups. In essence these larger organizations have developed a professional structure that facilitates contact with the press. Consider NOW as an example. Since its inception in 1966, NOW has pursued connections with the mainstream media. Betty Friedan, the first president of NOW, had access to New York public relations firms and hired them to design the first NOW press releases. In addition, early NOW members included freelance writers who had contacts in the publishing world and could sell articles about the movement to popular magazines (Tuchman 1978, 136–37). In contrast, radical feminist organizations that emerged in the late 1960s tended to shun the press, preferred small scale organizations that were not hierarchically organized, and lacked extensive resources (Echols 1989).[2]

While Friedan and other NOW leaders put themselves forward as movement spokespersons, radical groups often chided members who sought media attention. For example, The Feminists, a New York group of radical feminists formed in 1969, penalized Ti-Grace Atkinson for allowing the media to portray her as a group leader (Echols 1989, 181). In fact, members of radical feminist organizations in the late 1960s and early 1970s were opposed to feminists who presented themselves as self-appointed leaders of the women's movement and were dismayed at the publicity given to celebrity feminists, such as Gloria Steinem, who had not been active within the movement prior to her emergence on the national media scene in 1971.

Despite predictions from Hypothesis 3 of a strong media link between feminism and larger, professionally organized women's groups, the media's interest in social movement organizations that are willing to present a narrow set of demands may have led these larger organizations to avoid labeling themselves as feminist because of the term's association with a broader ideology and a more extensive set of demands. This leads directly to Hypothesis 4, which predicts that as organizations linked to the women's movement pursued and attained increased media access, they were increasingly unlikely to describe themselves to the media as feminist organizations and, thus, were increasingly unlikely to be described as feminist organizations in news articles. This leads to the paradoxical prediction that professionally organized women's groups were more likely to be referred to as feminist organizations in the early 1970s, when organizations pursued a mix of radical and conventional political strategies, than in the 1980s and 1990s, when women's organizations were pursuing the strategies of political insiders (Gelb 1989; Schlozman 1990; Spalter-Roth and Schreiber 1995).

It is not fair, however, to blame only women's organizations for failing to connect their activities to the women's movement. The media also play a role in minimizing the connection between the women's movement and women's organizations, regardless of their size or organizational style. As Ferree and Martin (1995, 16) point out, "Feminist organizations are no longer news. . . . Or, if the media do report on them, they rarely acknowledge the organizations' feminism." They attribute this, in part, to the fact that feminist organizations have become "unremarkable." In other words, the movement is no longer newsworthy because it is no longer new and does not pursue the kinds of flamboyant tactics and activities that made for good news copy in the late 1960s and early 1970s. An organization may get mentioned in an article on sexual harassment, for instance, but it may not be described as a feminist organization. Sympathetic journalists may contribute unwittingly to this public decoupling of feminism and women's organizations by avoiding the term feminist for organizations or individuals associated with the women's movement because of what they perceive to be the term's broad and possibly negative connotations (for a discussion about sympathetic journalists see Mills, chapter 2, and Tuchman 1978).

Research Design

This study examines use of the terms "feminist" and "feminism" in news articles on the women's movement. Hypotheses are tested by examining the frequency with which specific policy issues, women's organizations, and individuals associated with the women's movement have been explicitly labeled feminist or supportive of feminism. News stories are examined from two different sources: the *New York Times* and the major weekly news magazines—*Time*, *Newsweek*, and *U.S. News & World Report*. Analyses combine stories from both news sources.

The two news sources provide complementary coverage of the women's movement. In the next chapter Costain et al. provide information about the *New York Times*' coverage of the women's movement from the 1950s onward (see also Costain 1992). She notes that the *New York Times* provided a very balanced and comprehensive record of movement events; the only slight indication of bias that she detected was a tendency to report hard news about a social movement (demonstrations, riots) to a greater degree than soft news (speeches, internal debates). In contrast, news magazines are not obligated to provide comprehensive coverage of movement-related events. Thus, their coverage of the women's movement may have a different emphasis than the *New York Times* that is more in keeping with television news which shares their popular magazine format. Inclusion of news magazine articles seemed crucial in this project, because, in some ways, the news magazines may resemble more closely the format in which most people obtain news about the women's movement.

Data Base. The data base for this research consists of roughly 550 news print articles that were published between 1965 and 1993. Specifically, the data base includes all of the articles ($N = 276$) that appeared in *Time*, *Newsweek*, and *US News & World Report* and that were indexed in the *Reader's Guide to Periodical Literature* under one of the following ten headings: (1) Women: Employment, (2) Women: Equal Rights, (3) Women: Legal Status, Laws, etc., (4) Women: Social and Moral Issues, (5) Women: and Politics, (6) Women: In Politics, (7) Women: Political Activities, (8) Women's Liberation Movement, (9) Equal Pay for Equal Work, (10) Feminism.[3] There was a roughly equal mix of articles from the three news magazines. The data base also includes a sample of just under 300 ($N = 271$) articles from the *New York Times* that were published between 1965 and 1993 and indexed under the heading Women in the United States.[4]

Coding Scheme. The following information was coded for each article regardless of whether feminist or feminism was mentioned: (1) The primary and secondary issues that arose in the article, coded according to a scheme that contained approximately 150 different possible issues that were then aggregated into broad categories. (2) References to individuals mentioned as supportive of a feminist position on an issue (although feminist need not be mentioned explicitly), coded as a reference to one of approximately twenty-five individual feminists or seventy different kinds of people aggregated into broad categories. (3) References to organizations referred to as supportive of a feminist position on an issue, coded as a reference to one of ten specific feminist organizations or roughly sixty types of organizations aggregated into broad categories.

Each article was coded for the presence of the terms feminist and feminism. If either term was present, the article was coded further for the issues, specific individuals, types of people, and specific organizations or kinds of organizations mentioned as feminist or supportive of feminism. The same coding scheme was used to code issues, people, and organizations as for the article as a whole.[5]

Trends in References to Feminist and Feminism

The term "feminism" existed before the emergence of the second women's movement in the United States. In fact, the term was first coined in France in the 1880s, migrated to Britain in the 1890s, appeared in the United States in the early 1900s, and entered common parlance by the mid to late 1910s (Cott 1987). By the 1920s feminist had become a negative term connoting extremism and subsequently disappeared from popular view until the 1960s when it was resurrected to refer to women involved in the second women's movement (Cott 1987). The revival of feminist as a term to describe the movement and its followers was not without controversy, however. Some movement participants considered and initially rejected feminist as a term for the movement because in the words of Shulamith Firestone it suggested a "granite-faced spinster obsessed with the vote" or as noted by Anne Forer it sounded "unfeminine" (Echols 1989, 54).

The initial aversion to feminist among movement activists appeared to have dissipated by 1969. According to Echols, the term "feminism was eventually rehabilitated, but even many 'feminists' preferred the term 'radical feminism' because it differentiated them from the reformist branch of the women's movement" (Echols 1989, 54). Several radical organizations included feminist in their name. The Feminists was formed in June of 1969 by a group of defectors from the National Organization for Women (NOW), including Ti-Grace Atkinson; Shulamith Firestone and Anne Koedt formed the New York Radical Feminists in the fall of 1969; and Firestone published *The Dialectic of Sex: The Case for Feminist Revolution* in 1970 (Echols 1989). Thus by 1970 the term feminist was well established within the women's movement, although more commonly in use among radical than mainstream feminists.

Not surprisingly, given some activists' dissatisfaction with feminist as a term for the women's movement, feminist and feminism appeared infrequently in the news media prior to 1970. As can be seen in Table 10.1, a mere 10 percent of articles published before 1970 included one of the two terms. The frequency of feminist and feminism increased after 1970 and has stayed at the same level since, with the terms appearing in roughly 30 percent to 40 percent of all articles published in the 1970s, 1980s, and early 1990s. The news magazines have been somewhat more likely than the *New York Times* to make reference to feminists and feminism in articles on the women's movement. And references to feminist vastly out-

Table 10.1
References to Feminist and Feminism, 1965–93

		Percentage of Articles		
Year	*# of Articles*	% New York Times	*% News Magazines*	*% Both Sources*
1965–1969	61	7	13	10
1970–1974	119	33	43	40
1975–1979	90	21	38	30
1980–1984	122	34	50	43
1985–1989	80	34	49	41
1990–1993	75	17	68	44
Total	547	28	47	38

Note: Entries in the first column are number of articles; entries in the remaining columns are the percentage of all articles in which "feminist" or "feminism" was mentioned in the *New York Times* and news magazines, 1965–1993.

number references to feminism in news articles; feminist appeared in 36 percent of all articles published between 1965 and 1993 compared to only 11 percent of articles which mentioned feminism during the same period. Thus, as activists in the women's movement adopted feminist as a term of self-description, the media also employed the term to describe the movement, its ideas, and its adherents.

Defining and Simplifying the Feminist Agenda

To test the first hypothesis—the expectation that the media have tended to simplify the meaning of feminist and feminism in its coverage of the women's movement—I consider several strands of evidence using a mix of qualitative and quantitative techniques. First, the study examines the explicit definitions of feminist and feminism in news articles published in the late 1960s when readers were presumably unfamiliar with the terms and later in the 1970s and 1980s when the terms had gained widespread acceptance. Second, I explore whether feminist and feminism have been narrowly defined by linking them to a single issue or defined more broadly in line with the varied issue agenda pursued by the women's movement.

Prior to 1970, before feminist and feminism were everyday words, the terms appeared in five news articles in our data base. Three articles appeared in the *New York Times*, but none provided an explicit definition of feminism or feminist that might help readers understand their meaning. The first reference to feminist in our sample of articles from the *New York Times* was purely historical and appeared in a review of a book on the suffrage movement, referred to in the article as the feminist movement (Elizabeth Janeway, *New York Times* 1 August 1965). Two articles that referred to feminists appeared subsequently in 1968. One (Martha Wienman Lear 10 March 1968) described feminists as members of NOW, going on to explain that NOW supported full equality between men and women, although the article provided no additional definition of feminist. Further on in the article the author enumerated NOW goals in greater detail, from which one could infer that feminists supported expanded roles for women outside the home and, perhaps, greater equality within marriage.

The second *New York Times* article to mention feminist in 1968 was a letter to the editor written in response to the previous March 10th article (14 April 1968). Not surprisingly, the author of the letter did not define feminism but commented that she "read with a certain wry amusement, the impassioned arguments of the New Feminists [in the March 10 article] . . . and the equally impassioned rebuttals of the stay-at-home mothers" in subsequent letters to the editor. One might infer from this that feminists are in favor of women working outside the home, but it is difficult to intuit much more than this from the context of the letter.

Unlike the *New York Times*, the news magazines provided somewhat clearer definitions of feminist and feminism in the late 1960s that hinted at support for a broad principle if not qualifying as a statement of fully fledged ideology. There were two news magazine articles in the sample published prior to 1970 in which the words feminist or feminism appeared. These two articles provided straightforward, though very different, definitions of feminist. In an article on the new-found career plans of women graduating from Vassar, Radcliffe, and other women's colleges (*Newsweek* 13 June 1966) students described as feminist were seen as wanting to combine a career with marriage. The author defined feminism by describing the women as having a "changed ideal of feminism. They want to use their rights and their heads, but they cling with vengeance to *femininity*."

The second magazine article to mention feminists in the late 1960s appeared three years later in 1969 in a magazine article on radical feminism (Ruth Brine, *Time* 21 November 1969). Feminists in this article were described as differing "widely on many issues, but on one they are united: sexism must go." The article went on to describe various radical activities and groups, concluding with the statement that these groups have drawn attention to legitimate issues such as poverty among women, the need for greater wage equality, access to day care, and heightened self-esteem for women. As noted by Douglas (1994, 168), the tone of this article "oscillated wildly between dismissive ridicule and legitimation." At odds with the predictions of Hypothesis 1 that journalists tend to simplify the meaning of political terms, this article captures the complexity, diversity, and spirit of feminists and their agenda in the late 1960s.

Despite the increasing popularity of feminist and feminism in the 1970s and 1980s, few articles bothered to define the terms by stating their meaning explicitly. More commonly, readers had to infer the terms' meaning from their context. To illustrate this point, I draw examples from articles in which feminist or feminism appeared in the title, and which can be assumed to deal centrally with their meaning. In these articles, there were a few rare instances in which an author provided a specific definition of feminist or feminism by directly linking the words to a set of ideas that were broader than one or two specific issues. For example, in a letter to the editor (*New York Times* 7 February 1982), the author describes feminists as of diverse views although "united by a longing for justice and dignity for all people." In an article titled "Feminism's Identity Crisis" (*Newsweek* 1 March 1986) the authors define feminist in terms of what feminists have and have not accomplished. They accuse feminists of having ignored women's personal lives and claim that within feminism "family issues have taken a back seat to the Equal Rights Amendment, legal abortion and job opportunity."

More pointedly, an article titled "The War Against Feminism" (Nancy Gibbs, *Time* 9 March 1992) tackled explicitly the question of what feminism means and how its meaning has changed over time. The author states that in the 1970s feminism was "understood as an effort to secure for women the economic, politics, and social rights that men have always enjoyed." She argues that its meaning had shifted in the 1980s to mean "denigrating motherhood, pursuing selfish goals, and wearing a suit."

But these three articles are the exception to the rule. More commonly feminist and feminism are not defined as a broad set of ideas, indeed they often remain undefined. Even in an op-ed article titled "Feminism, a Dirty Word" (Paula Kamen, *New York Times* 23 November 1990), the author failed to define feminism clearly; she mentioned "its since-obscured ideals of justice and self-esteem" and implied it meant opposition to sexism, which she viewed as evident on college campuses in the form of eating disorders and acquaintance rape. But the reader received no further assistance from the author in explaining the meaning of feminism.

More commonly the meaning of feminist and feminism has to be gleaned from an article's text. Consider the following example from a magazine article titled "The New Feminism on Main Street" (Marguerite Michaels, *Time* 20 March 1972). In the article, the meaning of feminist can be inferred from the statements of women described as feminists, one of whom was quoted as saying "It makes me so mad to be always Mrs. Richard Bulkeley. I don't have a first name of my own. I'm a person too." The meaning of feminist can be gleaned from this quote but the definition is necessarily more narrow than a broad ideological statement, because it implies, at best, support for one or two specific issues. Learning about feminism from associations, implied by an article's context rather than from an explicit definition, lends support to Hypothesis 1. These implied associations usually connect one or two concepts to feminism, at best, but are less sweeping than an explicit ideological definition which might link feminism to the eradication of sexism or to a woman's desire to combine marriage with an independent life outside the home.

SIMPLIFYING THE FEMINIST AGENDA

Additional quantitative analysis of articles in our data base suggest that readers have varied associations from which to infer the meaning of feminist and feminism. The terms were often connected directly or indirectly to specific people, issues, and organizations even if they were not defined as broad ideology. Among news articles in this study, 42 percent of all articles which included the terms feminist or feminism used the terms in connection to a specific individual. Thirty-six percent of all articles used the terms to imply support of a specific issue; and 27 percent of articles used feminist or feminism to refer to a specific organization. In total, feminist or feminism were linked to a specific person, issue, or organization in 61 percent of all articles. Of course, that leaves 39 percent of articles in which the meaning of feminist or feminism remained vague and unclear.

Not surprisingly, the term feminist was often used to describe individual people. But the term was used almost as often to suggest support for specific policy issues. Is there any evidence, consistent with Hypothesis 1, that journalists have drawn the feminist agenda narrowly by linking feminists to one or two issues or to a selective issue domain? The answer is mixed and requires some elaboration. On the one hand, a range of issues arose in articles which referred to feminists or feminism. When articles that did and did not include the terms feminist or feminism were compared, articles containing the terms mentioned more issues than articles that did not (4.02 compared to 2.54). However, within a specific article coders found that, on average, only one issue was explicitly mentioned as an issue supported by feminists or linked to feminism. The safest conclusion to draw from this evidence is that the feminist agenda has been drawn broadly, since it would be reasonable for readers to infer that issues discussed in an article that mentioned feminism were indeed feminist issues. This finding contradicts Hypothesis 1.

On the other hand, in support of Hypothesis 1, there is evidence that the range of feminist issues has been construed narrowly in news articles about the women's movement. The percentage of articles that made mention of feminists or feminism in connection to one of nine broad issue areas, differed by issue area. These data are presented in Table 10.2. Feminist and feminism arose in more than 50 percent of articles that included some discussion of women's private roles—women's changing roles in the family, reproductive issues such as abortion and contraception, women's psychological well-being, and cultural issues such as references to new women's magazines or books by women. In contrast, references to fem-

Table 10.2
References to Feminist/Feminism Issues

	Mention Feminist/Feminism		*Link Issue to Feminist/Feminism*	
	Yes	*No*	*Yes*	*No*
Private roles				
Family and marriage (27%)	51	49	14	86
Reproductive issues (13%)	60	40	21	79
Women's well-being (10%)	51	49	4	96
Cultural issues (11%)	58	42	11	89
Public roles				
Work (37%)	37	63	11	89
Legal equality (33%)	37	63	14	86
Finances (17%)	45	55	15	85
Education (9%)	55	45	11	89
Politics (18%)	49	51	7	93

Note: Entries are percentages. Numbers in parentheses represent the percentage of all articles in which each issue was mentioned.

inist and feminism came up less often in articles that referred to work issues or women's legal rights.[6] Feminist or feminism were mentioned in less than 40 percent of articles which mentioned these issues. This finding is somewhat surprising in the light of criticism that U.S. feminists have ignored or downplayed issues that concern women's private, family roles to concentrate instead on issues affecting women's roles in the public sphere (Hewlett 1986).

For the most part, when issues were mentioned they were not linked to feminists or feminism. Even when articles touched on issue areas such as reproduction and cultural concerns that were likely to be accompanied by a reference to feminists or feminism, that reference rarely linked feminists explicitly to the issue under discussion. Thus, as seen in Table 10.2, a link was made between feminists and changing gender roles in only 14 percent of all articles that touched on this issue; reproductive issues were linked to feminists in 21 percent of all articles in which the issue arose. Of course, many of these articles mentioned the issue without referring to feminists. But even when feminists were mentioned, a reader had to go beyond the most obvious links in the text to forge a connection between feminists and the issue at hand.

In sum, the data provide mixed support for Hypothesis 1. As expected, journalists were unlikely to define feminist or feminism in broad ideological terms for their readers, although several articles defied this pattern by providing a more abstract definition of feminists. More commonly readers had to infer the terms' meaning from their context, especially through links to specific people, policy issues, or women's organizations. Moreover, articles that mentioned feminists and feminism appeared to construe the terms narrowly by mentioning them more often in the context of issues touching on women's private roles than their public roles at work or their rights within the legal system. Nonetheless, articles that mentioned feminist or feminism made reference to a number of policy issues and did not simply discuss feminism in connection to a single issue.

Feminist Superstars

The second hypothesis asserts that the media have singled out a small group of women as feminists, leaving unclear whether the term applies to ordinary women and men. Further analysis of news articles in our data base strongly supports this expectation. Each news article was coded for its reference to one of a number of prominent feminists; other individuals who were mentioned as supportive of a feminist position on a wide range of issues were coded within broad categories of people. Of the prominent feminists included in our check list, the four most commonly occurring individuals were Betty Friedan, whose name appeared in 10 percent of all news articles, Gloria Steinem (6 percent); Bella Abzug (6 percent); and Eleanor Smeal (5 percent).[7] These four women were rarely mentioned in a news article without the simultaneous appearance of feminist or feminism (Table 10.3). Thus, the words feminist or feminism appeared in between 70 percent and 80 percent of articles that mentioned Betty Friedan, Gloria Steinem, or Eleanor Smeal. The words feminist and feminism were also often included in articles that referred to other prominent feminist writers and activists, such as Kate Millet, Germaine Greer, and Susan Faludi.

But many individuals associated with a feminist position were not linked to feminism to the same degree as the most prominent feminist

Table 10.3
References to Feminist/Feminism Individuals

	Also Mention Femimist/Feminism		*Also Link Person to Feminist/Feminism*	
	% Yes	*% No*	*% Yes*	*% No*
Individuals on check list				
Eleanor Smeal (5%)	80	20	19	81
Other prominent activitists/ writers (4%)	80	20	37	63
Gloria Steinem (6%)	75	25	26	74
Betty Friedan (10%)	72	28	29	71
Bella Abzug (6%)	60	40	15	85
Prominent women politicians (10%)	54	46	8	92
Types of people: feminist issue supporters				
Artists/writers (5%)	72	28	21	79
Represent women's organization (17%)	58	42	19	81
Educators/academics (9%)	57	43	9	91
Suffrage activists (5%)	50	50	8	92
Other professionals (10%)	51	49	7	93
Politicians (23%)	41	59	6	94
Represent nonwomen's organizations (9%)	39	61	4	96
Regular people (11%)	40	60	10	90
Gender: feminist issue supporters				
Woman (53%)	48	52	22	78
Man (26%)	37	63	9	91

Note: Entries are a percentage of articles that mention the specific individual or types of people. Percentages in parentheses indicate the percentage of all articles in which the person or types of people were mentioned.

activists. Only 54 percent of articles which mentioned one of the individual women politicians on our check list also mentioned feminists or feminism. Even articles that mentioned Bella Abzug, a prominent feminist politician, were somewhat less likely to also mention feminists or feminism (60 percent) than articles that mentioned Friedan (72 percent) or Steinem (75 percent). Educators, professionals, and suffrage activists were linked to feminists and feminism to roughly the same degree as prominent women politicians. Between 50 percent and 58 percent of articles which mentioned individuals in one of these groups also referred to feminists or feminism. The types of individuals mentioned as supportive of a feminist position but least likely to be associated with feminism were politicians other than prominent women politicians, representatives of nonwomen's organizations, and regular people. Of the articles which mentioned individuals from one of these three groupings, only 40 percent also referred to feminists or feminism.

While individuals who support a feminist agenda were often mentioned in an article that also referred to feminists or feminism, relatively few articles clearly identified the individuals or categories of people presented in Table 10.3 as feminist. As an example consider a *New York Times* article by Anna Quindlen titled "Anticipating a Historic Occasion, Women Stream to Conference" (18 November 1977) about the 1977 Houston women's conference. The word feminist occurs in the article along with references to Bella Abzug and Eleanor Smeal. However, neither individual is called a feminist and the word is used only once in reference to "various antifeminist groups" who view the conference delegates as "representative only of the radical feminist point of view." It is unclear from the article's context whether Smeal, Abzug, or any of the other convention delegates should be considered feminists.

Of those articles in which individuals are clearly described as feminists or linked to feminism, movement leaders such as Friedan and Steinem, artists and writers, and representatives of women's organizations were more likely to be called feminist than women politicians, professionals, educators, representatives of nonwomen's organizations, and regular people. Smeal, Steinem, Friedan, and other prominent activists were identified as feminists in roughly 20 percent or more of all articles in which they were mentioned. In contrast women politicians (with the exception of Abzug), educators, suffrage activists, professionals, other politicians, representatives of nonwomen's organizations, and regular people were called feminists in 10 percent or less of all articles in which they were referred to.

In addition, it is clear from Table 10.3 that individual men were less likely to be mentioned as supportive of a feminist issue position than individual women. But even when a man was described or quoted as supporting a feminist position, he was much less likely to be described as a feminist than a woman holding similar views. In articles in which at least one woman was described or quoted as supporting a feminist position on an issue, the words feminist or feminism appeared in almost half (48 percent) of all articles. In contrast, only 37 percent of articles in which a man was described as holding a feminist position used the words feminist or feminism. In addition, 22 percent of all woman but only 9 percent of all men described as supporting a feminist position were clearly identified as a feminist or as supportive of feminism.

Overall, these results provide strong support for the second hypothesis. Since the inception of the second women's movement, feminists have been identified narrowly as a small subset of women involved in the women's movement. Most notably this designation has been reserved for prominent movement activists. Other individuals who support a feminist position on one or several issues are less likely to be identified as feminist, especially if they are male. Feminist is used even less frequently for individuals who support a feminist position but are politicians, regular individuals not associated with any specific profession or organization, or the representatives of nonwomen's organizations.

Feminism as an Organized Movement

The data provide some support for Hypothesis 3 and its prediction that the media have forged a strong link between feminism and larger, professionally organized women's groups. NOW has dominated news coverage of the women's movement during the last thirty years and has been most strongly identified in the media with feminism (Table 10.4). From a check list of ten specific women's organizations, NOW was by far the most commonly mentioned organization, appearing in 17 percent of all

Table 10.4
References to Feminist/Feminism Organizations

	Mention Feminist/Feminism		*Link Organization to Feminist/Feminism*	
Women's Organizations	*% Yes*	*% No*	*% Yes*	*% No*
NOW (17%)	72	28	29	71
Reproductive rights (2%)	71	29	22	78
Political rights (8%)	61	39	16	84
Radical/local/domestic violence/health (4%)	47	53	24	76
Business/work (4%)	41	59	9	91
Equal rights (7%)	40	60	10	90

Note: Entries are a percentage of articles that mention the specific organization or types of organizations. Percentages in parentheses indicate the percentage of all articles in which the organization or types of organizations were mentioned.

articles in the data base.[8] The only other organization to appear with any regularity was the National Women's Political Caucus (NWPC), which came up in 5 percent of all articles and is included in Table 10.4 with other organizations representing women's political rights. These results mirror Costain's (1992) findings on the dominance of NOW in news stories on the women's movement in the *New York Times.*

The prominence of NOW in news stories on the women's movement is not especially surprising. The collapse of radical organizations and the emergence of NOW as the most visible organization in support of women's equal rights in the early 1970s has already been documented (B. Ryan 1992). It is more surprising, however, that even when an organization was quoted or mentioned as supporting a feminist agenda, the organization was less likely than NOW to appear in an article that also mentioned feminist or feminism and was less likely to be described as a feminist organization. More than 60 percent of articles that mentioned NOW, reproductive rights groups such as NARAL, and political rights groups including the NWPC also mentioned feminists or feminism. In contrast, less than 50 percent of articles which mentioned business, work, or equal rights organizations as supporting a feminist position also mentioned feminists or feminism even though most of these organizations share NOW's centralized structure. For instance, equal rights organizations included centrally organized groups such as the League of Women Voters, The Women's Equity Action League (WEAL), and the Women's Legal and Defense Fund (Table 10.4). The contrast between the frequency with which feminist or feminism arose in articles mentioning NOW (72 percent) and other equal rights organizations (40 percent) is especially striking.

These findings run parallel to the incidence with which different organizations were described explicitly as feminist organizations. In more than 20 percent of all articles in which they appeared, NOW and reproductive rights organizations were linked directly to feminism. In contrast, business, work-related, and equal rights groups were linked explicitly to feminism in 10 percent or fewer of articles in which they were referred to as supporting a feminist position.

Hypothesis 3 predicted that well-organized women's groups would be more likely to gain media access than smaller, localized groups and therefore dominate media references to feminists. And NOW by virtue of its media prominence and strong links to the terms feminist and feminism is the women's organization most likely to be linked to feminism. But this finding does not provide support for Hypothesis 3 in any simple form, since other well-organized groups fighting for women's equal rights should have been just as likely as NOW to warrant the label feminist.

To complicate further the test of Hypothesis 3, fine-grained analysis of coverage of the women's movement in the late 1960s and early 1970s demonstrates that radical, decentralized organizations had greater access to the press than predicted. In fact, a comparable percentage of news magazine articles published between 1965 and 1973 referred to various radical groups (9 percent), most commonly Redstockings and WITCH, as referred to NOW (12 percent). Moreover, the term feminist was used as often for radical groups as it was for NOW between 1965 and 1973. During this period, feminist or feminism was specifically linked to NOW in 36 percent of all articles in which NOW arose and was linked to radical groups in 32 percent of all articles in which they were mentioned. The radical groups in Table 10.4 combine radical groups from the late 1960s and more recent groups that employ a decentralized structure—local, domestic violence, and health-related organizations. These organizations are described explicitly as feminist organizations almost as frequently as NOW, although articles mentioning them are much less likely to mention feminist or feminism.

Taken together, these results do not support Hypothesis 3 in any straightforward way. There is no evidence that well-organized groups dominated media coverage of the women's movement in its early years when the clearest distinction existed between radical, decentralized groups and more mainstream women's organizations (B. Ryan 1992; Spalter-Roth and Schreiber 1995). Despite NOW's greater media savvy and more central organization it did not receive a disproportionate share of media attention when compared to radical organizations. Whether radical groups wanted the attention or not, they were written about almost as often as NOW (of all articles between 1965 and 1973 NOW arose in 14 percent and radical groups in 10 percent). They were also referred to as feminist organizations with about the same frequency as NOW. What is most startling about media coverage of women's organizations is not that the term feminist has been reserved for well-organized groups with easy media access but that among these groups it is NOW who is most likely to be singled out as a feminist organization.

Findings on the likelihood of a given organization being linked to feminism need to be considered in the light of Hypothesis 4, which suggested that well-organized groups with connections to the media would increasingly shun the term feminist over time to fit in with journalists' demands. To provide journalists with a simple story uncomplicated by references to a broader ideology they would avoid identifying their organization as feminist.

To evaluate this prediction, I examined the extent to which women's organizations including NOW have been associated with feminism over time. I divided coverage of the second women's movement into three distinct time periods: the early days of the movement (1967–73), the fight for the ERA (1974–82), and the post-ERA period (1982–93). Analysis of the articles in which NOW is mentioned suggests that there has been some slight decline in the tendency to identify NOW as a feminist organization. In the late 1960s and early 1970s, 36 percent of the articles which mentioned NOW referred to it explicitly as a feminist organization. This dropped somewhat to 27 percent in the late 1970s and early 1980s and remained steady at 28 percent in the 1980s and early 1990s.

Since references to organizations other than NOW were markedly less frequent, I examined trends in their link to feminism by combining references to all organizations representing women's reproductive rights, political rights, business and work-related concerns, and equal rights. References to radical, local, domestic violence, and health organizations were excluded from this grouping, because I was interested in groups with a more centralized structure and greater possible access to the media. When analyzed in this way, there was also evidence of a very slight decline in the incidence with which women's groups other than NOW were called feminist organizations. In the late 1960s and early 1970s, 13 percent of the articles which mentioned other women's organizations referred to them explicitly as feminist organizations. This declined very slightly to 8 percent in the late 1970s and early 1980s and 6 percent in the 1980s and early 1990s.

Thus there is very slight evidence for Hypothesis 4, that organized women's groups have been less likely to be labeled as feminist organizations in recent years. However, this trend cannot be linked to women's organizations in any clear way. If anything, women's organizations may have used the term feminist increasingly in the 1980s and early 1990s when quoted on women's issues. In articles that used the terms feminist or feminism in the late 1960s and early 1970s, the terms appeared in a quote in only 17 percent of all articles; this percentage had increased to 26 percent in the 1980s and early 1990s. While not all of these quotes can be attributed to spokepersons for the women's movement, the increase is partly due to a rise in the number of quotes in which feminist is used in a positive sense. While a positive quote was recorded in only ten percent of articles mentioning feminist or feminism between 1965 and 1973, this had increased to fifteen percent in the 1980s and early 1990s.[9] Contrary to Hypothesis 4, there seemed to be an increase over time in the use of feminist and feminism by individuals supporting a feminist agenda.

Conclusions

How have the media defined feminist and feminism? More narrowly, it appears, than the breadth of people, organizations, and issues inherent within the women's movement. Only some of the individuals and organizations that make it into news stories on the women's movement are designated as feminist. Specifically, the terms are reserved for a small group of media spokepersons, such as Gloria Steinem and Betty Friedan, or limited to NOW and other organizations fighting for women's reproductive rights. This emphasis occurs despite the large number of feminist organizations that exist at both the national and local political levels and the more varied groups of people and organizations that are referred to in many of the articles as supportive of a feminist agenda (Ferree and Martin 1995). In addition, feminism is used somewhat less often to refer to the expansion of women's roles outside the home than for women's private concerns with changed family roles and the assurance of reproductive rights.

These findings lend greater credence Hypothesis 1 and 2—that journalists have simplified the meaning of feminist and reserved the term for a handful of preferred movement activists—than to Hypotheses 3 and 4—which suggest that women's organizations have consciously restricted their use of the term feminist to fit the neds of journalists. There was little or no empirical evidence to support the view that women's organizations have toned down their message and shunned the use of terms such as feminist to gain or keep access to the media. If anything, direct quotes from individuals who use the word feminist seem to have actually increased in the 1980s. Nor was there any evidence that radical groups were less able to gain media access than mainstream organizations in the late 1960s and early 1970s. Despite predictions that media-friendly women's organizations would gain the lion's share of attention from the press, considerable attention was given by the media to radical organizations.

These findings indicate that journalists are subject to various pressures that can shape or frame their presentation of the news, and in this case their use of political terminology. In order to simplify a story, journalists may reserve the term feminist for specific individuals and organizations to avoid cumbersome political definitions. To create the appearance of conflict, they may imply that feminists are at odds with ordinary men and women. There is clear evidence that journalists draw from a small pool of colorful and flamboyant individuals to speak for the women's movement. Their tendency to regard these individuals as feminists may reduce their tendency to apply the word to others who are mentioned or quoted as supporting feminist issues. In this way journalists' own understanding of what feminism means may further color the issues, individuals, and organizations which they label as feminist (Gans 1980).

But one might ask if this is anything more than a matter of trivial semantics. Does it matter that a position in favor of women's equal rights is labelled a feminist position? I believe it does. By avoiding the term feminist for ordinary men and women; by depicting work-related concerns as less fully central to a feminist agenda; and by linking feminism to NOW but not the myriad of current feminist organizations the media are not representing the full range of feminist concerns. Based on these findings, it would be unfair to fault ordinary men and women for viewing feminism as a narrow movement that does not represent ordinary men and women and that is uninterested in their concerns.

Notes

1. In this research, I focus on references to feminism and feminist because they are the terms used most commonly in the articles included in this study to

refer to the women's movement. There were frequent references to women's liberation in news articles from 1970 till 1974 but the term largely disappeared after 1974. Infrequent references to the women's movement occur throughout the period of study (1965–93).

2. It would be wrong to suggest, however, that NOW and other larger feminist organizations found it easy to obtain positive media coverage. They did not. Tuchman (1978b) describes how in the early days of the movement its members "complained that male editors would not take them seriously" (p. 137) and indeed ridiculed the movement with tongue-in-cheek headlines and frivolous coverage.

3. These categories were chosen because they were obviously tied to the women's movement and had been used more or less continuously between 1965 and 1993 or when no longer in use (for example, the women's liberation movement) were cross-referenced with one of the other categories.

4. A random sample was drawn from the total list of articles indexed under the heading. The sample was not a simple random sample, but was rather stratified by five-year blocks. Fifty articles were chosen from each five-year time period to smooth out irregularities that might arise from having too few articles at a given time point. Thus, articles from the *New York Times* provide an accurate sample of each five-year period and are weighted in accordance with their sampling ratio to gain an accurate picture of *New York Times*' coverage over the entire twenty-nine-year period. As documented by Costain (1992, Figure 5–3, p. 102), coverage of the women's movement by the *New York Times* was sparse in the 1960s, rose sharply and peaked in the mid-1970s, and declined thereafter. All articles—op-ed pieces, editorials, and letters to the editor—indexed under Women and the United States were included in the sample. The major difference between articles from the two sources is the omission from the *New York Times* of articles on women and politics and work-related issues which were indexed separately under their own subheadings. The bulk of abortion articles are omitted from the data base since they are indexed under separate headings by both news sources.

5. Coding was performed by fifteen raters who coded five articles in common, all of which contained the term feminist. Interrater reliability was high across all broad categories of issues, individuals, and organizations coded in the article as a whole and as linked to feminist or feminism. The average percent agreement was 90% or higher for each of the categories listed in Tables 2–4.

6. The nine broad issue areas reflected an aggregation of a number of specific issues. Family and marriage included changing gender roles at home, day care, family leave, and the concerns of single mothers; reproductive issues included abortion and contraception; women's well-being was a single category that included issues which touched on women's psychological and overall well-being; cultural concerns included reference to women's contribution to the arts, movies, and books about women, the emergence of women's magazines, pornography, how to refer to women, and the portrayal of women in the media. Work-related issues included gender discrimination and unequal hiring practices, general issues concerning women and work, sexual harassment, and less frequently affirmative action; the ERA dominated issues that came up under women's legal equality; women's finances included equal pay and comparable worth, women's pensions, and access to credit; women and education included a mix of concerns about gender discrimination in the education system and general issues concerning women and education; women and politics included general issues concerning women in politics, specific women politicians, and the gender gap among voters.

7. The complete list of individual names was compiled from a preliminary reading of articles in the sample. The names that occurred most commonly were included in the check list. Other individuals whose name came up in articles were coded under headings for types of people. Individual women leaders and writers in the second women's movement included in our check list included Andrea Dworkin, Susan Faludi, Shulamith Firestone, Betty Friedan, Germaine Greer, Anita Hill, Catherine MacKinnon, Kate Millet, Gloria Steinem, and Naomi Wolf; Abigail Adams, Hillary Clinton, and Eleanor Roosevelt were included as first ladies associated with the women's movement; Susan B. Anthony and Elizabeth Cady Stanton represented women active in the first women's movement; Bella Abzug, Shirley Chisholm, Geraldine Ferraro, Martha Griffiths, Elizabeth Holtzman, Eleanor Holmes Norton, and Patricia Schroeder represented women in Congress who had been active on women's issues.

8. The women's organizations included in the check list included several organizations representing women's equal rights in addition to NOW: the League of Women Voters, the Women's Equity Action League (WEAL), the Women's Rights Project of the American Civil Liberties Union, MS. Foundation, and the Women's Legal Defense Fund. Organizations representing women's reproductive rights included the National Abortion Rights Action League (NARAL) and Planned Parenthood. The National Women's Political Caucus was included as an organization representing women's political rights and the American Association of University Women (AAUW) was included as an organization representing women's educational rights.

9. Coders rated whether each conveyed a positive, negative, or neutral impression of feminist or feminism. When a quote was recorded, average percent agreement on its direction was seventy-nine percent.

11

Framing the Women's Movement

Anne N.Costain, Richard Braunstein, and Heidi Berggren

The women's movement could not have mobilized successfully without substantial press coverage. Movements arise when excluded groups, acting together, succeed in creating enough political leverage to advance their interests through noninstitutionalized means (McAdam 1982; Tarrow 1994). Communication on a broad scale is necessary for this mobilization to take place. Movements possess neither the centrality to the political process nor the resources to guarantee that they will be heard without media coverage. Press coverage is particularly crucial in the early period of mobilization, since this is the time when organizers must work hardest to overcome the illogic of collective action for many individuals, who are drawn to the movement, but are reluctant to spend time and resources without some promise of meaningful return (Olson 1965). Because the costs of participating in a movement will rarely be offset by any distribution of private goods, these individuals must come to believe that they will be educated, meet like-minded people, or make a difference in creating an important social good before they will contribute significantly to movement success (Wilson 1973; Tarrow 1994; Ferree 1992; Gamson 1992). The media may help overcome this start-up problem by reporting the objectives and accomplishments of movements.

The Concept of Framing

Movements need a particular kind of coverage from the press. In order to mobilize the core of activists, the larger pool of adherents, and the still vaster number of sympathizers, the movement must have a message powerful enough to win adherents. Successful movements do several things. They identify serious social problems; they provide an explanation for the problem; finally, they propose remedial actions. This process is part of what can be called "framing" or "frame construction" (see the introduction; Snow and Benford 1988, 1992; Snow et al. 1986; Gamson 1988). In essence, framing provides a story which helps individuals interpret the world around them and their place in it. For social movements, framing takes place as dissatisfaction and anger among individuals get reinterpreted as a public rather than a private problem. For example, studies found American women in the fifties and sixties were discontented with their lives (Keniston and Keniston 1964; Rossi 1964; Chafe 1972; Amundsen 1971). Women used the publication of Betty Friedan's book, *The Feminine Mystique* in 1963, to take this problem which had "no name" and tied it to the narrow scope of career and life options then available to them (Friedan 1974 [1963]). Women were told that they were justified in being dissatisfied with their lives and that they, in conjunction with a broader women's movement, needed to pressure society and government to change conditions which kept women from participating in a full range of activities outside the home. This was the general message that the American women's movement offered in response to women's discontent.

Since most grievances are not acted upon, it is a particular challenge for movements to break individuals out of a pervasive inertia (Piven and Cloward 1979). Individuals need help in making sense out of situations which they previously found unacceptable and frustrating, but felt powerless to change (Snow and Benford 1988, 1992). The message of the women's movement had to provide a coherent frame, telling women what to change to improve their condition and how to do it. Frames play a large role in empowering previously passive individuals to act collectively. Work by sociologists on movement framing parallels analysis of news framing (Gans 1979; Gitlin 1980; Tuchman 1978b), as well as schema theory in cognitive psychology (Hastie 1984, 1986; Conover and Feldman 1991). All these perspectives begin with the view that individuals process complex information using a set of simplifying assumptions. In the case of the women's movement, a frame, such as civil rights, helps women to see that laws keeping them off juries or out of schools or public accommodations set the stage for them to be treated as second-class citizens. The agenda for change would then be to change laws treating women differently from men.

The links between emerging movements, the media, and government are critical and not well understood. Theoretically, the social movement has worked out in advance the frame it wants the media to transmit to the public at large. Its story is clear, laying out the nature of the problem, the blame for the problem, and the solution to the problem (along with the movement's role in guiding the public toward that solution). The movement's task is simply to get the media to pass along this analysis of events. In reality, the broad scope and spotty organization of incipient movements means that they rarely have arrived at any consensus on a frame during their early years. Only a static and doctrinaire movement would be likely to preconstruct a frame to take to the press and the public. This tentativeness within movements probably serves them well, for just as Presidents and Congress send up trial balloons to see what ideas find favor with the public, movements similarly go through long periods of self-definition. The public can express its support or opposition to various tactics and solutions identified by the movement, in the process, educating it about how to win popular support. Social movement–linked organizations may even converge around competing ways of conceptualizing problems or seeking solutions. One perspective is likely to predominate only after negotiation, competition, and sometimes simply the passage of time. Sidney Tarrow (1994) observes that the media push movements to arrive at some consensus about their message. Without media presence, this consensus might be unachievable. The media are important vehicles for these efforts to test the waters of public approval.

Various media act somewhat independently in these dramas as well. They possess their own simplifying frames in reporting news stories. The media want to send out stories which appeal to individuals as ways to simplify complex events. Two generic frames that are popular are conflict and human interest. In the first, the reporter, in his or her story, emphasizes the battle between two or more sides to a conflict. In the early years of the women's movement and currently as the "Year of the Woman" is contrasted with the rise of "angry white men," the "war between the sexes" is a favorite frame of the press. Many stories are couched as "what women want" versus "what men want." It is unlikely that any significant group within the women's movement wanted its story framed this way, but the media were comfortable couching women's movement events in this format. Similarly, human interest was an appealing framework that turned up in some of the news coverage of the women's movement. Interesting or sometimes even bizarre activists in the women's movement were singled out for features. The press, in the early days of the movement, often appeared to be designating movement leadership. Betty Friedan appeared as "mother" of the movement. Gloria Steinem, Kate Millett, and others were selected by the media as "spokespersons for the movement." The press singled out the personal lives and goals of individuals as representative of the movement as a whole, often including detailed discussions of their marital status. This human interest media frame contributed to conflict within the women's movement, which feared that a number of press-designated leaders would begin to tell all women what to do. To many within the movement, this was replicating a male hierarchical structure with a few leaders commanding followers. Feminism argued for a flatter organizational chart with women encouraged to make decisions for themselves (Freeman 1974, 1975).

A third, somewhat less distorting frame favored by the media for the women's movement was that of the civil rights movement. Since the media had already educated a large number of Americans about why a group of citizens might want equality and legal rights, a civil rights frame could now be applied to women as well. Many early analyses of the women's movement stress its similarity to the civil rights movement (Bird 1968; Chafe 1972, 1977; Freeman 1975). These works emphasize how women recognized their second-class citizenship after listening to the grievances voiced by the black civil rights movement. This frame, along with the conflict and human interest frames, was "on the shelf" and ready for application to the women's movement.

The civil rights frame might have emerged as a "master" frame for the women's movement. Master frames are introduced by a successful movement as an innovative new way to understand and resolve persistent problems. They resonate powerfully in a culture. Since social movements appear in clusters during particular periods of time, analysts have observed that the creation of an innovative frame early in a period of activity (such as the legal equality or civil rights frame in the 1950s) may spur the emergence and growth of other groups which can plausibly adopt this frame. This may lead to an ongoing cycle of protest (Snow and Benford 1992; Tarrow 1994). The creation of a civil rights frame by African Americans in the fifties and sixties was innovative and left an available master frame for the women's movement to adopt. The other preexisting frames for the women's movement, the protracted conflict between women and men, and the individual unhappiness of a number of women, had limited long-term appeal. By contrast, a frame based on legal equality and individual rights as a citizen resonates strongly in a culture with a cherished Constitution and historic commitment to a policy-setting system of courts.

Government and political parties also had a strong stake in the kind of frame constructed for the women's movement. For many years, the Republican Party had seen women's issues as ones of individual equality. Party activists felt that women who could compete successfully against men as lawyers, doctors, or laborers should be allowed to do so. This belief in a sort of free enterprise individualism undergirded the Republican Party's early support for an equal rights amendment to the U.S. Constitution (Costain 1991). From the 1930s until 1980, the Republican Party platform routinely endorsed equal rights for women.[1] In common with other libertarian elements in the party philosophy, the Republican Party asserted that women should attain economic and social positions based on their own capabilities, not on the artificial basis of government fiat or legislative statutes. The Democratic Party had adopted a different perspective, taking its lead from labor unions and social reformers. They argued that the collective well-being of women was the government's responsibility. Government should protect women from working nightshifts, standing all day without breaks on assembly lines, and from lifting weights that might strain them physically (Harrison 1988). In the 1960s these positions left both parties rather uncomfortable. The Democratic Party was in the process of establishing itself as the great party of civil rights, yet not for women. The Republican Party was trying to take a more moderate role on civil rights, slowing the Democratic Party's push for immediate change. Republicans did not want to be on the cutting edge of advocating the extension of rights for women.

Because of the number of available frames for a women's movement, ranging from the war between the sexes to use of the Constitution and courts to make a wider place for women in U.S. society, the process of constructing a collective frame for the women's movement was dynamic, complex, and probably not a great deal different from the experiences of other large-scale, highly politicized movements within American society. The movement, the media, the public, and the government all had stakes in the outcome. A frame once established produces real consequences. Frames limit the tactical repertoire available to a movement. For example, once the civil rights movement in America adopted a master frame that enshrined legal reform and nonviolent civil disobedience, violence seemed like a betrayal of core values of the movement. Frames also do more, determining the centrality of competing groups within a particular movement and drawing cleavage lines between political parties, which may be fought out in electoral campaigns. Because the stakes are high, the process is dynamic and often prolonged.

Methods

To assess the creation of a frame for the women's movement, we first used the *New York Times Index* to compile a list of all articles indexed under Women-United States or Women-General that were published between 1955 and mid-April of 1995.[2] We drew the articles from the *Times* since it is the only American paper with an index extending back to the 1950s. We divided this period into four eras (1955–64, 1965–74, 1975–84, and 1985–95), using random numbers to select 50 articles from each.[3] We content-analyzed these 200 *Times* articles using QSR NUDIST, a program which can locate phrases, synonyms, and close mentions of individual words and phrases as well as performing standard word counts.[4] By analyzing the content of the articles from each period, we got a picture of change over time, as well as observing how the *Times* transmitted women's issues to the public. In interpreting the results, it should be mentioned that newspapers tend to report "hard news," such as protest demonstrations, congressional votes, and public marches more routinely than "soft news," including speeches, position papers, and internal disagreements over social movement tactics (Snyder and Kelly 1977). This means that the balance of activities reported is likely to be tipped unrealistically, on the one hand, toward confrontational politics or, on the other, toward institutional politics. This bias should, however, affect all periods equally.

We sampled four separate ten-year periods, rather than looking at the period as a whole, because we believe that framing is a process. There is seldom adoption of an instant frame. We wanted to see the competition among alternative frames as well as the emergence of a dominant frame. Second, we wished to contrast "premovement" frames with those which appeared as part of a politically influential movement. Therefore, we divided the years into separate time periods.

The time from *1955 to 1964* preceded the formal emergence of a women's movement in America, whose birth is most often dated from the formation of NOW (the National Organization for Women) in 1966. By sampling from this period, we have an overview of the issues and perspectives in American society which led up to the appearance of a new movement. By contrast, from *1965 to 1974*, the women's movement was simultaneously gathering support in a radical women's liberation wing and in an older, more mainstream, women's rights wing (Freeman 1975; Hole and Levine 1971; Deckard 1975). The women's movement was both mobilizing and experiencing internal competition for members and resources during this decade.

The next period, from *1975 to 1984*, was the high point of the women's movement nationally and, in some ways, its low point as well. During this time, pressure was intense to add an equal rights amendment (ERA) to the American Constitution. By 1982, the ERA ratification effort had collapsed and the most public phase of the women's movement was over.

Finally, the years from *1985 to 1995* are ones in which feminism and women's issues were still high on America's political agenda, but the direction of change was being debated among movement adherents and opponents alike. The common focus provided by the ERA had disappeared, as issues of family, sexual harassment at work, and child care all occupy public attention.

Along with examining the presentation of news stories in this period, we have linked these data to another set of data, compiled by one of the authors, on women's news events from *1955* to *1985* (Costain 1992). This data set consists of coded data on events falling under the subject headings Women-General and Women-United States which were reported in the *New York Times.* This set differs from the previous one because it catalogs actions only, not commentary on events, or any *Times*-generated materials such as letters, replies, opinion-type stories in the Sunday sections, surveys, or editorials. In combination with the more complete list of articles, it provides a contrast between what was happening in society and politics and how it was reported by the *Times.* Together the data sets suggest how actions may influence interpretation.

The *New York Times* "Frames" the Women's Movement

Before the Movement: 1955–64

In the earliest period, there was no predominant frame with which to examine women (see Table 11.1). Issues of work and family were most com-

Table 11.1
Frequency of Frames Utilized, 1955–95

	Number of Articles (%)[a]			
Type of Frame	*1955–64*	*1965–74*	*1975–84*	*1985–95*
Civil Rights/ERA	12 (23)	25 (50)	38 (76)	25 (50)
Work/job	25 (50)	28 (56)	30 (60)	41 (82)
Family	22 (44)	21 (42)	25 (50)	35 (70)
Women's movement	3 (6)	21 (42)	15 (30)	23 (46)

[a]Percentages sum to more than 100 since some articles contain more than one frame.

mon, with fully half of the articles sampled in the *Times* employing a framework of women and work.[5] Within this perspective, most stories examined which women worked outside the home, why, and what kinds of work they were doing. The *Times*, under the headline "Mothers Replacing the Career Woman," reported demographic data showing that 60 percent of employed women were married and that women make up 30 percent of the labor force (*New York Times* 18 January 1956, 13). By the 1960s, marriage was so common that only 7 percent of American women in their thirties had never married (*New York Times* 22 September 1963, VI, 34). As this entry of married women into the work force continued, there was increasing debate over their appropriate role. In the midfifties at a Labor Department conference on manpower, Secretary James Mitchell urged women to be ready to join the work force if needed (*New York Times* 11 March 1955). He observed that, "Besides the 20,000,000 women not at work . . . there are 11,000,000 more women available for work in case our economy has to expand for a national emergency." His comments were quickly criticized. Dr. Florence Kluckhohn of Harvard noted that it was "psychologically ridiculous" to expect women to hold themselves aloof from actually working to prepare for a national emergency which may never come. Women scholars also disagreed with a psychiatrist on a panel called "Horizons for Women" who observed that the growing proportion of women with young children who worked was motivated "by neurotic competition."

In addition to probing why women worked, *Times*' articles also featured women in nontraditional roles, such as longshorewoman and business executive (*New York Times* 23 July 1955, 32; 3 January 1960 VI, 11). The ambiguities in these roles were probed. For example, an article by Marya Mannes with the page-filling title, "Female Intelligence: Who Wants It? There is Plenty of It; the Nation Needs It—But Our Social Scheme Discourages It," discussed the contradictions between national leaders who urged women to develop their intellect so that the nation would be ready in case of conflict with the Russians and the social climate which discouraged such achievement by females (*New York Times*

3 January 1960, VI, 11). In addition, the *Times* reported on each of a series of luncheons hosted by first lady, Lady Bird Johnson at the White House to honor "women doers," noting somewhat ambiguously, that guest lists included career women along with the wives of prominent men (*New York Times* 17 January 1964, 22). It was evident during this decade that a major "women's story" or frame was the entry of women into the work force.

The other way of looking at women that was prevalent during the late fifties and early sixties was within families.[6] Forty-four percent of the articles sampled referred to women and the family. A number of these articles examined women and employment, including those discussed previously describing the increasing number of married women with children entering the work force. Other articles were more traditional, for example, discussing the influence families had on individual women of achievement (*New York Times* 19 April 1964, 9; 23 December 1964, 17; 22 September 1963, 71). Finally, a few articles noted the malaise of married women who were housewives. Although the coverage of women and work traced the trend that more women were entering the workplace, articles on women in the family seemed uncertain about how families and women were changing. When the Young Women's Christian Association (YWCA) conducted a poll of girls and women ranging between twelve and thirty-five, the organization had a family life consultant, Mrs. Helen Southard, provide the group's "official" interpretation of the results (*New York Times* 24 April 1957, 37). In brief, the YWCA felt that women who were married, unemployed, and had children were least likely to desire to change their lives. Southard, speaking for the Y, observed that it was also evident that women over thirty-five, with children in school, were often discontented, wishing part-time jobs, "so that they can prepare themselves to be both economically and emotionally independent of their progeny in their later years."

The third most prevalent mention was related to equal rights for women.[7] The twelve articles utilizing a rights frame generally referred either to the United Nations'–sponsored convention on political rights for women, the proposed Equal Rights Amendment (ERA) to the U.S. Constitution, or to references linking women's rights to the broad civil rights struggle in America. During this period, President Eisenhower became the first President to mention the Equal Rights Amendment in a State of the Union message, giving it his endorsement.

Finally, only three of the sample of articles from this period mentioned a women's movement or the activity of feminists.[8] In this premovement period in America, these articles either used feminism as a negative referent, or dealt with communist invocation of a worldwide women's movement (*New York Times* 7 July 1963, 2).

Emergence of a Movement: 1965–74

The period from 1965 to 1974 continued the diffuse focus on women's concerns. The frames shifted rank somewhat.[9] The greatest number of articles continued to examine women and work (constituting 56 percent of all the articles sampled). Now, women's rights was the second most frequently addressed subject at 50 percent. Forty-two percent of the stories (twenty-one each) discussed the family or the women's movement. As these percentages indicate, most of the articles sampled addressed two or more of these issues. For example, a significant number of the stories concerned the impact of feminism on work. These range from discussions of the demands of early feminists for equal pay for equal work, to a secretary's description of how she used the women's movement to get male workers to stop making sexist comments as she left the office for lunch each day (*New York Times* 21 August 1970, 29; 15 July 1974, 31). Most of the articles on women and work, however, discussed discrimination on the job. The issues ranged from unequal pay to differential promotion policies and conditions of employment (see, for example, *New York Times* 21 August 1972, 33; 27 June 1968, 38; 3 October 1974, 48; 28 May 1973, 14; 7 May 1968, 40). In this period, there were also discussions of how women were coping with work and family (*New York Times* 20 August 1969, 50; 20 February 1972, 94; 26 January 1974, 37).

The women's rights category had expanded and developed considerably following the emergence of a women's movement. The *New York Times* covered in detail the debates over the desirability of passing an Equal Rights Amendment to the American Constitution. Stories in the *Times* traced governmental actions, including the passage of the ERA by Congress in 1972, organized support for the amendment among groups like NOW, and the historic background of the ERA (*New York Times* 7 May 1968, 40; 28 May 1973, 14; 1 June 1974, 18; 21 August 1970, 29). Under the category of rights, there was discussion of a U.N. resolution on political rights for women as well as advocacy of stronger legal rights for married women (*New York Times* 20 December 1967, 8; 27 June 1968, 38). Rights discourse joined discussion of employment and family as a way to frame women's issues.

The family continued to be an important frame in this period. Although it had lost ground relative to rights, discussion of family still surfaced in 42 percent of the articles sampled. Many of these articles debated the role of mothers and fathers in the socialization of young children. On the one hand, they emphasized the importance of contact with parents for the development of children, on the other, they probed the limited availability of child care for families with working mothers (see, for example, *New York Times* 13 February 1972, VI, 12; 19 May 1974, 2; 13 October 1973, 30; 27 August 1970, 30; 13 November 1971, 14).

A number of *Times* stories examined current and historic feminism (*New York Times* 21 August 1970, 29; 21 August 1972, 33; 13 February 1972, VI, 12; 26 January 1974, 37; 17 November 1974, 14; 1 June 1974, 18). While these articles were not always positive, feminism had moved from routine usage as a term of disapprobation, to being taken seriously as a perspective worth understanding. The emergence of a women's movement and the reappearance of feminism forced this reexamination.

In summary, by the end of the second period, women's rights and work were receiving most attention, with family and the women's movement close behind. The movement had arrived and the *Times* was still trying to figure out how to respond to it. There were several available frames for the movement, but none had been selected as a single structure to present women's story.

The Peak of a Movement: 1975–84

This next period comes as close as any to possessing a single frame. Seventy-six percent of the articles (thirty-eight of the sample of fifty) addressed women's rights. More than half of these articles dealt with the ERA. The rest positioned women's rights in the broad context of expanding civil rights within the United States and human rights internationally. Politicians and women's activists argued that women must have equal access to a democratic political process insuring them equality. In this period also, opponents of the ERA, including Phyllis Schlafly and Senator Sam Ervin urged rejection of legal equality for women (*New York Times* 14 June 1978, 18; 26 June 1977, 32; 20 March 1975, 13). Both insisted that men's and women's social circumstances were too different to make equal treatment desirable.

For the first time, work dropped in importance, becoming only the second most frequently mentioned subject in articles on women. Still, discussion of women and work appeared in fully 60 percent of the stories sampled. A number of the articles on work also explored women's legal rights as workers. With ever more women joining the work force, issues of discrimination on the job, equal pay for equal work, and access to nontraditional occupations were featured (*New York Times* 30 April 1981, C2; 14 January 1980, 12; 1 July 1981, 2). The other type of issue which arose frequently was that of balancing work and family (*New York Times* 30 November 1977, 1; 23 January 1981, 23; 27 January 1981, D5). At a conference called "The Jewish Woman in a Changing Society," Betty Friedan discussed the common interests of women and men in bringing about changes in the workplace. She observed:

> Something profound and major is happening with men. Its symptoms include the mid-life crisis, their refusal in increasing numbers to accept job transfers for family reasons. Together men and women will demand child care services, new forms of housing, flextime, parental leaves and other services. (*New York Times* 1 November 1979, C1).

There were also stories featuring personal accounts of how families juggled parenting and jobs.

> Nancy Jones wanted it both ways. "I love corporate America," she said, "but I love my family, too." When Mrs. Jones became pregnant in 1974, she

> wanted more than the usual six-to-eight-week disability leave given to women recuperating from childbirth. So Manufacturers Hanover Trust, her employer for the previous 10 years, gave her five months off and promised that she would get her job back when she returned.
>
> The arrangement worked, and Mrs. Jones did the same thing when she had another child two years later. Now a vice president at Bankers Trust, Mrs. Jones thinks the breaks were necessary for her personal life and her career. (*New York Times* 27 January 1981, D5)

Fully half of the articles from this period mentioned the family. In addition to discussing issues of family and work, many of them also looked at the likely impact of the ERA on families. A marcher in a pro-ERA demonstration in West Virginia lamented that

> [T]here's an economic fear that the ERA would allow men to walk off and leave their families. Personally, I think that if a man wants to walk off and leave, he'll do it anyway, and without the ERA a woman doesn't have much protection. (*New York Times* 14 January 1980, 12)

The women's movement itself was discussed in the fewest number of articles, but this still included 30 percent of our sample. Some of the stories, such as the report of Betty Friedan's speech to the Jewish women's conference, cited above, examined new initiatives and directions for the women's movement to take (*New York Times* 1 November 1979, C1. See also, *New York Times* 29 December 1976, 8; 30 November 1977, 1). Others were open attacks on feminism and the women's movement (*New York Times* 26 April 1975, 25; 5 February 1976, 38).

This period had far more coverage of women than the other three (1,705 articles as contrasted with 881 articles in the next most active period—1965–74). Women's rights had become the overarching category applied to problems of work and family. If this were the last period we looked at, we might speculate that a civil rights master frame had been established for the women's movement and that the failure of the ERA to win ratification would force that frame to be refocused away from a constitutional amendment, but still toward a clear goal of legal equality. With the benefit of hindsight, it now appears that a different dynamic was under way. The failure of the ERA to win ratification ended the effort to contain issues of work and family under the umbrella of legal rights. In the current period, we see a struggle to define women's place in society, pitting the frames of work and family against each other.

The Post-ERA Movement: 1985–95

The two subjects of work and family had never lost importance in this forty-year time span. In the current period, they structure most of the discussion of women. While the overall coverage has fallen by more than half, from 1,705 articles to 412, fully 82 percent of the articles we sampled dealt with issues of employment. Seventy percent of the articles discussed family. The strongest theme in the articles on women and work in this time period is the pressure women are under with full-time employment outside the home and, frequently also, primary responsibility for child care and housework inside the home. Unlike earlier articles, which dealt with the tension between husband and wife over her reentry to the job market, in this period, men seemed to accept the need for a working wife, but expected her to continue with her domestic duties as well (*New York Times* 15 April 1990, VI, 24; 11 December 1994, XII, 3; 9 December 1992, C16; 2 June 1986, II, 5; 22 July 1987, A23).

Many of the articles on family were the same as those on work. Specifically, they examined the way parents must juggle demands from family and work (*New York Times* 9 December 1992, C16; 2 June 1986, B5; 6 July 1986, VI, 14). The most common topic addressed by these articles was the need for adequate child care (*New York Times* 14 August 1989, B6; 15 April 1990, VI, 24; 22 April 1990, VII, 18). Two other concerns filled out the 70 percent of the articles dealing with family. Those were domestic violence and the growth of single parent families *(New York Times* 25 August 1991, XII, 4; 5 August 1993, C1; 4 September 1991, D2). This last issue, in particular, was one championed by proponents of "family values." Many of these political conservatives blamed the women's movement for the breakup of the American family through rising divorce rates. Similarly, domestic violence against children and spouses was often regarded, at least partially, as an outgrowth of the rapid change in women's participation in the labor force. Within the category of women in the family are bundled, on the one hand, a desire for more corporate and community responsibility for the well-being of children and, on the other, a more conservative agenda seeking to move women out of the job market and strengthen the traditional family.

Discussion of women's rights still appeared in half the articles sampled. Some of these were reports of observances commemorating important events in the history of women's rights, such as the granting of suffrage through the Nineteenth Amendment and the first national women's rights conference held in Seneca Falls, New York in 1848 (*New York Times* 15 April 1990, VI, 24; 25 August 1991, XII, 4; 18 November 1994, B1). Articles also continued to discuss the pros and cons of ERAs in federal and state constitutions (*New York Times* 12 December 1986, B8; 20 July 1984, I, 1; 19 October 1986, VII, 7).

Work and family, often joined in a single discussion, form the current frame for women's issues in the *New York Times.* The countermovement which grew up in the wake of the earlier women's movement, objecting to its characterization of American society and of women's interests, was responsible for much of the emphasis on family. By contrast, the women's rights movement was pushing to keep women, work, and child care as a frame.

The pattern of news coverage during these forty years, then, is a shifting one, lacking a strong central focus. In the period leading up to the emergence of a women's movement, issues of work and family predominated. When the new women's movement appeared, issues of civil rights, work, and family all grew in importance. At the movement's height, we see a rights focus, or frame, structuring most of the coverage of women, including consideration of work and family issues. With the failure of the states to ratify the Equal Rights Amendment to the Constitution, family and work again become major foci for understanding women's shifting social role.

Initiating Change

A question which emerges from the shifting frame of the women's movement is how these changes of focus were brought about. Another data set that we had available to us allowed us to provide at least a partial answer (Costain 1992). Data had been collected and coded from the period 1955 to 1984 on reported news events in the *New York Times* that were related to women's rights, very broadly defined. The data on these events differ from the current sampling of stories in the *Times* because they excluded all Times-generated material, including editorials, book reviews, and opinion columns. They also counted activities or events related to women only once, regardless of the amount of press coverage. Finally, these data were not a sample, but the totality of events from these decades. Table 11.2 summarizes the numbers of news events in each of the subjects that emerged as important foci for coverage of women. It is quickly evident that concrete actions on civil rights overwhelmed each of the other areas through 1984. Table 11.3 shows which groups initiated these actions.

Civil rights actions were overwhelmingly initiated by the women's movement (including individual feminists and organized groups within the movement), political parties, and the government. Despite the fact that, on the surface, this table might suggest that civil rights/ERA activity was largely a result of government action, this is primarily an artifact of the way news is defined. If NOW holds a rally supporting the ERA,

Table 11.2
Number of Women's Events Reported, 1955–84

Subjects	*1955–64*	*1965–74*	*1975–84*
Civil Rights/ERA	27	164	482
Work/job	28	32	28
Family	12	1	8
Women's movement	3	21	44

Source: *Nexis/Lexis* and *New York Times.*

Table 11.3
Initiators of Women's Events by Subject, 1955–84

Initiators	*Civil Rights/ERA*	*Work/Job*	*Family*	*Women's Movement*
Women's movement	140	22	1	30
Government body	307	21	2	9
Counter-movement	22	0	0	3
Political parties/candidates	52	3	0	4

the *Times* may or may not choose to cover it. When a state legislature passes the ERA, Congress holds hearings on women's legal rights, or the Supreme Court decides a case in which a woman charges that an Idaho state law preferring males as executors of estates violates the U.S. Constitution, the *Times* will cover it. The overview reveals that emphasis on the civil rights of women yielded both government action and news stories which, in turn, probably encouraged greater utilization of the civil rights perspective.

Conclusions

Only in the period from 1975 to 1984 is there evidence of a master frame for the women's movement. More than three-quarters of the articles in this period discussed women's problems as ones of denial of civil or citizenship rights. The ERA with its guarantee that neither the national nor state governments could deprive women of their constitutionally guaranteed rights was seen as a possible way of incorporating women more fully and equally into society. When the ERA failed to win ratification, civil rights lost ground as a framework. Since many of women's dissatisfactions related to either work or family, these frames, which had been present throughout these forty years, again rose to the fore.

Work has always been a difficult political framework within the United States. The strong beliefs in entrepreneurial capitalism and relatively unregulated free markets, which precluded socialism from gaining ground in America, made it difficult for work to be accepted as a frame for changing women's condition (Lipset 1968). Except for the era of the Great Depression, Americans have been reluctant to sanction direct government intervention in the economy in response to political needs. Yet the most significant demographic changes leading up to the advent of the women's movement were economic. Between 1955 and 1985 the full-time labor force in the United States went from under one-third women to nearly 45 percent women (Spitze 1988). Issues of access to jobs, acceptable conditions in the workplace (including protection from sexual intimidation and accommodation of workers' parental roles) and of just compensation for work, are all important, but lack easy political solutions.

If work is a difficult frame to motivate a political movement, the family is not much easier. The antifeminists have led the way in arguing that many problems of women and families would be resolved if women left the work force and returned full time to caring for their homes and children. This would require reversing more than forty years of U.S. experience with women entering the work force. There is also a built-in limitation to this political thrust. For women to stop working, without massive subsidization of families by government, would mean a serious decline in the standard of living for American families. The political conservatives who are at the forefront of antifeminism object on principle to the kind of government intervention in the American economy that might make this a politically feasible reality. Alternately, the countermovement could argue for economic sacrifice in the interest of preserving traditional families. No group politically has had much success arguing for a severe and sustained drop in the American standard of living. This is one of the realities that the most adamant back-to-nature environmentalists have run up against.

By tracing the shifting frames applied to women's issues during the last forty years, we see the failed effort, with ERA, for the women's movement, with governmental cooperation, to establish a civil rights master frame. This failure leaves many issues of work and family seeking an alternative action-oriented frame. Since both work and family have been looked at historically, within the United States, as categories of issues which are best left private, either through the invisible hand of the marketplace or the unencumbered realm of love and intimacy, framing these issues is a significant challenge for the women's movement, the countermovement formed to challenge it, or the government which needs to respond to societal discontents. The *New York Times*, as representative of the quality print media within the United States, seemed to have reflected this lack of consensus, not contributed to it. Generic media frames did not show up strongly in the content analysis we did. The media appeared to push women's issues toward a few foci, including the civil rights frame, but women's story never subsumed the reality of an ongoing political struggle.

Notes

1. In 1980, the Republican Party removed support for the ERA from the party platform with the backing of presidential nominee Ronald Reagan.

2. From 1955 to 1983, we included articles indexed under Women-United States or Women-General, omitting only letters to the editor and articles which were either private in nature (for example, a columnist writing about starting to date again after her divorce) or that had little relevance to the United States. (An example of this last type would be a report on small businesses started by women in India.) Letters to the editor were excluded because we were most concerned

about the way the *Times* presented news about women rather than reactions to the *Times'* presentation. Beginning in 1984, the *Times* replaced the two earlier categories with a single category, "Women," which we then used. We continued to remove letters to the editor, private articles, and those stories from other countries without any United States tie-in. Articles dealing with the United Nations and U.N. agencies, International Women's Year, and foreign heads of governments and their spouses were kept because of their likely impacts on American domestic and foreign policy.

3. We decided to draw an equal sample for each period, even though the total number of articles varied considerably (1955–64 lists 253 articles, 1965–74 has 881, 1975–84, 1,705, and 1985–95, 412), because we want to compare the framing of the movement across the periods. We also observed that, beginning in 1980, there was a significant jump in the numbers of articles indexed under Women - United States. We contacted Harvey Holmes, the chief indexer for the *New York Times.* He informed us that in 1980 the *Times* restructured its index to make it more complete. This restructuring makes it difficult to compare categories numerically before and after 1980.

4. QSR NUDIST 3.0 (Non-numerical Unstructured Data Indexing) allows qualitative data to be evaluated through searches for word patterns. The fact that man or woman is used several hundred times in documents may be much less significant than the frequency with which women's rights, equality, and equal rights, for example, are used in articles about women.

5. We used the following keywords to identify articles dealing with women and work: work (which also flags working, worker, workplace, and other words containing work, job, employment, discrimination, and pay). Because of the inclusiveness of the category, articles were skimmed to make sure that work was one of the subjects covered. References such as, "I will work for the party's [presidential] ticket," were discarded.

6. The keywords: family/families, child/children, parent, mother, and father were employed to locate subject matter concerning families. References such as to Father Theodore Hesburgh were eliminated.

7. To locate materials discussing women's rights, we used keywords: equal (which also brings up equality, equally, etc.), civil rights, amend (which includes amendment, amended, etc.), constitution, and rights. In this category, too, we eliminated unrelated references. As an example, an article identified because of the sentence, "Cows of this breed are equally malevolent" was taken out of the category.

8. The keywords: women's movement, feminist, and feminism were singled out to find articles discussing women's movement activities.

9. The same keywords were used in each of the four areas, work, rights, family, and women's movement during each period.

12

Talk Radio and Gender Politics

Andrew Kohut and Kimberly Parker

Talk radio has become a powerful political force in recent years. In 1994 talk radio listeners turned out to vote in much higher numbers than other eligible voters. They carried the conservative message of talk radio with them into the ballot boxes—helping to sweep a new Republican majority into Congress. And when the massive GOP freshman class gathered for their congressional orientation in December 1994, their keynote speaker was none other than Rush Limbaugh.

While the nature and effects of talk radio have been explored extensively elsewhere,[1] an important element of the talk radio phenomenon has gone largely unnoticed. That element is the gender gap which underlies nearly all aspects of talk radio. Work at the *Times Mirror Center* has consistently found that men are more likely to listen to talk radio than are women; they are more likely to call into talk radio shows; and they are more likely to support the conservative, antigovernment agenda which pervades so much of talk radio today.

The gender gap is evident not only in terms of attitudes and participation; it can also be seen in the *content* of talk radio. Women play a less significant role in talk radio than men: they are less likely to be talk radio hosts, and they are less likely to call into talk radio shows. When women do participate, they focus on issues pertaining to their own personal lives and relationships, whereas men talk about government and the economy. In short, talk radio is an outlet for the political views of conservative men. It is much less an outlet for the political views of women, liberal, conservative, or otherwise.

This chapter explores the gender gap in talk radio, examining women's attitudes toward talk radio and their rates of participation, as well as the role that women and women's issues play on the talk radio airwaves.

Gender and Politics

In order to put gender and talk radio into perspective, it is important to look more broadly at the role gender plays in American politics today. As Ladd explains in chapter 6, men and women hold differing political views, values, and preferences, and talk radio is a forum that expresses and reinforces these differences. A 1994 *Times Mirror* survey of the national political landscape showed dramatic contrasts in the values of men and women. These values gaps are reflected in their divergent attitudes toward the major issues of the day and more broadly about the proper role of government in American society. The gender gap is played out and reinforced on talk radio—much of which has become a forum where male attitudes and preferences dominate while the female point of view is, at best, overlooked and often criticized.

While the gender gap is not the only dividing line in the American electorate, its significance should not be overshadowed by the presence of other social and economic cleavages. Differences in race, socioeconomic status, region, and religion have an impact on values and political attitudes. But among these various "gaps" within the electorate, the gender gap warrants special consideration. With the exception of the racial gap, which pervades nearly all aspects of public opinion, the gender gap is more consistent, predictable, and less based in self-interest than socioeconomic, religious, and geographical group differences. In addition, the political consequences of the gender gap are in some respects potentially much greater than these other gaps, since each gender group represents approximately half of the electorate.

Politics and Party Identification

The gender gap has widened in the last decade. This trend is perhaps most apparent in party identification and attitudes toward the two major political parties. Over the last eight years, men have moved away from the Democratic Party and toward the Republican and Independent parties. At the same time women have remained more loyal to the Democratic Party (Table 12.1).

Table 12.1
Party Identification and the Gender Gap, 1995

	Men	*Women*	*(Gap)*
Republican	31	30	(1)
Democrat	24	34	(10)
Independent	42	32	(10)

Data are from "More Clinton Leadership Wanted—Now The GOP Faces Cynical, Dissatisfied Public." *Times Mirror Center for the People & The Press*, April 13, 1995, Washington, DC.

Men and women differ significantly in their attitudes toward President Clinton, the Republican Congress, and many divisive policy issues of the day. Women tend to be more supportive of Bill Clinton than men. This gender gap has fluctuated over the course of the Clinton presidency, but at the end of his third year, Clinton enjoys a strong base of support among women, while most of his detractors are men.

In attitudes toward the Republican Congress, the gender gap is even wider. Men are more likely than women to say they approve of the policies and proposals of the Republican leaders in Congress. And men are more likely to give favorable ratings to Newt Gingrich and the Contract with America. At the end of the first 100 days of the 104th Congress, large gaps were found between men and women in their attitudes toward specific Republican policy proposals. Many of these proposals dealt with hot-button issues which are discussed frequently on talk radio, and many involve the central dilemma of what the proper role of government should be in this country today.

The Values Gap

Men and women differ not only in party affiliation and policy preferences, but also in the values that underlie their political views and beliefs. In an age of increasing antigovernment sentiment, women are less hostile toward government than men. They are less likely to see the government as wasteful and inefficient and more likely to believe the government does a better job than it is given credit for.

At the same time, women are more likely to believe too much power is concentrated in the hands of a few big companies and that business corporations make too much profit. Women also differ from men in their attitudes toward the poor and the needy. Women tend to be more sympathetic to the plight of minorities and poor people in this country and more likely to think the government has a responsibility to help them. Women are more tolerant of homosexuality than men. They tend to be more supportive of environmental protection efforts than men and are less militaristic. Women also tend to be less satisfied with their own financial circumstances and are more economically constrained than men.

Finally, while men and women express nearly equal levels of political alienation, men are significantly more cynical than women, not only about government but about a whole host of major American institutions. A 1995 *Times Mirror* survey which measured public cynicism toward federal officials, state and local officials, business leaders, religious leaders, and military leaders found that nearly one-third of men could be characterized as highly cynical, compared to only 20 percent of women. Middle-aged men appear to be the most cynical group in the electorate today. They are often credited with the Republican victory in 1994. They also form the core of the talk radio audience.

These values gaps are persistent and have widened somewhat, much as the political forces in Washington have become more polarized. All the values items mentioned above are taken into account in building the *Times Mirror* political typology—a system of classifying voters into distinct, homogeneous groups which goes beyond breakdowns by party identification. Not surprisingly, men and women are clustered in different groups within this typology. Men are strongly dominant in the right end of the political spectrum, women are found in larger numbers in all four of the Independent groups and all three of the liberal-leaning groups (Table 12.2).

The Knowledge Gap

Men and women also differ in their levels of awareness and knowledge, both about the political process and about specific policies and proposals being debated in the political arena. Previous research has shown that women are less interested in the substance of conventional politics; they are less likely to feel they can make an impact on the political process; and as a result, they are less likely to participate in formal political activity beyond voting. In contrast, men feel themselves better informed and more knowledgeable about government.[2]

These gender differences in political involvement are manifested in the manner and extent to which men and women are engaged by talk radio. Men are not only more interested in the brand of politics that dominates the air waves, but they are also more aware and generally interested in political subjects.

Table 12.2
The *Times-Mirror* Typology by Gender, 1995

Typology Group	*Men*	*Women*	*(Gap)*
The "Right"			
Enterprisers	*60*	40	(20)
Moralists	48	*52*	(4)
Libertarians	*65*	35	(30)
The "Center"			
New economy Independents	41	*59*	(18)
The embittered	40	*60*	(20)
Bystanders	46	*54*	(8)
Seculars	46	*54*	(8)
The "Left"			
New Democrats	41	*59*	(18)
New Dealers	48	*52*	(4)
Partisan poor	43	*57*	(14)

Source: Data are from *Times Mirror Center for The People & The Press*, April 13, 1995.

Talk Radio

In 1993 the *Times Mirror Center for The People & The Press* conducted a major survey about the new modes of participation in American politics. Much of this survey focused on talk radio, detailing how many people listen, the reasons why they listen, and what their views are. The study also included a sample of radio talk show hosts, examining their attitudes and beliefs. This survey and numerous follow-up polls serve as the basis for much of the analysis that follows.

The Talk Radio Audience

The size of the talk radio audience in this country today is substantial. Nearly one in five adult Americans listens to talk radio regularly, and as many as half say they listen at least sometimes.[3] The typical talk radio listener is more conservative, better educated, more antigovernment, more likely to be a male, and more critical of the Clinton administration than the average American. All of these differences play to the gender gap. The average American man fits the political and attitudinal profile of the typical talk radio listener much more closely than his female counterpart.

The talk radio audience differs most dramatically from the public at large in terms of its political orientation. Republicans are nearly twice as likely as Democrats to report regularly listening to talk radio (24 percent vs. 13 percent, respectively). Overall, 53 percent of Republicans say they listen to talk radio either regularly or sometimes, compared to 41 percent of Democrats and 45 percent of Independents. The same pattern holds true with ideology. Conservatives are almost twice as likely to be regular listeners as are liberals (22 percent vs. 12 percent). More than half of all conservatives say they listen either regularly or sometimes, compared to 38 percent of liberals and 44 percent of those who fall in between.[4]

In terms of their political attitudes, regular listeners tend to be more critical of Bill Clinton's job performance, more negative about his economic program, and more hostile to him personally than the public at large. They are not particularly fond of the first lady either. Talk radio listeners are more likely to rate Hillary Clinton unfavorably than are nonlisteners. Regular listeners could also be described as rabidly antigovernment. Those who not only listen to talk radio but also *call in* to express their views are the most extreme in their antigovernment sentiment.

Talk radio listeners are also more politicized than the average American. In the weeks leading up to the 1994 election, regular listeners were almost twice as likely to say they planned to go to the polls as nonlisteners (63 percent vs. 34 percent).[5] And they did indeed vote at a higher rate than nonlisteners (65 percent vs. 55 percent later reported voting). In addition, more than twice as many regular listeners reported voting for Republicans in the 1994 races (63 percent) than for Democrats (25 percent).[6] These postelection findings confirmed again that talk radio, along with the Christian Right, was one of the important elements spurring Republicans and conservatives to the polls in November 1994. They also raise an important question: if talk radio listeners were more likely to vote in 1994 than nonlisteners, and if more men than women tune into talk radio, are women's voices and preferences being expressed effectively in the political arena today?

Talk radio listeners differ from the public at large not only in terms of their politics but also in their attentiveness to the news and their awareness of current events. Regular talk radio listeners are more likely to read a daily newspaper regularly (88 percent vs. 73 percent of the general public).[7] They are also more likely on average to closely follow the breaking news stories of the day. Reflecting their media habits, regular talk radio listeners are more knowledgeable about current events, both domestic and international.

Women and Talk Radio

The Male Audience vs. the Female Audience

Women have made up a smaller share of the political talk radio audience in sixteen successive nationwide surveys conducted by the *Times Mirror Center*. In a recent poll, some 50 percent of men reported listening to talk radio regularly or sometimes, compared to 42 percent of women. But the gap is even bigger for regular listenership: 25 percent of men say they listen regularly compared to 15 percent of women. And while only 23 percent of men said they *never* listen to talk radio, fully a third of women say they never listen.[8]

Not only do fewer women tune into talk radio, those women who do listen fairly regularly differ in important ways from their male counterparts. And the ways in which they differ are all reflective of the gender gap. The male talk radio audience is affluent, conservative, and strongly antigovernment. The female audience, while slightly more conservative than the overall female population, is more diverse.

With regard to party identification and ideology, the differences between the male and female talk radio audiences are striking. While the talk radio audience, generally speaking, is dominated by Republicans and conservatives, that dominance is stronger among men than among women. Some 44 percent of Republican women, compared to 41 percent of Democratic women and 41 percent of Independents, listen to talk radio at least sometimes. Among men, 56 percent of Republicans are talk radio listeners, compared to 48 percent of Independents and only 45 percent of Democrats.[9] A similar pattern is evident for ideology. Male listeners are mostly conservative, while among women listeners, the gap is not nearly so large.

Men and women who listen to talk radio differ not only on these basic demographic and political characteristics, they also express divergent attitudes toward political figures and policy issues. While all talk radio listeners are less likely than the public at large to rate Bill Clinton favorably, men who listen regularly are more likely than regular female listeners to give the president a "very unfavorable" rating. The same evaluations are made of the first lady (Table 12.3).

Thus while the attitudes and opinions of male and female listeners depart from those of nonlisteners in the same direction, the departure is greater for men. Male listeners are more strongly negative toward Bill Clinton, the Democratic Party, the government, and the liberal agenda than are male nonlisteners. Female listeners, while they may lean more toward the conservative end of the political spectrum than female nonlisteners, express a more balanced set of attitudes and opinions. In other words, women who listen to talk radio are more representative of the public at large than are the men who listen. This pattern can be seen on issues ranging from environmental protection to term limits for members of Congress.

Table 12.3
The Audience for Talk Radio by Gender

	Listen to Talk Radio	
	Men	*Women*
Regularly	25	15
Sometimes	25	26
Rarely	26	25
Never	23	32
Political Views of Regular Listeners		
Party ID		
Republican	39	34
Democrat	18	33
Independent	37	28
Bill Clinton Ratings		
Favorable	35	42
Unfavorable	63	55
Newt Gingrich Ratings		
Favorable	44	36
Unfavorable	44	53
Hillary Clinton Ratings		
Favorable	33	43
Unfavorable	65	55
Better Approach to Balancing Budget		
Clinton & Democrats	23	33
Republicans	63	51

Source: Data are from *Times Mirror Center*, August 24, 1995.

The pattern holds as well when we look at the values of male and female talk radio listeners. In general, men are more conservative, more Republican, and more antigovernment than women, and men who listen to talk radio express those viewpoints in more extreme terms than men who do not listen. Women who listen to talk radio are more liberal, more compassionate, and more supportive of government than men who listen, and in that sense they do not differ drastically from the women who do not listen.

One way in which male and female talk radio listeners are quite similar is in their level of political vocalization. On a wide range of political activities, both men and women listeners show substantially higher rates of participation than men and women nonlisteners. Regardless of their different outlooks, values, and agendas, both male and female talk radio listeners use the political system to express their views more frequently than those who are not faithful listeners.

Survey data belie the notion that listeners rely mostly on talk radio for their information. Both male and female talk radio listeners are greater consumers of most types of media than the public at large. They are especially more likely to utilize public affairs–oriented media such as the *News Hour with Jim Lehrer*, *C-SPAN*, and the Sunday morning talk shows like *Meet the Press.*

Gender Issues and Talk Radio Audiences

Most radio talk show hosts say their audiences overall are more antigovernment in orientation and more conservative in their ideology than the

Table 12.4
Political Participation by Gender

	Women		*Men*	
	All Women	*Regular Listeners*	*All Men*	*Regular Listeners*
Written a letter to an elected official	27	43	28	43
Attended a public hearing	20	33	30	44
Contributed money to a political candidate	13	21	22	32
Called or sent a letter to your representative in Congress	28	41	30	50
Attended a city or town council meeting	27	38	35	44

Note: Percentage who did each during the last 12 months.
Source: "The Vocal Minority in American Politics." *Times Mirror Center for The People & The Press*, July 16, 1993, Washington, DC.

general public. The hosts believe that feminists are underrepresented by those who call into their shows. And polling data reveal that men are both more likely to call into talk radio shows (by a margin of 14 percent to 9 percent) and more likely to make their views heard on the air.

In a recent interview with the *Washington Post*, female talk show host Diane Rehm reinforced these findings with evidence from her own show. Rehm, whose *National Public Radio* show explores a wide range of issues with a fairly balanced tone, says her data show that while close to half of her listeners are women, more than 90 percent of her calls come from men.[10] The talk radio audience is more conservative than the public at large when it comes to gender issues. Regular listeners are more likely to have an unfavorable opinion of the women's movement and more likely to say women have too much say in the way the government in Washington is run. They are also less likely to support affirmative action programs for women and minorities.

Women and Women's Issues on the Airwaves: The Content of Talk Radio

While exact figures are difficult to obtain, it is safe to say that more men than women are hosts of radio talk shows across the nation. Among the 410 talk radio shows listed in the 1995 edition of *Talk Show Selects*, male hosts outnumber female hosts by a ratio of more than five-to-one.[11]

This may be changing, however, as women have made inroads into the broadcasting business in recent years, and several women have gained national recognition as talk radio hosts. Some women's political organizations, feeling shut out of the talk radio scene, have launched a campaign of sorts to get their own messages on the airwaves in an effort to counter the conservative dominance of talk radio. The Women's National Democratic Club recently distributed a tip sheet to its members called "How to Talk Back to Talk Radio." The group encouraged its members to challenge conservative talk radio hosts and express alternative points of view.[12] And Congresswoman Pat Schroeder (a Democrat from Colorado) has urged the League of Women Voters to get into the talk radio business, "to counteract the Republicans and Rush Limbaugh."[13]

In an effort to learn more about the content of talk radio and the role women play on the air, the *Times Mirror Center* monitored two very different types of talk radio shows. One was the *Rush Limbaugh Show*, the prototypic male, conservative radio talk show; and the other, in sharp contrast, a female-hosted, moderate program, the *Susan Bray Show*.[14] A content analysis of the two shows focused on a few basic issues: (1) whether and how women's issues are discussed on talk radio; (2) how many women call into talk radio shows and what they talk about; (3) and whether there are significant differences between talk radio shows run in the "classical" conservative mold and those which take a more middle-of-the-road approach.[15]

The results of the analysis were revealing. Women's issues are not a central topic in either talk radio format, and women are less likely to call into talk radio shows than men for both formats. When women do call in, they are more interested in talking about their personal lives than about public policy or current events. Most importantly, conservative talk radio differs significantly from more moderate formats. Our conclusion is that when a show is dominated by a conservative male host, the content and tone of the show plays into and reinforces the gender gap. The two shows were monitored for six weeks during the spring and summer of 1995. A total of 306 individual segments were coded, of which 100 (33 percent) featured female callers and 190 (62 percent) featured male callers. Overall, male callers outnumbered female callers by a nearly two to one mar-

Table 12.5
Content Analysis of Talk Radio by Gender of Host

	Rush Limbaugh	*Susan Bray*
Gender of callers		
Male	77	52
Female	19	42
General topic		
Politics	20	*
Personal relationships	3	32
The media	18	*
Health & medicine	7	9
Consumer issues	*	7
Crime/drugs	*	7
Major player		
Clinton administration	26	1
Congress	10	0
Groups (specific)	6	2
Groups (nonspecific)	19	36
Individuals (specific)	29	54
Host position toward major player		
Critical	58	17
Neutral	6	18
Supportive	29	59
Caller position toward major player		
Critical	58	27
Neutral	0	4
Supportive	23	57

gin. And the gender gap was wider on the *Rush Limbaugh Show*. Only 19 percent of the Rush Limbaugh segments coded involved female callers; 77 percent involved male callers. On the more moderate female hosted show, 45 percent of the calls came from women; although the majority, 54 percent, still came from men.

Further comparisons between the *Rush Limbaugh Show* and the more moderate female hosted show reveal some important insights into the nature and content of conservative talk radio and the perspective of those who call and listen. The content of the *Rush Limbaugh Show* was more political and the tone more critical than the *Susan Bray Show*. The latter dealt with a wider variety of issues and was more neutral in tone.

The two shows differ not only because of the hosts' respective agendas but also because of the disposition of the callers. Some 20 percent of the calls coming into the *Rush Limbaugh Show* dealt with government or legislative issues, compared to less than 1 percent of the calls to the more moderate female hosted show. On the other hand, 30 percent of the calls to the *Susan Bray Show* dealt with personal lives or relationships compared to only 3 percent of the calls to Limbaugh.

The Limbaugh segments were much more likely to focus on Bill Clinton, his administration, or the Congress than was true for the other show—again indicative of the political nature of Limbaugh's show. The Limbaugh callers were more likely to focus their comments on political leaders and more likely to assume a critical tone than were callers to the Bray show. In more than half of the Limbaugh segments, the caller's tone toward the "major player" was mostly critical.[16] This compares to only about 20 percent among the callers to the female hosted show. The Limbaugh callers were especially critical of the Clinton administration when discussing policy issues.[17]

The hosts also differed in their tone and attitude. Rush Limbaugh's tone was overwhelmingly negative, whether he was talking about the Clinton administration or some other group or institution. Susan Bray, on the other hand, was more supportive of her subjects.

While these two shows do not represent the universe of talk radio, they do provide some insight into the manner in which women participate in this medium. Women are clearly less likely than men to call into a show that focuses on politics and assumes a confrontational tone. They prefer to discuss their personal lives and relationships and are less inclined to rail against the powers that be. While those women who did call into Rush Limbaugh's show expressed a more negative tone than the women who called into the *Susan Bray Show*, there were simply fewer of them.

In terms of the general topics discussed on both shows, issues which might be of particular interest to women did not dominate either agenda during the study period. Women were more likely than men to bring up so-called women's issues on both of the radio shows.[18] Only 13 of the 306 segments involved male callers talking about women's issues. Those calls dealt mostly with the Shannon Faulkner situation and reproductive health issues. Shannon Faulkner began a legal battle in 1993 to gain admittance to the Citadel, an all-male military academy in South Carolina. She succeeded in 1995 and became the first female student to enroll at the school, though medical complications forced her withdrawal shortly after orientation.

By far the most popular topic of conversation among women was personal relationships. More than a third of the calls initiated by women dealt with this topic. This compares to only 12 percent of all the calls initiated by men. Ten percent of the female callers talked about issues relating to health and medicine. The rest of the calls ranged in subject matter from ethnic and racial issues, to the environment, to political and legislative affairs. While men were less interested than women in talking about their personal lives, they were more interested in talking about governmental and legislative issues, the media, constitutional issues, and the economy.

Women were less interested in discussing "big stories" in the news than were men. The stories dominating the news agenda during May and June 1995 prompted more calls and comments from men than from women. This is no doubt tied to the fact that women were more likely to discuss their personal lives than external topics such as government or the economy; 83 percent of women's calls did not involve a big story. The big stories most often discussed by male callers were the congressional debate over the balanced budget amendment and the 1996 presidential race.

While talk radio hosts are sometimes portrayed as being hostile to women or unsympathetic to women's issues, we found both hosts to be more complimentary than confrontational toward their female callers. Of the 100 women's calls we monitored, nearly 70 percent had a mostly complimentary tone between host and caller. Only 7 percent could be characterized as confrontational or antagonistic. Rush Limbaugh was slightly more hostile to his female callers than was Susan Bray. Even so, Limbaugh's tone was largely complimentary. A more confrontational tone was heard between male callers and the female host. Nearly 30 percent of the segments involving a male caller and Susan Bray could be characterized as antagonistic or confrontational in tone. This compares to only 15 percent of the calls involving Limbaugh and a male listener.

When policy issues were discussed on the air, hosts and callers tended to be more critical than supportive of the Clinton administration's position. Very few women called in to discuss policy. Only 16 of the 306 segments involved women talking about policy issues. However, those who did call to talk policy were largely critical of the Clinton administration's position.

Conclusions

The gender gap in talk radio is a function *not* of the medium but rather of the message. Women tend to be less conservative in their values and policy preferences than men, and they tend to know less about government and to be less interested in politics. Importantly, they are less hostile toward government and public officials than men. Accordingly, most women are not drawn to a talk radio show such as Rush Limbaugh's which focuses largely on politics, reinforces conservative policy views, and complains bitterly about the liberal establishment. Women are more attracted to shows hosted by a political moderate which deal with a broad range of subjects and allow them to talk about the issues most on their minds—their own lives and relationships. Clearly it is not the conservative agenda alone that inhibits women from listening to talk radio. Today's talk radio is not only too conservative for many women, it is too conventionally political.

Notes

1. See "Radio: The Forgotton Medium," *Media Studies Journal* Summer 1993.

2. Michael X. Delli Carpini and Scott Keeter, "The Gender Gap in Political Knowledge." *The Public Perspective* (July/August 1992): 23.

3. Based on average audience size found in sixteen *Times Mirror* surveys conducted from May 1993 through April 1995.

4. Data are from *The New Political Landscape. Times Mirror Center for The People & The Press*, July 1994, Washington, DC.

5. "Democrats Recover but GOP's Turnout Edge Looms Large." *Times Mirror Center for The People & The Press*, 28 October 1994, Washington, DC.

6. "More About White Males from the Exit Polls—Public Gives Press 'C' for Campaign Coverage." *Times Mirror Center for The People & The Press*, 27 November 1994, Washington, DC.

7. *Times Mirror Center*, 28 October 1994.

8. "Support for Independent Candidate in '96 Up Again," *Times Mirror Center for The People & The Press*, 24 August 1995, Washington, DC.

9. *Times Mirror Center*, 24 August 1995.

10. Kim Masters, "She's Got America by the Ear," *The Washington Post*, 11 July 1995.

11. *Talk Show Selects: A Guide to the Nation's Most Influential Television and Radio Talk Shows* 1995 Edition. Among the 410 talk radio shows listed where the gender of the host could be determined, 334 has male hosts, 60 had female hosts, and 16 were cohosted by a male-female team.

12. Stephanie Fliakas, "Go On, Call Those Radio Shows," Gannett News Service, 26 May 1995.

13. Fred W. Lindecte, "Schroeder Lambastes Limbaugh; Coloradan Urges Shows to Offset 'Rush' Radio," *St. Louis-Dispatch*, 7 March 1995, 2B.

14. The *Susan Bray Show* is a current events/general interest program, featuring both guests and calls from listeners. Produced by WWDB-FM Radio, it reaches the Philadelphia metropolitan area, a market that includes portions of New Jersey and Delaware, as well as Pennsylvania. It is not syndicated and is designed to be a local show. It airs weekdays between 9:00 and 12:00 noon (EST).

15. Lee Ann Brady, of the *Times Mirror Center for The People & The Press*, designed the coding scheme for the talk radio content analysis, supervised the research, and provided us with the data.

16. The major player is defined as the principal newsmaker or "protagonist" in each story and can be an individual or an organization.

17. Only segments involving female callers, male callers discussing women's issues, or host commentaries dealing with women's issues were coded for major player, position toward major player, and position toward Clinton administration on a policy issue.

18. For the purposes of this study, "women's issues" encompassed abortion, child care, affirmative action, job discrimination, pay equity, reproductive health, welfare reform, and sexual harassment.

13

How Can Media Coverage of Women Be Improved?

Maurine H. Beasley

Efforts to improve the media coverage of women in politics need to be understood in the larger context of the practices of the news media and professional codes that provide official guidelines governing the standards of American journalism. After considering the effectiveness of existing standards this chapter proposes three sets of recommendations for good practice aimed at individual journalists and educators, news organizations, and women in politics. These recommendations may be viewed within the context of the new phenomenon called civic journalism.

Professional Practice and Codes

Journalists contend that they adhere to professional standards that enable them to perform an essential, autonomous role in a democratic society. Organized groups of journalists have evolved standards and codes of ethics that define professional journalism in the United States (Konner 1995, 10). The two oldest codes—those of the *American Society of Newspaper Editors* (ASNE) and the *Society of Professional Journalists* (SPJ)—have been influential in the formation of similar codes by hundreds of news organizations.

The idea of journalism as a profession devoted to public service was enshrined in the first ethics code developed in 1923 by the *American Society of Newspaper Editors.* Known as the *Canons of Journalism*, the code stated that "the primary function of newspapers is to communicate to the human race what its members do, feel, and think." As a way of "finding some means of codifying sound practice and just aspirations of American journalism," the canons set forth seven principles and described them briefly: responsibility; freedom of the press; independence; sincerity, truthfulness, and accuracy; impartiality; fair play; and decency. Acknowledging the existence of journalism that violated these standards, the canons expressed "hope that deliberate pandering to vicious instincts will encounter effective public disapproval or yield to the influence of a preponderant professional condemnation" (Mott 1962, 726–27).

The canons were supplanted in 1975 by the *American Society of Newspaper Editors' "Statement of Principles."* This contained six articles titled responsibility, freedom of the press, independence, truth and accuracy, impartiality, and fair play (Fink 1988, 287–88). Gone was the section on "decency" and any mention of "pandering to vicious instincts," along with consideration of possible public disapproval.

Three years after the ASNE code was drawn up, the *Society of Professional Journalists* adopted a *Code of Ethics.* It was subsequently revised in 1973, 1984, and 1987 to cover broadcasters as well as print journalists. SPJ refers to its code today as "the nation's most widely invoked code for individual journalists and news organizations" (Black, Steele, and Barney 1993, 7). The code remains under the process of revision. It begins with a statement that the society accepts "the sacred duty to serve the people by providing information and by guaranteeing a public forum in which issues of common concern can be addressed." Under "principles and standards" it lists six main headings—truth, comprehensiveness, privacy, loyalty, confidences, and freedom—and ends with a pledge that the society will encourage the establishment of local ethics codes by news organizations in conjunction with professional journalists and the public (SPJ report 1995, 50).

The 1987 SPJ Code contained one clear example of sex-specific language. Perhaps this reflected the history of the 14,000-member society, which is the nation's largest organization of individual journalists. The organization, started in 1909 as a male-only fraternity for journalism students, did not vote to accept women until 1971. The 1987 code stated, "Journalists acknowledge the newsman's ethic of protecting confidential sources of information" (Black, Steele, and Barney 1993, 5).

By contrast, journalistic codes of ethics in Europe, most of which have been drawn up or revised in recent years, have addressed more directly the issue of discrimination based on gender, race, and other categories in terms of reporting the news. A recent study of journalistic codes adopted by journalists and publishers in twenty-six European countries divided principles enumerated in the codes into six categories. Four dealt with accountability in terms of the public, sources and referents, state, and employers, while the remaining two stressed protection of professional integrity and the status and unity of the journalistic profession (Laitila 1995, 7–9). A subgroup of principles in the area of accountability to the public was classified under the heading of the responsibility of journalists as creators of public opinion. In this area twenty-five of the codes prohibited discrimination on the basis of race/nationality/religion and twenty-three prohibited it on the basis of sex and social class (Laitila 1995, 10–11). These codes came from a variety of countries: Belgium, Bulgaria, Catalonia, Croatia, Czech Republic, Denmark, Finland, France, Germany, Greece, Hungary, Ireland, Italy, Netherlands, Norway, Portugal, Russia, Slovak Republic, Slovenia, Spain, Sweden, Turkey, and the United Kingdom, which has two separate codes (Laitila 1995, 11).

No reference to discrimination appeared in the canons, principles, or SPJ code prior to its latest proposed revision. In a departure from earlier versions, the proposed code holds under the section on comprehensiveness that journalists have "the affirmative duty to report on all significant aspects of global society, including its constituent groups." It urges journalists "to tell the story of the diversity and magnitude of the human experience boldly, even when it is unpopular to do so." It states that journalists must "be vigilant and courageous about holding those with power accountable, especially the media themselves," and "avoid stereotypes in covering issues of race, gender, age, religion, ethnicity, geography, sexual orientation and social status." Journalists also are told to "strive to give voice to all segments of society in public discourse" (Bolton 1995).

The proposed revision eliminates the term "objectivity" that figured prominently in earlier versions of the SPJ code in spite of widespread questioning of this concept. In a eulogy to Douglass Cater, a former editor and college president who died in 1995, Edwin M. Yoder, a veteran journalist, noted that Cater had led a movement against objectivity as a professional ideology some thirty years earlier. At that time Cater contended adherence to objectivity had resulted in reporting without disclaimers outrageous charges by Senator Joseph McCarthy that Communists had infiltrated the U.S. government (Cater 1955, 111). Instead of objectivity, according to Yoder, journalists now subscribe to a convention of "corrective journalism." He described it this way: "If, today, a U.S. senator asserts that the sky was blue on Labor Day, a diligent reporter will check the back weather reports. And it was actually gray, you can bet that fact will be reported early in the story . . ." (Yoder 1995, A19). A philosophy of "corrective journalism" appears allied to SPJ's proposed emphasis on comprehensiveness as a goal of reporting.

While the professional codes in themselves do not appear biased against women or any other group, it seems from this brief overview that they have changed belatedly, and rather grudgingly, over the years to incorporate women into the practice of journalism. What they clearly establish is the ideological basis for the news media to see itself as a guardian of the social order. As the ASNE principles put it, "The American press was made free not just to inform or just to serve as a forum for debate, but also to bring an independent scrutiny to bear of the forces of power in the society, including the conduct of official power at all levels of government" (Fink 1988, 287). While this stands out as an essential element in a democratic political system, one also might wish that the codes specifically pledged the news media to give attention to the relatively powerless elements of society, which include women. The proposed revision of the SPJ code, however, appears to deal with concerns that have been raised repeatedly by feminists and other critics.

Developing Alternative Guidelines

In the face of continuing negative portrayals, women have fought for better depiction in the media during the last quarter-century. Among their endeavors have been formulation of media guidelines for improved treatment of women. The most comprehensive were created by the National Commission on the Observance of International Women's Year in 1975.

To see how far women have—or have not—come today in terms of the news media, it is instructive to look at the total of ten guidelines. Two dealt with employment, three with news definitions, two with respect, and three with the specifics of language. Employment guidelines urged as an ultimate goal "the employment of women in policy-making positions in proportion to their participation in the labor force" as well as employment "at all job levels" with equal pay and opportunity for training and promotion.

News guidelines called for news definitions to be "expanded to include more coverage of women's activities locally, nationally, and internationally." They also asked for special attempts to "seek out news of women," which was said to figure in less than 10 percent of the articles defined as news, and that news be placed "by subject matter, not sex," an apparent endorsement of the move at that time to do away with women's pages. Guidelines pertaining to respect forbade using women's bodies "in an exploitative way to add irrelevant sexual interest in any medium," and the presentation of "personal details when irrelevant to a story." Language guidelines said women should choose their own courtesy titles, "Ms., Miss, or Mrs.," be called "women, not girls," if at least sixteen years of age or older, and not be referred to as "broad," "chick," or the like. They also advocated substituting gender-free terms for those with specific gender reference (firefighter instead of fireman, etc.) and treating women's activities and organizations "with the same respect accorded men's activities and organizations," avoiding sensationalism and concentration on "fights" (National Commission on the Observance of International Women's Year 1976).

To some degree the news media responded. Many newspapers dropped "Mr.," "Miss," and "Mrs." before surnames, or, if they continued to use courtesy titles, referred to women as "Ms." Print and broadcast stylebooks were revised to discourage references to stereotypical comments about a woman's appearance, such as use of hackneyed phrases like "petite blonde" (Beasley and Gibbons 1993, 289–305). In 1977 the *As-*

sociated Press stylebook, the single most widely used guide, stated that "women should receive the same treatment as men in all areas of coverage. Physical descriptions, sexist references, demeaning stereotypes and condescending phrases should not be used" (Associated Press 1977, 240). Yet, the examples of usage given in the stylebook itself abound in stereotypical examples such as these to help users distinguish between the words compliment and complement: "The ship has a complement of 200 sailors and 20 officers. The hat compliments her dress" (quoted in Beasley and Gibbons 1993, 299).

As previous chapters in this book have made clear, any examination of today's news media shows that the spirit of the guidelines, far more important than the letter, is not always followed. True, much blatant sexism has gone. But women still do not have parity with men in either political participation or portrayal in the news media.

Assessment of Women's Progress

Any assessment of why women have not made more progress runs up against a phenomenon described in a 1978 style guide. As the *Washington Post Deskbook on Style* put it, "Sexism—the arbitrary stereotyping of men and women and their roles in life—breeds and reinforces inequality. But some words and forms are so historically and culturally imbedded that they defy efforts to eradicate them" (Webb 1978, 41). The guide called for journalists "to write and edit with a sense of equality, appropriateness, and dignity for both sexes" (Webb 1978, 42). A revised edition of the same style guide eliminated references to "imbedded" words but discussed the problem of attempting to avoid sex-based language. It argued that the effort to adjust language to social change "has presented a new set of difficulties that we have not yet resolved" before concluding that "the basic idea is to treat all persons the same in all areas of coverage and to avoid condescension and stereotypes" (Lippman 1989, 190–91).

As far as women's participation in the news media itself is concerned, improvements have occurred since 1970 (see chapter 1 by Weaver and chapter 2 by Mills). In terms of employment, there are high-profile women in the news business—women like Cathleen Black, former publisher of *USA Today* and current president and chief executive officer of the Newspaper Association of America; and Sandra Mims Rowe, editor of the Portland *Oregonian*. There are feminist columnists like Ellen Goodman, a Pulitzer Prize–winner who is syndicated by the *Boston Globe*. Yet one of the most powerful women, Katharine M. Graham, chairman of the executive committee of the *Washington Post* company board, contends that there are too few women setting policy. Recalling her own "unique" experiences in taking over the *Post* company after the suicide of her husband, Graham told Radcliffe College alumnae in 1994, "There are still not enough women at the highest levels. In journalism, as in all fields, there's a difference between having the authority to make decisions and the power to make policy" (quoted in Terry 1995, 32).

Large numbers of women news executives, producers, and editors might make changes in the portrayal of women, including those in politics, because they would be open to different ideas of news. Clearly the newspaper industry today lags behind other segments of the job market in the promotion of women who might bring fresh approaches. According to the most recent survey of women publishers and editors conducted by the National Federation of Press Women, about 8.7 percent of the nation's publishers were women in 1992 as were 19.4 percent of executive editors. This percentage represented an average yearly growth rate of about 1 percent over the sixteen-year period of the survey. While women represent 30 percent of newspaper executives or managers, the comparable statistics for the U.S. work force as a whole is 36 percent (Terry 1995, 33). The total percentage of women journalists is not growing significantly, because women move into—and then out of—the field (see chapter 1 by Weaver).

With many women on the lower ranks in news organizations, they have relatively little opportunity to press for more equitable treatment of women in the news even if they have not been socialized themselves into prevailing models of professional practice. A statistical profile of newsrooms found that 67 percent of the women are reporters or copy editors, "positions relatively low in prestige, pay and power." It pointed out that "three-quarters of African-American women, 97 percent of Latino women and 78 percent of Asian-American women are reporters or copy editors, compared to 57 percent of white men" (Pease and Smith 1991, 11).

Developing New Guidelines

New guidelines for the coverage of women are needed that address three groups: (1) individual journalists and educators, (2) news organizations, and (3) women involved in the political process. Today it is imperative to reexamine traditional forms of news content and presentation.This is particularly true if the media want to retain women as members of their audience.

Recommendations for Journalists

Individual journalists, broadcasters, producers, and editors, along with journalism educators, could consider whether the following recommendations could improve coverage:

1. In line with the thinking of the proposed revised Society of Professional Journalists ethics code, recognize that objectivity is an unattainable goal. Instead of adhering to outworn definitions of news, seek to frame news stories within the configuration of a diverse society that is no longer solely the province of white males. Recognize that professional

codes are living entities that have changed in the past and should change in the future to articulate standards that address contemporary issues.

2. Work to change worn-out definitions of news that treat men and women differently. Often these definitions have been taught in the nation's schools of journalism and mass communication, which graduate some 33,000 students annually, 60 percent of whom are women. One of the most widely used reporting textbooks has included this definition of news—"women, wampum, and wrongdoing." It explained that Stanley Walker, a New York city editor of the 1930s who coined this definition, "meant that news was concerned with sex, money and crime—the topics people secretly desired to hear about" (Mencher 1991, 49).

3. Include women in news stories in the context of political decision making. Unfortunately, the professional approach to journalism, which has been based on obtaining information from official sources and experts, tended to exclude women from discussions of public policy, since relatively few hold policy-making positions. An analysis of guests on a long-time broadcast news program, *Meet the Press*, from its inception in 1947 through 1989 found that 96.3 percent were male (cited in Beasley and Gibbons 1993, 288). Surely pools of available experts can be broadened to include more women to contribute to public discussion.

4. Refrain from using biased language or physical descriptions. As the author of a new reporting text expressed it, "When you write about a woman, do not include descriptive details about her appearance unless you would also include descriptive details about a man's appearance" (Rich 1994, 370). She cited suggestions on avoiding sexism taken from *The Gannetteer*, a publication for employes of Gannett newspapers that include *USA TODAY*. Among them:

- Avoid using masculine pronouns (in place of "everyone should eat his biscuit," say, "everyone should eat a biscuit"), words that refer to one sex or the other (substitute tutor for governess), and words starting or ending with man (in place of fireman use firefighter);
- Avoid stereotypes of mothers implied in phrases such as "old wives' tale," or "tied to her apron strings" as well as adjectives that dwell on sexual attributes such as "suggestive" and "feisty" in the case of women, since such terms are rarely, if ever, applied to men;
- Beware of news stories that emphasize the "first" woman to win an election, work in a certain occupation, etc., [since stories of this nature unwittingly may convey a sense of amazement at a woman's achievement]. Similarly, phrases such as "smart and dedicated woman" should be avoided [since they give the impression that a woman with these qualities is unusual] (Rich 1994, 371–72).

The Media Industry

Individual journalists can try to rethink their practices, but they work within larger organizations that shape the context of news production. Therefore the news media industry also needs to consider its practices, and whether the following recommentations could improve coverage:

1. Make treatment of women an issue subject to the consideration given by businesses in general to their relationship with their customers. According to Kristin McGrath, president of Minnesota Opinion Research Inc., newspapers are losing women readers faster than male readers because "papers are seen as having a male personality" (McGrath 1993, 102–4). She cited figures that showed over the two decades from 1972 to 1991 daily newspaper readership by women dropped 19 percentage points compared to 14 percentage points for men. McGrath attributed this decline in part to the composition of newsrooms, noting journalism still is practiced by males for males (McGrath 1993, 101).

2. Continue efforts to hire, retain, and promote women as well as minorities so that a variety of voices are brought into the news process. More women should be made political writers and commentators and encouraged to give their views on public policies. The industry should work with journalism schools to improve the climate for women entering the newsroom. Part of the reason women move out of journalism lies in working conditions seen as particularly taxing to them—along with low starting pay, long hours, lack of on-site child care, and a general feeling that women reporters are not taken as seriously as males. Efforts to enhance working conditions are needed to help women break through the so-called glass ceiling that is seen as keeping them from moving into top jobs (Oring and Dank 1995, 35).

3. Recognize that the news industry has a civic commitment to oppose covert, as well as overt, sexism and racism and to uphold the democratic process in return for its enjoyment of First Amendment privileges. News of women in politics should be treated as integral aspects of the newspaper's dialogue with the public and receive the same kind of attention as news of men in politics.

4. Avoid repeated reliance on official sources, most of whom are male, and spokespersons for long-standing organizations in order to broaden public debate. With women candidates now coming from all parts of the political spectrum, some hold points of view different from those of news sources linked to the "woman's movement." Therefore, it is insufficient to equate coverage of women in politics with traditional organized activity. What is needed is reporting that recognizes women are not necessarily like-minded, but that they still are a legitimate presence in politics.

5. Eliminate excuses for sexist language and portrayals in style books, but address issues of bias plainly. As Carl Sessions Stepp, senior editor of the *American Journalism Review*, commented, "The best motivator is not necessarily a prescriptive code, but a powerful argument that exposes how language stereotypes and demeans women and offers some logical alternatives. Over time, I think this will work."[1]

Women Candidates and Politicians

Lastly, women running for office, women in positions of leadership, and campaign managers need to consider what they can do to influence coverage. The following recommendations could prove effective:

1. Recognize at the onset of the campaign process that women candidates have a history of separate, and unequal, media treatment compared to males and prepare personal strategies to deal with it. As Nan Robertson, a Pulitzer Prize–winning reporter for the *New York Times*, expressed it, "Women are held up to different standards than men in almost all areas outside the home—standards involving clothes, voice, hair style."[2]

2. Try to keep media attention focused on areas of strength. According to Frank Wilkinson, communications director for EMILY's (Early Money Is Like Yeast) List, women have to cope with more critical coverage than men candidates. "It's considered perfectly acceptable to belabor [appearance] when it's a woman. No one would give two paragraphs to what kind of suit a man was wearing," he said. Disagreements between women candidates, Wilkinson said, are played up as unseemly scratching matches, whereas male candidates engage in "legitimate debate." The husbands of women candidates undergo much more scrutiny than male candidates' spouses because it is assumed the men are "big manipulators" and "important advisers" to their wives, he continued. Also there is an assumption that "if a woman candidate has young children somehow she's not a good mother by running for office whereas with a male candidate it's never an issue." Rumors that single women are lesbians may or may not be given credence by the news media, Wilkinson said, but "single male candidates are not subject to the same rumor mill generally."[3]

3. Speak for yourself as much as possible. Recognize that one of the reasons for the popularity of talk shows is that they allow individuals to express personal views instead of being bound to the conventions of the news media. The principle that "people should speak for themselves" has been set forth by Donna Allen of the Women's Institute for Freedom of the Press in Washington, DC: "We believe that the surest way to dispel stereotypes, to achieve accuracy, and to add more, new factual information, is for people to make their own case directly to the public and thus to define themselves." The institute believes that the role of the journalist should be a limited one—"we believe that neither the person with the information nor the public needs an intermediary reporter to be an interpreter—but only to help the person get her own account down on paper, on the air, or into some other medium" (*Media Report to Women* 1976).

4. Interest a foundation in setting up a program to promote improved coverage of women's political participation. Perhaps recognition could take the form of annual prizes. Another option might be to establish a fellowship program aimed at preparing midcareer journalists to better

cover political developments to show their effect on women.[4] As noted previously, women now are given limited credibility in the public arena. Female experts may appear in the news when the topic is abortion or affirmative action, but "when the topic is war, foreign policy, the environment, or national purpose, female voices, and feminist voices, in particular, are ignored" (Douglas 1994, 277). Women still are not full participants in the democratic political process.

Conclusions: Reforms and Civic Journalism

As this book has shown, the mass media convey a series of mixed messages. The issue of changing the coverage of women in politics fits within the new civic journalism movement in the United States. Born partly out of frustration with the news media's role in the campaign of 1988 in which candidates emphasized negative messages, the movement calls for journalists to help mobilize other citizens in mutual efforts to solve community problems. It opens editorial pages to ordinary citizens and solicits comments from those lacking a claim to being experts. A key element is to encourage vote turnout and citizen participation in politics (Shepard 1994, 30–31).

If journalism is truly interested in a new dimension of community responsibility, it needs to look at the relatively low percentage of women who seek public office and ask why there are not more. Those who identify themselves as "public journalists" have decided that "journalism ought to make it as easy as possible for citizens to make intelligent decisions about public affairs, and to get them carried out" (Charity 1995, 3). As one part of this goal, it seems reasonable to reexamine the coverage of women in politics and see how it can be shaped to facilitate, rather than hinder, the full participation of women in political life. A flourishing and healthy American democracy requires the talents of all its citizens. Many factors are responsible for women's marginalization in public life, but we can conclude that the media bear some responsibility for this situation.

Notes

1. Comments by Carl Stepp, College Park, MD, 21 September, 1995.
2. Telephone interview with Nan Robertson, College Park, MD, 12 September 1995.
3. Telephone interview with Frank Wilkinson, College Park, MD, 25 September 1995.
4. Some of these guidelines are similar to, but not identical with, those advanced in Robinson and Saint-Jean 1991, 161–62.

References

Adams, Charles Frances (ed.) 1840. *Letters of Mrs. Adams.*

Adams, Henry. 1879. *The Life of Albert Gallatin.* Philadelphia.

Aldrich, John H. 1995. *Why Parties?* Chicago: University of Chicago Press.

Allen, Donna and Martha Leslie Allen. 1976. *Media Report to Women.* "Female Journalism Is Something Different." 4(1):2.

Almanac. 1993. "Women in the Civilian Labor Force." In *The 1993 Information Please Almanac.* Boston: Houghton Mifflin.

Amateur Athletic Foundation of Los Angeles. 1991. "Coverage of Women's Sports in Four Daily Newspapers."

Amundsen, Kirsten. 1971. *The Silenced Majority.* Englewood Cliffs, NJ: Prentice-Hall.

Ansolabehere, Stephen and Shanto Iyengar. 1991. "Why Candidates Attack: Effects of Television Advertising in the 1990 California Gubernatorial Campaign." Presented at the Annual Meeting of the Western Political Science Association Seattle.

Ansolabehere, S. and S. Iyengar. 1994. "Riding the Wave and Exercising Ownership Over Issues." *Public Opinion Quarterly* 58: 335–57.

Ansolabehere, S. and S. Iyengar. 1995. *Going Negative.* New York: Free Press.

Ansolabehere, Stephen, Roy Behr, and Shanto Iyengar. 1993. *The Media Game: American Politics in the Television Age.* New York: Macmillan.

Anthony, Carl Sferrazza. 1990. *First Ladies, The Saga of the Presidents' Wives and Their Power.* Vol. I: *1789–1961.* Vol. II: *1961–1990.* New York: Quill, William Morrow.

Ashmore, Richard D. and Frances K. Del Boca. 1979. "Sex Stereotypes and Implicit Personality Theory: Towards a Cognitive-Social Psychological Conceptualization." *Sex Roles* 5:219–48.

Ashmore, Richard D., Frances K. Del Boca, and Arthur J. Wohlers. 1986. "Gender Stereotypes." In The Social Psychology of Female-Male Relations: A Critical Analysis of Central Concepts, ed. Richard D. Ashmore and Frances K. Del Boca. Orlando, FL: Academic Press, Inc.

Associated Press Stylebook and Libel Manual. 1977. New York: The Associated Press.

Baehr, Helen and Gillian Dyer. 1987. *Boxed In: Women and Television.* New York: Pandora.

Banaji, M. R. and A. G. Greenwald. 1995. "Implicit Gender Stereotyping and Judgments of Fame." *Journal of Personality and Social Psychology* 68: 181–98.

Bate, Barbara and Anita Taylor. 1988. *Women Communicating: Studies of Women's Talk.* Norwood, NJ: Ablex.

Baumer, D. L. and H. J. Gold. 1995. "Party Images and the American Electorate." *American Politics Quarterly* 23: 33–61.

Beasley, Maurine H. 1987. *Eleanor Roosevelt and the Media.* Urbana and Chicago: University of Illinois Press.

Beasley, Maurine. 1993. "Covering Today's Women." *American Journalism Review* 15(4):1–7.

Beasley, Maurine H. and Shiela J. Gibbons. 1993. *Taking Their Place: A Documentary History of Women and Journalism.* Washington, DC: American University Press.

Beasley, Maurine H. and Kathyrn T. Theus. 1988. *The New Majority: A Look at What the Preponderance of Women in Journalism Means to the Schools and to the Professions.* Lanham, MD: University Press of America.

Becker, Ingrid. 1995. "Pulitzer Women Tell How They Did It," *JAWS Newsletter*, p. 6.

Beckman, Peter and Francis D'Amico (eds.) 1994. *Women, Gender and World Politics: Perspectives, Policies and Prospects* Westview, CT: Bergin and Garvey.

Berelson, Bernard, Paul Lazarsfeld, and William McPhee. 1954. *Voting: A Study of Opinion Formation in a Presidential Campaign.* Chicago: University of Chicago Press.

Bergen, Lori A. 1991a. "Testing the Relative Strength of Individual and Organizational Characteristics in Predicting Content of Journalists' Best Work." *Ph.D. dissertation*, Indiana University-Bloomington.

Bergen, Lori A. 1991b. "Journalists' Best Work." In *The American Journalist*, ed. David H. Weaver and G. Cleveland Wilhoit. 2nd Edition. Bloomington, IN: Indiana University Press.

Berger, Gilda. 1986. *Women, Work and Wages.* New York: Franklin Watts.

Bird, Caroline. 1968. *Born Female: The High Cost of Keeping Women Down.* New York: David McKay.

Black, Jay, Bob Steele, and Ralph Barney. 1993. *Doing Ethics in Journalism: A Handbook With Case Studies.* Greencastle, IN: Sigma Delta Chi Foundation and the Society of Professional Journalists.

Blondel, Jean. 1987. *Political Leadership: Towards a General Analysis.* London: Sage.

Boller, Paul F., Jr. 1988. *Presidential Wives.* New York: Oxford University Press.

Bolton, Dan. 1995. *SPJ Convention Draft Code of Ethics.*

Bonk, Kathy. 1988. "The Selling of the Gender Gap." In *Politics of the Gender Gap*, ed. Carol Mueller. Newbury Park, CA: Sage.

Borquez, Julio, Edie Goldenberg, and Kim Kahn, "Press Portrayals of the Gender Gap." In *Politics of the Gender Gap*, ed. Carol Mueller. Newbury Park, CA: Sage.

Bowman, William W. 1974. "Distaff Journalists: Women as a Minority Group in the News Media." Ph.D. dissertation, University of Illinois at Chicago Circle.

Boxer, Barbara. 1994. *Strangers in the Senate*. Washington DC National Press Books.

Broverman, Inge, Susan R. Vogel, Donald M. Broverman, Frank E. Clarkson, and Paul S. Rosenkrantz. 1974. "Sex Role Stereotypes: A Current Appraisal." *Journal of Social Issues* 28: 59–78.

Braden, Maria. 1993. *She Said What? Interviews with Women Newspaper Columnists*. Lexington, KY: University Press of Kentucky.

Brown, Mary Ellen. 1990. *Television and Women's Culture: The Politics of the Popular*. London: Sage Publications.

Buchanan, Bruce. 1991. *Electing a President: The Markle Commission's Report on Campaign '88*. Austin: University of Texas Press.

Bumiller, Elisabeth. 1995. "Through the Gates of Health, Elizabeth McCaughey Transformed the Debate, Not to Mention Herself." *Washington Post*, 12 July: D1,6.

Burrell, Barbara C. 1994. *A Woman's Place Is in the House: Campaigning for Congress in the Feminist Era*. Ann Arbor, MI University of Michigan Press.

Burrell, Barbara C. 1995. "Women's and Men's Campaigns for the U.S. House of Representatives, 1972–1982: A Finance Gap?" *American Politics Quarterly* 13: 251–72.

Campbell, Angus, Philip E. Converse, Warren E. Miller, and Donald E. Stokes. 1960. *The American Voter*. New York: Wiley.

Campbell, Christopher P. 1995. *Race, Myth and the News*. Thousand Oaks, CA: Sage Publications.

Campbell, Donald and Julian Stanley. 1963. *Experimental and Quasi-Experimental Design*. New York: Rand McNally.

Caroli, Betty Boyd. 1987. *First Ladies*. New York: Oxford University Press.

Carroll, Susan J. 1995. "A Mixed Verdict: The Impact of Women in Congress on the Crime Bill." Paper presented at the Annual Meeting of the Midwest Political Science Association, Chicago, April 5–8.

Carroll, Susan J. 1997. *Women and American Politics: Agenda Setting for the 21st Century*. Forthcoming.

Carroll, Susan. 1994. *Women as Candidates in American Politics*. Indiana: University of Indiana Press.

Carroll, Susan, Debra L. Dodson, and Ruth B. Mandel. 1991. "The Impact of Women in Public Office: An Overview." CAWP, Eagleton Institute of Politics, Rutgers University. Center for the American Woman and Politics.

Carroll, Susan and Ronnee Schreiber. 1996. "Media Coverage of Congressional Women." *Women, Media, and Politics*, ed. Pippa Norris. New York: Oxford University Press.

Carter, Kathryn and Carole Spitzack (eds.) 1989. *Doing Research on Women's Communication: Perspectives on Theory and Method.* Norwood: NJ: Ablex.

Cater, Douglass. 1959. *The Fourth Branch of Government.* Boston, MA: Houghton Mifflin.

Chafe, William. 1972. *The American Woman: Her Changing Social, Economic, and Political Roles, 1920–1970.* New York: Oxford University Press.

Chafe, William. 1977. *Women and Equality: Changing Patterns in American Culture.* New York: Oxford University Press.

Charity, Arthur. 1995. *Doing Public Journalism.* New York: Guilford Press.

Children's Beat, The. 1995. Newsletter of the Casey Journalism Center for Children and Families. University of Maryland at College Park, p. 1.

Clark, Allen C. 1914. *Life and Letters of Dolly Madison.* Washington, DC: Press of W.F. Roberts.

Cohen, Akiba A. and Gadi Wolfsfeld (eds.) 1993. *Framing the Intifada: People and Media.* Norwood, NJ: Ablex.

Collison, Michele. 1987. "More Young Black Men Choosing Not to Go to College." *The Chronicle of Higher Education*, December 9: 1, A26–A27.

Congressional Record, 1993, 24 February.

Conover, Pamela and Stanley Feldman. 1991. "Where is the Schema? A Critique." *American Political Science Review* 84: 1364–69.

Cook, Elizabeth, Sue Thomas, and Clyde Wilcox. 1994. *The Year of the Woman: Myths and Realities.* Boulder, CO: Westview.

Cook, Timothy E. 1989. *Making Laws and Making News: Media Strategies in the U.S. House of Representatives.* Washington, DC: Brookings.

Costain, Anne N. 1992. *Inviting Women's Rebellion: A Political Process Interpretation of the Women's Movement.* Baltimore: Johns Hopkins University Press.

Costain, Anne. 1991. "After Reagan: New Party Attitudes Toward Gender." *Annals of the American Academy of Political and Social Science* 515: 114–25.

Cott, Nancy F. 1987. *The Grounding of Modern Feminism.* New Haven: Yale University Press.

Council of Europe. 1984. *Proceedings of the Seminar on the Contribution of the Media to the Promotion of Equality between Women and Men.* Strasbourg: Council of Europe.

Covert, Catherine L. 1981. "Journalism History and Women's Experience: A Problem in Conceptual Change." *Journalism History* 8 (1):2–5.

Craig, Steve (ed.) 1992. *Men, Masculinity and the Media.* Newbury Park, CA: Sage.

Creedon, Pamela J. (ed.) 1993a. *Women in Mass Communication.* Newbury Park, CA: Sage.

Creedon, Pamela J. 1993b. "Framing Feminism—a Feminist Primer for the Mass Media." *Media Studies Journal* 7(1): 68–81.

Crigler, Ann N. (1997). *Making Sense of Politics: Constructing Political Messages and Meaning.* Ann Arbor, MI: University of Michigan Press.

D'Amico, Francine and Peter R. Beckman (eds.) 1995. *Women in World Politics.* Westport, CT: Bergin and Garvey.

Darcy, Robert, Susan Welch, and Janet Clark. 1994. *Women, Elections and Representation.* Lincoln, NE: University of Nebraska Press.

Deaux, Kay and Laurie L. Lewis. 1984. "Structure of Gender Stereotypes: Interrelationships Among Components and Gender Label." *Journal of Personality and Social Psychology* 46: 991–1004.

Deckard, Barbara. 1975. *The Women's Movement: Political, Socioeconomic, and Psychological Issues.* New York: Harper & Row.

Delli Carpini, Michael X. and Bruce Williams. 1994. "Methods, Metaphors, and Media Research: The Uses of Television in Political Conversation." *Communication Research* 21(6): 782–812.

Dines, Gail and Jean M. Humez (eds.) 1995. *Gender, Race and Class in Media.* Thousand Oaks, CA: Sage.

Dodson, Debra L. 1995. "The Impact of Women on Health Care Reform: The Case of the 103rd Congress." Paper presented at the Annual Meeting of the American Political Science Association, Chicago, April 6–8.

Dodson, Debra L. and Susan J. Carroll. 1991. *Reshaping the Agenda: Women in State Legislatures.* New Brunswick, NJ: Center for the American Woman and Politics.

Dodson, Debra L., Susan J. Carroll, Ruth B. Mandel, Katherine E. Kleeman, Ronnee Schreiber, and Debra J. Liebowitz. 1995. *Voices, Views, Votes: The Impact of Women in the 103rd Congress.* New Brunswick, NJ: Center for the American Woman and Politics.

Donovan, Josephine. 1990. *Feminist Theory: The Intellectual Traditions of American Feminism.* New York: The Continuum Publishing Company.

Douglas, Susan J. 1994. *Where the Girls Are: Growing Up Female with the Mass Media.* New York: Times Books.

Douglas, Susan. 1991. "The Representation of Women in the News Media." *Extra*, March–April:2.

Echols, Alice. 1989. *Daring to Be Bad: Radical Feminism in America, 1967–1975.* Minneapolis: University of Minnesota.

Eddings, Barbara Murray. 1980. "Women in Broadcasting (U.S.) De Jure, De Facto." *Women's Studies International Quarterly* 3: 1–13.

Ehrenreich, Barbara. 1995. "A Term of Honor." *Time*: 23 Jan.

Entman, Robert M. 1991. "Framing U.S. Coverage of International News." *Journal of Communication* 41(4): 6–28.

Entman, Robert M. 1993a. "Framing: Towards Clarification of a Fractured Paradigm." *Journal of Communication* 43(4).

Entman, Robert. 1993b. "Freezing Out the Public: Elite and Media Framing of the U.S. Anti-Nuclear Movement." *Political Communication* 10(2): 155–73.

Epstein, Laurily Keir (ed.) 1978. *Women and the News.* New York: Hastings House.

Faludi, Susan. 1991. *Backlash: The Undeclared War Against American Women.* New York: Crown Publishers.

Feldmann, Linda. 1995. "Winner in '96 Will Need the Women's Vote." *Baltimore Sun*: April 23.

Ferree, Myra Marx and Beth B. Hess. 1994. *Controversy and Coalition: The New Feminist Movement Across Three Decades of Change.* New York: Twayne Publishers.

Ferree, Myra Max and Patricia Yancey Martin. 1995. "Doing the Work of the Movement: Feminist Organizations." In *Feminist Organizations: Harvest of the New Women's Movement*, ed. Myra Max Ferree and Patricia Yancey Martin. Philadelphia: Temple University Press.

Ferree, Myra. 1992. "The Political Context of Rationality: Rational Choice Theory and Resource Mobilization." In *Frontiers in Social Movement Theory*, ed. Aldon Morris and Carol Mueller. New Haven: Yale University Press.

Fink, Conrad C. 1988. *Media Ethics in the Newsroom and Beyond.* New York: McGraw-Hill.

Fiorina, Morris P.1981. *Retrospective Voting in American National Elections.* New Haven: Yale University Press.

Fitzpatrick, Kellyanne. 1995. "Gender Gap Politics: The Republican Warning." *Campaigns and Elections. 258* October–November 1995.

Fowler, Tillie. 1995. Personal Interview.

Fox, Mary Frank. 1988. "Women and Higher Education: Gender Differences in the Status of Students and Scholars." In *Women: A Feminist Perspective*, ed. Jo Freeman. 4th Edition. Mountain View, CA: Mayfield Publishing Company.

Francovic, Kathleen. 1983. "Sex and Politics: New Alignments, Old Issues." *P.S.* 15: 441.

Frankovic, Kathleen. 1988. "The Ferraro Factor, The Women's Movement, the Polls, and the Press." In *Politics of the Gender Gap*, ed. Carol Mueller. Newbury Park, CA: Sage.

Freeman, Jo. 1974. "The Tyranny of Structurelessness." In *Women in Politics*, ed. Jane Jaquette. New York: John Wiley.

Freeman, Jo. 1975. *The Politics of Women's Liberation: A Case Study of an Emerging Social Movement and Its Relation to the Policy Process.* New York: David McKay.

Friedan, Betty. 1963. *The Feminine Mystique.* New York: W.W. Norton.

Friedan, Betty. 1974 [1963]. *The Feminine Mystique.* New York: Dell.

Fuchs, Victor R. 1988. *Women's Quest for Economic Equality.* Newbury Park, CA: Sage.

Gallagher, Margaret. 1985. *Women in the Media.* Strasbourg: Council of Europe.

Gallup Report, 1984. 228: 2–14.

Gamson, William A. 1988. "Political Discourse and Collective Action." In *From Structure to Action: Comparing Social Movement Research Across Cultures*, eds. B. Klandersman et al. Greenwich, CT: JAI Press, pp. 219–44.

Gamson, William A. and Modigliani. 1987. "The Changing Culture of Affirmative Action." In *Research in Political Sociology*, ed. Richard D. Braungart. Greenwich, CT: JAI Press, Vol. 3, pp. 137–77.

Gamson, William A. and Gadi Wolfsfeld. 1993. "Movements and Media as Interacting Systems." *Annals of the American Academy of Political and Social Science* 528: 114–25.

Gamson, William A., David Croteau, William Hoynes, and Theodore Sasson. 1992. "Media Images and the Social Construction of Reality." *American Review of Sociology* 18:373–93.

Gamson, William. 1986. *Talking Politics.* New York: Cambridge University Press.

Gamson, William. 1968. *Power and Discontent.* Homewood, IL: Dorsey.

Gamson, William. 1988. "Political Discourse and Collective Action." *International Social Movement Research* 1: 219–44.

Gamson, William. 1992. "The Social Psychology of Collective Action." In *Frontiers in Social Movement Theory*, ed. Aldon Morris and Carol Mueller. New Haven: Yale University Press.

Gans, Herbert J. 1980. *Deciding What's News: A Study of CBS Evening News, NBC Nightly News, Newsweek and Time.* New York: Vintage.

Gans, Herbert J. 1995. *The War Against the Poor: The Underclass and Antipoverty Policy.* New York: Basic Books.

Garramone, Gina. 1984. "Voter Responses to Negative Political Ads." *Journalism Quarterly* (61): 250–59.

Gelb, Joyce. 1989. *Feminism and Politics: A Comparative Perspective.* Berkeley: University of California Press.

Gelb, Joyce. 1995. "Feminist Organization Success and the Politics of Engagement." In *Feminist Organizations: Harvest of the New Women's Movement*, ed. Myra Max Ferree and Patricia Yancey Martin. Philadelphia: Temple University Press.

Genovese, Michael A. (ed.) 1993. *Women as National Leaders.* Newbury Park, CA: Sage.

Giddings, Paula. 1984. *When and Where I Enter: The Impact of Black Women on Race and Sex in America.* New York: William Morrow.

Gilligan, Carol. 1982. *In a Different Voice: Psychological Theory and Women's Development.* Cambridge, MA: Harvard University Press.

Gitlin, Todd. 1980. *The Whole World Is Watching.* Berkeley: University of California Press.

Gitlin, Todd. 1994. *Inside Prime Time.* London:Routledge.

Goffman, Erving. 1974. *Frame Analysis: An Essay on the Organization of Experience.* New York: Harper & Row.

Goldin, Claudia.1990. *Understanding the Gender Gap: An Economic History of American Women.* New York: Oxford Univ. Press.

Goldstein, Joel H. 1984. *The Effects of the Adoption of Women Suffrage: Sex Differences in Voting Behavior—Illinois, 1914–21.* New York: Praeger Publishers.

Graber, Doris. 1989. *Mass Media and American Politics.* Washington, DC: Congressional Quarterly Press.

Graber, Doris A. 1984. *Processing the News: How People Tame the Information Tide.* New York: Longmans.

Greenberg-Lake, *The Analysis Group.* no date. "Campaigning in a Different Voice." EMILY's List. Washington, DC.

Gunter, Barrie. 1995. *Television and Gender Representation.* London: John Libbey.

Gutin, Mara G. 1989. *The President's Partner: The First Lady in the Twentieth Century.* Westport, CT: Greenwood Press.

Hall, Mimi. 1994. "A Whitman Sampler: N.J. Gov. Inspires GOP." *USA Today* 6 Oct.

Hallin, Daniel. 1990. "Sound Bite News." In *Blurring the Lines*, ed. Gary Orren. New York: Free Press

Harding, Sandra. 1991. *Whose Science? Whose Knowledge?* Ithaca, NY: Cornell University Press.

Harris, Louis. 1991. *Steelcase Office Environment Index.* Louis Harris & Associates.

Harrison, Cynthia. 1988. *On Account of Sex: The Politics of Women's Issues, 1945–1968.* Berkeley: University of California Press.

Harrison, Teresa M., Timothy D. Stephen, William Husson, and B.J. Fehr. 1991. "Images Vs. Issues in the 1984 Presidential Election: Differences Between Men and Women." *Human Communication Research* 18(4):290–297.

Harwood, Richard. 1995. "The Media's Healthy Dinosaurs." *Washington Post* 13 Sept.

Hastie, Reid. 1984. "Causes and Effects of Causal Attribution." *Journal of Personality and Social Psychology* 46: 44–56.

Hastie, Reid. 1986. "A Primer of Information-processing Theory for the Political Scientist." In *Political Cognition*, ed. Richard R. Lau and David O. Sears. Hillsdale, NJ: Erlbaum. Hastings House.

Heller, Deane and David Heller. 1961. *Jacqueline Kennedy.* Derby, CT: Monarch Books.

Hershey, Marjorie. 1989. "The Campaign and the Media." In *The Elections of 1988*, ed. Gerald Pomper. Chatham, NJ: Chatham House.

Hewlett, Sylvia Ann. 1986. *A Lesser Life: The Myth of Women's Liberation in America.* New York: David Morrow.

Hirsch, Paul M. 1977. "Occupational, Organizational, and Institutional Models in Mass Media Research." In *Strategies for Communication Research*, eds. Paul M. Hirsch, Peter V. Miller, and F. Gerald Kline. Thousand Oaks, CA: Sage.

Hole, Judith and Ellen Levine. 1971. *Rebirth of Feminism.* New York: Quadrangle.

Holloway, Laura Langford. 1881. *The Ladies of the White House.* Philadephia.

Houston Chronicle, 1993, 29 May.

Hovland, C. 1959. "Reconciling Conflicting Results from Experimental and Survey Studies of Attitude Change." *American Psychologist* 14: 8–17.

Howell, Sharon. 1990. *Reflections of Ourselves: The Mass Media and the Women's Movement, 1963 to the Present.* New York: Peter Lang.

Huddy, Leonie. 1994. "The Political Significance of Voters' Gender Stereotypes." *Research in Micropolitics* 4: 169–193.

Huddy, Leonie and Nayda Terkildsen. 1993a. "The Consequences of Gender Stereotypes for Women Candidates at Different Levels and Types of Office." *Political Research Quarterly* 46(3): 503–26.

Huddy, Leonie and Nayda Terkildsen. 1993b. "Gender Stereotypes and the Perception of Male and Female Candidates." *American Journal of Political Science* 37(1):119–48.

Hunt-Jones, Conover. 1977. *Dolley and the Great Little Madison*. Washington, DC: AIA Foundation.

Inter-Parliamentary Union. 1994. *Distribution of Seats between Men and Women in the 178 National Parliaments Existing as at 30 June 1994*. Geneva: Inter-Parliamentary Union.

Iyengar, Shanto and Donald R. Kinder. 1987. *News That Matters*. Chicago: University of Chicago Press.

Iyengar, Shanto. 1991. *Is Anyone Responsible? How Television Frames Political Issues*. Chicago: University of Chicago Press.

Jacobson, G. C. and S. Kernell. 1983. *Strategy and Choice in Congressional Elections*. New Haven: Yale University Press.

James, Marquis. 1937. *Andrew Jackson: Portrait of a President*. New York: Grosset and Dunlap.

Jamieson, Kathleen Hall. 1989. *Eloquence in an Electronic Age*. New York: Oxford University Press.

Jamieson, Kathleen Hall. 1995. *Beyond the Double Bind: Women and Leadership*. New York: Oxford University Press.

Janis, Irving. 1982. *Groupthink*. New York: Houghton Mifflin.

Jelen, Ted G. 1994. "Carol Moseley-Braun: The Insider as Insurgent." *In The Year of the Women: Myths and Realities*, eds. Elizabeth Adell Cook, Sue Thomas, and Clyde Wilcox.

Jennings, M. K. and R. G. Niemi. 1981. *Generations and Politics: A Panel Study of Young Adults and Their Parents*. Princeton: Princeton University Press.

Johnson, Sammye and William G. Christ. 1989. "Women Through 'Time': Who Gets Covered." *Journalism Quarterly* 65:889–97.

Johnston, Anne and Anne Barton White. "Communication Styles and Female Candidates: A Study of Political Advertising During the 1986 Senate Elections." *Journalism Quarterly* 71(1): 321–29.

Johnstone, John W.C., Edward J. Slawski, and William W. Bowman. 1976. *The News People*. Urbana, IL: University of Illinois Press.

Jurney, Dorothy. 1986. "Tenth annual survey reports women editors at 12.4 percent," *American Society of Newspaper Editors Bulletin*, pp. 4–7, 10.

Just, Marion, Ann Crigler, Dean Alger, Tim Cook, Montague Kern, and Darrell West. (1996). *Crosstalk: Citizens, Candidates and Media in a Presidential Campaign*. Chicago: University of Chicago Press.

Just, Marion. 1995. "Talk is Cheap: Improving the Voter Information Process in Light of the 1992 Campaign," In *Improving the Electoral Process*, eds. William B. Mayer, Michael Dukakis. Twentieth Century Fund.

Kahn, Kim Fridkin and Edie N. Goldenberg. 1991. "Women Candidates in the News: An Examination of Gender Differences in U.S. Senate Campaigns." *Public Opinion Quarterly* 55(2):180–99.

Kahn, Kim Fridkin. 1991a. "Senate Elections in the News: Examining Campaign Coverage." *Legislative Studies Quarterly* 16: 349–374.

Kahn, Kim Fridkin. 1991b. "The Media: Obstacle or Ally of Feminists?" *Annals of the American Academy of Political and Social Sciences* 515(2): 104–13.

Kahn, Kim Fridkin. 1992. "Does Being Male Help? An Investigation of the Effects of Candidate Gender and Campaign Coverage on Evaluations of U.S. Senate Candidates." *Journal of Politics* 54: 497–517.

Kahn, Kim Fridkin. 1993. "Gender Differences in Campaign Messages: The Political Advertisements of Men and Women Candidates for U.S. Senate." *Political Research Quarterly* 46(3): 481–503.

Kahn, Kim Fridkin. 1994a. "The Distorted Mirror: Press Coverage of Women Candidates for Statewide Office." *Journal of Politics* 56(1): 154–74.

Kahn, Kim Fridkin. 1994b. "Does Gender Make a Difference? An Experimental Examination of Sex Stereotypes and Press Patterns in Statewide Campaigns." *American Journal of Political Science* 38(1): 162–95.

Kaid, Lynda Lee and Dorothy K. Davidson. 1986."Elements of Videostyle: Candidate Presentation Through Television Advertising." In *New Perspectives on Political Advertising*. eds. Lynda Lee Kaid, Dan Nimmo and Keith R. Sanders. Carbondale, IL: Southern Illinois University Press.

Kathlene, Lyn, Susan E. Clarke, and Barbara A. Fox. 1991. "Ways Women Politicians Are Making A Difference." *Gender and Policymaking: Studies of Women in Office*, ed. Debra L. Dodson. CAWP, Eagleton Institute of Politics, Rutgers University.

Keen, Judy. 1995. "GOP's No. 2 Spot Nothing to Talk About." *USA TODAY* 24 August.

Keniston, Ellen and Kenneth Keniston. 1964. "An American Anachronism: The Image of Women and Work." *American Scholar* 33: 355–75.

Kern, Montague and Marion Just. 1995. "The Focus Group Method, Political Advertising, Campaign News and the Construction of Candidate Images." *Political Communication* 12:127–45.

Kern, Montague. 1989. *Thirty-Second Politics.* New York: Praeger-Greenwood.

Kern, Montague. 1993. "The Advertising Driven 'New' Mass Media Election and the Rhetoric of Policy Issues." In *Media and Public Policy*, ed. Robert Spitzer. Westport, CT: Praeger-Greenwood, pp. 133–50.

Kinder, Donald R. 1983. "Presidential Traits." Pilot Study Report to the 1984 NES Planning Committee and NES Boards.

Kirkpatrick, Jeane. 1995. "In Their Own Words." In *Women in World Politics*, eds. Francine D'Amico and Pete Beckman. Westport, CT: Bergin and Garvey.

Kittay, Eva Feder and Diana T. Meyers. 1987. *Women and Moral Theory.* Totowa, NJ: Rowman and Littlefield.

Klein, Ethel. 1984. *Gender Politics.* Cambridge: Harvard University Press.

Knight-Ridder Women Readers Task Force. 1991. "How Newspapers Can Gain Readership Among Women . . . And Why It's Important."

Kohlberg, Lawrence. 1984. *Essays on Moral Development.* Vol. 1. *The Psychology of Moral Development.* New York: Harper & Row.

Konner, Joan. 1995. "Is Journalism Losing Its Professional Standards?" Text of speech delivered at a conference on *Ethics and Standards: New Rules for Journalism*, Hamburg, Germany. 3 July.

Krueger, Richard. 1988. *Focus Groups: A Practical Guide for Applied Research.* Newbury Park, CA: Sage.

Ladd, Everett Carll and Karlyn Keene Bowman. 1982. "Women and Men: Is a Realignment Underway?" *Public Opinion* 21–40.

Ladd, Everett Carll. 1995. "The 1994 Congressional Elections: The Realignment Continues." *Political Science Quarterly* 110(1):1–23.

Lafky, Sue A. 1991. "Women Journalists." In *The American Journalist*, ed. David H. Weaver and G. Cleveland Wilhoit. 2nd Edition. Bloomington, IN: Indiana University Press.

Laitila, Tiina. 1995. "The Journalistic Codes of Ethics in Europe." Paper presented at the International Association for Mass Communication Research conference, Portoroz, Slovenia. 28 June.

Lazarsfeld, Paul, Bernard Berelson, and Hazel Gaudet. 1948. *The People's Choice.* New York: Columbia University Press.

Lederman, Linda Costigan. 1990a "Assessing Education Effectiveness: The Focus Group Interview as a Technique for Data Collection." *Communication Education* 38: 117–27.

Lederman, Linda Costigan. 1990b. "An Exploration of the Modification of the Focus Group Technique: Participants Trained to Bring Information with Them." Paper presented at the 40th Annual Conference of the International Communication Association, Dublin, Ireland.

Leeper, Mark. 1991. "The Impact of Prejudice on Female Candidates: An Experimental Look at Voter Inference." *American Politics Quarterly* 19: 248–61.

LeVeness, Frank P. and Jane P. Sweeney. 1987. *Women Leaders in Contemporary U.S. Politics.* Boulder, CO: Lynne Rienner.

Lewin, Kurt. 1947. "Frontiers in Group Dynamics." *Human Relations* 1: 2–38.

Linville, P. W., P. Salovey, and G. Fischer. 1986. "Stereotyping and Perceived Distributions of Social Characteristics: An Application to Ingroup-Outgroup Perception." In *Prejudice, Discrimination, and Racism* eds. J. F. Dovidio and S. L. Gaertner. New York: Academic Press, pp. 165–208.

Lippman, Thomas W. 1989. *The Washington Post Deskbook on Style.* New York: McGraw-Hill.

Lipset, Seymour. 1968. *Agrarian Socialism.* Garden City, NY: Anchor.

Loe, Victoria. 1994. "Meet a few Pulitzer Prize Women," *JAWS* Newsletter, p. 1.

Logan, Mrs. John A. 1901. *Thirty Years in Washington or Life and Scenes in Our National Capital.* Hartford, CT: A.D. Worthington & Co.

Lont, Cynthia M. (ed.) 1995. *Women and Media: Content / Careers / Criticism.* Belmont, CA: Wadsworth Publishing Company.

Lovenduski, Joni and Pippa Norris. 1993. *Gender and Party Politics.* London: Sage Publications.

Lovenduski, Joni and Pippa Norris (eds.) 1996. *Women in British Politics.* Oxford: Oxford University Press.

Madison, Dolly. 1886. *Memoirs and Letters.* Boston.

Markus, Gregory B. 1982. "Political Attitudes During an Election Year: A Report on the 1980 NES Panel Study. *American Political Science Review* 76: 538.56n.

Marzolf, Marion. 1977. *Up from the Footnote: A History of Women Journalists.* New York: Hastings House.

McAdam, Doug. 1982. *The Political Process and the Development of Black Insurgency.* Chicago: University of Chicago Press.

McDermott, Monika. "Voting Cues in Low Information Elections: Candidate Gender as a Social Information Variable in Contemporary U.S. Elections." American Journal of Political Science. forthcoming.

McGlen, Nancy E. and Karen O'Conner. 1995. *Women, Politics and American Society.* Englewood Cliffs, NJ: Prentice Hall.

McGrath, Kristin. 1993. "Women and Newspapers." *Newspaper Research Journal* 14(2): 95–109.

McQuail, Denis. 1992a. *Mass Communication Theory: An Introduction.* Beverly Hills, CA: Sage.

McQuail, Denis. 1992b. *Media Performance.* London: Sage Publications.

Media Report to Women. 1976. "Female Journalism: Is Something Different." 4(1): 3.

Media Report to Women. 1995. "Slipping From the Scene: Front-Page News Coverage of Women Declines." 23(2):2–3.

Media Studies Journal. 1993. "The Media and Women: Without Apology." Special Issue. Winter.

Mencher, Melvin. 1994. *News Reporting and Writing.* 6th Edition. Dubuque, IA: Wm. C. Brown.

Merton, Robert, Marjorie Fiske, and Patricia L. Kendall. 1956. *The Focused Interview.* New York: Bureau of Applied Social Research. Columbia University Press.

Miller, Arthur, Martin Wattenberg, and Oksana Malanchuk. 1986. "Schematic Assessments of Presidential Candidates." *American Political Science Review* 79: 359–372.

Miller, Jean Baker. 1976. *Toward a New Psychology of Women.* Boston, MA: Beacon Press.

Mills, Kay. 1988. *A Place in the News: From the Women's Pages to the Front Pages.* New York: Columbia University Press.

Mitchell, Stewart (ed.) 1947. *New Letters of Abigail Adams.* Boston.

Montgomery, Lori and Marc Selinger. 1995. "Detroit Congresswoman Sinks to Bottom of Capitol Hill Heap." *Philadelphia Inquirer.* 24 August.

Morgan, David L. 1988. *Focus Groups as Qualitative Research.* Newbury Park, CA: Sage.

Morrow, Lance. 1984. "Why Not a Woman?" *Time* 4 June:18–22.

Mott, Frank Luther. 1962. *American Journalism, A History: 1690–1960.* New York: Macmillan.

Mowlana, Hamid. 1985. *International Flow of Information: Global Report and Analysis.* Paris: UNESCO, 1985.

Nasar, Sylvia. 1992. "Women's Progress Stalled? Just Not So." *New York Times* 18 October.

National Commission on the Observance of International Women's Year. 1976. "Ten Guidelines for the Treatment of Women in the Media." Leaflet L-1. Washington, DC: International Women's Year Secretariat, U.S. Department of State.

National Women's Political Caucus Survey. 1987. Washington, DC.

Nelson, Anson and Fanny. 1892. *Memorials of Sarah Childress Polk.* New York.

Nelson, Barbara and Najma Chowdhury. 1995. *Women and Politics Worldwide.* New Haven: Yale University Press.

Neuman, W. Russell, Marion R. Just, Ann N. Crigler. 1992. *Common Knowledge: News and the Construction of Political Meaning.* Chicago, IL: University of Chicago Press.

Nicolosi, Terry Hitchins and Jose L. Ceballos. 1992. *Official Proceedings of the 1992 Democratic National Convention.* Washington DC.

Nie, Norman H., Sidney Verba, and John R. Petrocik. 1976. *The Changing American Voter.* Cambridge, MA: Harvard University Press.

Nimmo, Dan and Robert Savage. 1976. *Candidates and Their Images.*Pacific Palisades: Goodyear.

NORC (National Opinion Research Center). 1991. *General Social Survey*, April. Chicago, IL: University of Chicago Press.

Norris, Pippa and Joni Lovenduski. 1995. *Political Recruitment: Gender, Race and Class in the British Parliament.* Cambridge: Cambridge University Press.

Norris, Pippa. 1988. "The Gender Gap: A Cross-National Trend?" *The Politics of the Gender Gap*, ed. Carol M. Mueller. Newbury Park, CA: Sage Publications.

Norris, Pippa. 1994. "The Impact of the Electoral System on Election of Women to National Legislatures." In *Different Roles, Different Voices*, eds. Marianne Githens, Pippa Norris, and Joni Lovenduski. New York: HarperCollins.

Norris, Pippa. 1996a. "Gender Realignment in Comparative Perspective." In *The Future of the Australian Party System*, ed. Marian Simms. Melbourne: Allen and Unwin.

Norris, Pippa. 1996b. "Gender Voting: Theoretical Frameworks and New Approaches." In *Women and American Politics: Agenda Setting for the 21st Century*, ed. Susan Carroll.

Norris, Pippa. 1996c. "Mobilising the Women's Vote: The Gender-Generation Gap in Voting Behaviour." *Parliamentary Affairs* 46(2).

Norris, Pippa. 1996d. "The Restless Searchlight: Network New Framing in the Post Cold War World." *Political Communication* 13(1)357-370.

Okin, Susan Moller (1990). "Thinking like a Woman." In *Theoretical Perspectives on Sexual Difference*, ed. Deborah L. Rhode. New Haven: Yale University Press.

Olson, Mancur. 1965. *The Logic of Collective Action.* Cambridge, MA: Harvard University Press.

Oring, Sheryl, and Danko, . 1995. "Kissing the Newsroom Goodbye." *American Journalism* Review. June: 31–35, 43.

Otto, Jean. 1993. "A Matter of Opinion," *Media Studies Journal* 7(1–2); 159–163.

Overholser, Geneva. 1989. 'Female journalists help newspapers expand their view of the world.' *Editorially Speaking.*

Parenti, Michael. 1986. *Inventing Reality: The Politics of the Mass Media.* New York: St. Martin's Press.

Paterson, Judith. 1986. "Among the Hats and Gloves: The Double Message on the Women's Pages." Paper presented at the American Journalism Historians Association convention, St. Louis, MO, 4 Oct.

Patterson, Thomas and Robert D. McClure. (1976). *The Unseeing Eye: The Myth of Television Power in National Elections.*New York: Putnam.

Patterson, Thomas. 1980. *The Mass Media and Elections.* New York: Praeger.

Pease, Ted and J. Frazier Smith. 1991. *The Newsroom Barometer: Job Satisfaction and the Impact of Racial Diversity at U.S. Daily Newspapers.* No. 1, Monograph Series. Athens: Ohio University.

Peterson, Paul V. 1979. "Enrollment Surges Again, Increases 7 Per Cent to 70,601." *Journalism Educator* 33(4): 3.

Petrocik, John. 1996. "Issue Ownership in Presidential Elections with a 1980 Case Study." *American Journal of Political Science* 40(3).

Pfau, Michel, R. Parrott, and B. Lindquist. (1992). "An Expectancy Explanation of the Effectiveness of Political Attack Spots: A Case Study." *Journal of Applied Communication Research* 90 (3): 235–54.

Piven, Frances and Richard Cloward. 1979. *Poor People's Movements* New York, NY: Vintage.

Poole, K.T. and L.H. Zeigler, (1985). *Women, Public Opinion and Politics.* New York: Longman.

Popkin, Samuel L. 1991. *The Reasoning Voter: Communication and Persuasion in Presidential Campaigns.* Chicago: University of Chicago Press.

Press, Andrea L. 1991. *Women Watching Television: Gender, Class and Generation in the American Television Experience.* Philadelphia: University of Pennsylvania Press.

Public Opinion. 1979, January/February. "The Modern Woman: How Far Has She Come." 35–39.

Rakov, Lana F. and Kimberlie Kranich. 1991. "Women as Sign in Television News." *Journal of Communication* 4:8–23.

Remini, Robert V. 1971. "Election of 1828." In *History of American Presidential Elections,* Vol. 1, ed. Arthur M. Schlesinger, Jr. et al. New York: Chelsea House, McGraw-Hill.

Rich, Carole. 1994. *Writing and Reporting News: A Coaching Method.* Belmont, CA: Wadsworth Publishing.

Robertson, Nan. 1992. *The Girls in the Balcony: Women, Men and the New York Times.* New York: Random House.

Robinson, Gertrude J. and Armande Saint-Jean, with Christine Rioux. 1991.

"Women Politicians and Their Media Coverage: A Generational Analysis." In *Women in Canadian Politics: Toward Equity in Representation*, ed. Kathy Megyery. Vol. 6 Research Studies, Royal Commission on Electoral Reform and Party Financing and Canada Communication Group - Publishing, Supply and Services Canada. Toronto: Dundurn Press.

Robinson, Michael. (1994). "Three Faces of American Media." In *Media Power in Politics*, ed. Doris A. Graber. 3rd Edition. Washington, DC: Congressional Quarterly Press, pp. 248–63.

Rojahn, K. and T. Pettigrew. 1992. "Memory for Schema-Relevant Information: A Meta-Analytic Resolution." *British Journal of Social Psychology* 31: 81–109.

Romano, Lois. 1995. "Top Chicks Cheer Chung." In "The Reliable Source" column, *Washington Post* 2 June.

Rosenwasser, Shirley Miller and Norma G. Dean. 1989. "Gender Role and Political Office." *Psychology of Women Quarterly* 13: 77–85.

Rossi, Alice. 1964. "Equality Between the Sexes: An Immodest Proposal." *Daedalus* 93: 607–52.

Ruble, T.L. 1983. "Sex Stereotypes: Issues of Change in the 1970's." *Sex Roles* 9: 397–402.

Rule, Wilma and Pippa Norris. 1992. "Anglo and Minority Women's Underrepresentation in Congress: Is the Electoral System the Culprit?" *United States Electoral Systems: Their Impact on Women and Minorities*, eds. Wilma Rule and Joseph F. Zimmerman. New York: Greenwood Press.

Rush, Ramona and Donna Allen. 1989. *Communications at the Crossroads: The Gender Gap Connection*. Norwood, NJ: Ablex.

Russell, Susan H. et al. 1991. *Profiles of Faculty in Higher Education Institutions*,1988. Washington, DC: National Center for Education Statistics, U.S. Department of Education.

Rutland, Robert A. 1987. *James Madison and the Founding Fathers*. New York: Macmillan.

Ryan, Barbara. 1992. *Feminism and the Women's Movement*. New York: Routledge.

Ryan, Charlotte. 1991. *Prime Time Activism*. Boston: South End Press.

Sanders, Marlene and Marcia Rock. 1988. *Waiting for Prime Time: The Women of Television News*. New York: Harper & Row.

Sapiro, Virginia. 1981–82. "If Senator Baker Were a Woman: An Experimental Study of Candidate Images." *Political Psychology* 2: 61–83.

Sapiro, Virginia. 1983. *The Political Integration of Women*. Urbana: University of Illinois Press.

Schilpp, Madelon Golden and Sharon M. Murphy. 1983. *Great Women of the Press*. Carbondale, IL: Southern Illinois University Press.

Schlozman, Kay L. 1990. "Representing Women in Washington: Sisterhood and Pressure Politics." In *Women, Politics and Change*, ed. Patricia Gurin and Louise Tilly. New York: Russell Sage.

Schorer, Jane. 1991. The Story Behind A Landmark Story of Rape." *Washington Journalism Review*, pp. 20–26.

Schorr, Daniel. 1995. "Publishing the Unabomber: Responsible or Reckless?" *Washington Post.* 24 September.

Sears, Donald. O. 1983. "The Persistence of Early Political Predispositions: The Roles of Attitude Object and Life Stage." In *Political Socialization, Citizenship Education, and Democracy*, eds. L. Wheeler and W.J. McGuire. New York: Teachers College Press.

Seelye, Katharine Q. 1995. "Democrats Fleeing to G.O.P. Remake Political Landscape." *New York Times* 7 October.

Sellers, Charles. 1957. *James K. Polk.* Princeton: Princeton University Press.

Shapiro, Robert Y. and Harpeet Mahajan. 1986. "Gender Differences in Policy References: A Summary of Trends from the 1960s to the 1980s." *Public Opinion Quarterly* 50: 42–61.

Shepard, Alicia C. 1994. "The Gospel of Public Journalism." *American Journalism Review* September:28–35.

Shoemaker, Pamela J. and Stephen D. Reese. 1991. *Mediating the Message: Theories of Influence on Mass Media Content.* White Plains, NY: Longman.

Siebert, Fred S., Theodore Peterson, and Wilbur Schramm. 1956. *Four Theories of the Press.* Chicago: University of Illinois Press.

Sigal, Leon V. 1973. *Reporters and Officials.* New York: Oxford University Press.

Sigelman, Lee and Carol K. Sigelman. 1984. "Sexism, Racism and Ageism in Voting Behavior: An Experimental Analysis." *Social Psychology Quarterly* 45:263–69.

Small, Melvin. 1994. *Covering Dissent.* New Brunswick, NJ: Rutgers University Press.

Smith, Erna. 1994. *Transmitting Race: The Los Angeles Riot in Television News.* Cambridge, MA: Joan Shorenstein Center.

Smith, Martha Bayard. 1906. *The First Forty Years of Washington Society.* New York: Ed. Gailard Hunt.

Smith, Nancy Kegan and Mary C. Ryan (eds.) 1988. *Modern First Ladies.* Washington, DC: National Archives and Records.

Smith, Tom W. and Lance A. Selfa. September/October 1992. "When Do Women Vote for Women?" *The Public Perspective* 30–31.

Snow, David and Robert Benford. 1988. "Ideology, Frame Resonance, and Participant Mobilization." *International Social Movement Research* 1:197–217.

Snow, David and Robert Benford. 1992. "Master Frames and Cycles of Protest." In *Frontiers in Social Movement Theory*, ed. Aldon Morris and Carol Mueller. New Haven: Yale University Press.

Snow, David, Burke Rochford, Steven Worden, and Robert Benford. 1986. "Frame Alignment Process, Micromobilization, and Movement Participation." *American Sociological Review* 51: 464–81.

Snyder, David and William Kelly. 1977. "Conflict Intensity, Media Sensitivity, and the Validity of Newspaper Data." *American Sociological Review* 42:105–23.

Solomon, William S. and Robert W. McChesney. 1993. *Ruthless Criticism: New Perspectives in U.S. Communication History.* Minneapolis: University of Minnesota Press.

Sommers, Christina Hoff. 1994. *Who Stole Feminism?* New York: Touchstone/Simon & Schuster.

Spalter-Roth, Roberta and Ronnee Schreiber. 1995. "Outsider Issues and Insider Tactics: Strategic Tensions in the Women's Policy Network During the 1980s." In *Feminist Organizations: Harvest of the New Women's Movement*, ed. Myra Max Ferree and Patricia Yancey Martin. Philadelphia: Temple University Press.

Spitze, Glenna. 1988. "The Data on Women's Labor Force Participation." In *Women Working*, ed. Ann Stromberg and Shirley Harkess. 2nd Edition. Mountain View, CA: Mayfield.

SPJ report "Working Draft of Revised Code of Ethics." 1995. *The Quill.* July/August.

Stangor, C. and D. McMillan. 1992. "Memory for Expectancy-Congruent and Expectancy-Incongruent Social Information: A Meta-Analytic Review of the Social Psychological and Social Developmental Literatures." *Psychological Bulletin* 111: 42–61.

Stanley, Harold W. and Richard G. Niemi. 1994. *Vital Statistics on American Politics.* Washington, DC: CQ Press.

Statistical Abstract of the United States. 1992. Washington, DC: U.S. Bureau of the Census.

Tarrow, Sidney. 1983. *Struggling to Reform: Social Movements and Policy Change During Cycles of Protest.* Ithaca, NY: Western Societies Program, Cornell University.

Tarrow, Sidney. 1989. *Struggle, Politics, and Reform: Collective Action, Social Movements, and Cycles of Protest.* Ithaca, NY: Western Societies Program, Cornell University.

Tarrow, Sidney. 1994. *Power in Movement: Social Movements, Collective Action and Politics.* Cambridge: Cambridge University Press.

Terry, Carolyn. 1995. "Breaking Through: Special Report." *Presstime.* March:31–36.

Thane, Elswyth. 1960. *Washington's Lady.* New York: Dodd, Mead.

Thomas, Sue. 1991. "The Impact of Women on State Legislative Policies." *The Journal of Politics* 53: 958–976.

Thomas, Sue. 1994a. "Women in State Legislatures: One Step at a Time." In *The Year of the Woman: Myths and Realities*, eds. Elizabeth Adell Cook, Sue Thomas, and Clyde Wilcox. Boulder, CO: Westview.

Thomas, Sue. 1994b. *How Women Legislate.* New York: Oxford University Press.

Thoveron, G. 1987. *How Women Are Represented in Television Programmes in the EEC.* Brussels: Commission of the European Community.

Tidmarch, Charles M., Lori J. Hyman, and Jill Sorkin. 1984. "Press Issue Agendas in the 1982 Congressional and Gubernatorial Election Campaigns." *Journal of Politics* 46: 1227–1242.

Tolleson-Rinehart, Sue. 1994. "The California Senate Races: A Case Study in the Gendered Paradoxes of Politics." In *The Year of the Woman: Myths and Realities*, eds. Elizabeth Adell Cook, Sue Thomas, and Clyde Wilcox.

Tolleson-Rinehart, Sue and Jeanie R. Stanley. 1994. *Claytie and the Lady: Ann Richards, Gender, and Politics in Texas.* Austin: University of Texas Press.

Tong, Rosemary. 1989. *Feminist Thought.* Boulder, CO: Westview.

Trent, Judith S. and Robert V. Friedenberg. 1983. *Political Campaign Communication: Principles and Practices.* New York: Praeger Publishing.

Trent, Judith and Robert Friedenberg. 1991. *Political Campaign Communication.* New York: Praeger Publishing.

Trent, Judith S. and Teresa Chandler Sabourin. 1993. "When the Candidate Is a Woman: The Content and Form of Televised Negative Advertising." In *Communication and Sex Role Socialization*, eds. Cynthia Berryman-Fink, Deborah Ballard-Reisch, and Lisa H. Newman. New York and London: Garland Publishing.

Tuchman, Gaye, Arlene Kaplan Daniels, and James Benet. 1978. *Hearth and Home: Images of Women in the Mass Media.* New York: Oxford University Press.

Tuchman, Gaye. 1978a. "The Newspaper as a Social Movement's Resource". In *Hearth & Home: Images of Women in the Mass Media*, ed. Gaye Tuchman, Arlene Kaplan Daniels, and James Benet. New York: Oxford University Press.

Tuchman, Gaye. 1978b. *Making News: A Study in the Construction of Reality.* New York: Free Press.

Turner, Justine G. and Linda Levitt Turner (eds.) 1987. *Mary Todd Lincoln: Her Life and Letters.* New York: Fromm International Publishing Co.

U.S.Commission on Civil Rights. 1977. *Window Dressing on the Set: Women and Minorities in Television.* Washington, DC: U.S. Government Printing Office.

U.S. Commission on Civil Rights. 1979. *Window Dressing on the Set: Women and Minorities in Television:An Update.* Washington, DC: U.S. Government Printing Office.

UNESCO. 1980. *Women in the Media.* New York: UNIPUB.

UNESCO. 1989. *World Communication Report.* Paris. UNESCO.

United Nations. 1995a. *The World's Women:Trends and Statistics.* New York: United Nations.

United Nations. 1995b. *Platform for Action: Fourth World Conference on Women, Beijing.* New York: United Nations.

Valentino, Nicholas A. 1995. "Gender vs. Partisanship in the Year of the Woman: Beginning to Untangle the Effects on Vote Choice." Paper presented at the annual meeting of the American Political Science Association, Chicago, August 31–September 3.

Van Dijk, Teun A. 1995. "The Mass Media Today: Discourses of Domination or Diversity?" *The Public Javnost* [publication of the European Institute for Communication and Culture (Euricom)] 2(2):27–45.

Van Zoonen, Liesbet and Annabel Sreberny Mohammdi (eds.) 1996. *Women's Politics and the Media.* Cresskill, NJ: Hampton Press.

Von Hippel, W., D. Sekaquaptewa, and P. Vargas. 1995. "On the Role of Encoding Processes in Stereotype Maintenance." In *Advances in Experimental Social Psychology*, ed. M. Zanna. Volume 27. New York: Academic Press, pp. 177–254.

Voss, Melinda. August 1991. "Pulitzers Price Women." *JAWS Newsletter*, p. 1.

Wadsworth, Anne Johnston, Philip Patterson, Lynda Lee Kaid, Ginger Cullers,

Drew Malcomb, and Linda Lamirand. 1987. " 'Masculine' vs. 'Feminine' Strategies in Political Ads: Implications for Female Candidates." *Journal of Applied Communication Research.*

Ward, Hiley. 1985. *Professional Newswriting.* New York: Harcourt Brace Jovanovich.

Weaver, David H. and G. Cleveland Wilhoit. 1986. *The American Journalist: A Portrait of U.S. News People and Their Work.* Bloomington: Indiana University Press.

Weaver, David and G. Cleveland Wilhoit. 1991. *The American Journalist: A Portrait of U.S. News People and Their Work*, 2nd edition. Bloomington: Indiana University Press.

Weaver, David and G. Cleveland Wilhoit. 1992. November. *The American Journalist in the 1990s.* Preliminary Report, The Freedom Forum, Arlington, VA.

Weaver, David H. and G. Cleveland Wilhoit. 1996. *The American Journalist in the 1990s: U.S. News People at the End of an Era.* Mahwah, NJ: Lawrence Erlbaum.

Webb, Robert A. 1978. *The Washington Post Deskbook on Style.* New York: McGraw-Hill.

West, Darrell. (1993). *Air Wars.* Washington, DC: Congressional Quarterly Press.

Westneat, Danny. 1993. "A Woman's Perspective in the Senate." *Journal American.* 9: C.

Wilcox, Clyde. 1994. "Why Was 1992 the 'Year of the Woman'? Explaining Women's Gains in 1992." In *The Year of the Woman: Myths and Realities*, eds. E. A. Cook, S. Thomas, and C. Wilcox. Boulder, CO: Westview, 1–24.

Wilhoit, G. Cleeland and Weaver, David. 1994. *U.S. Journalists at work, 1971–1992.* Paper presented at the annual meeting of the Association for Education in Journalism and Mass Communication, Atlanta, GA.

Williams, John E. and Deborah L. Best. 1990. *Measuring Sex Stereotypes: A Multination Study.* Newbury Park: Sage Publications, Inc.

Williams, Leonard. 1994. "Political Advertising in the 'Year of the Woman': Did X Mark the Spot?" In *The Year of the Woman: Myths and Realities*, eds. Elizabeth Adell Cook, Sue Thomas, and Clyde Wilcox. Boulder: Westview.

Wilson, James Q. 1973. *Political Organizations.* New York: Basic Books.

Winfield, Betty H. 1981. "Anna Eleanor Roosevelt Shines a Light on Herself and Women Journalists." *Journalism History* 8 (2): 54–58, 63–67.

Winfield, Betty Houchin. 1988. "Anna Eleanor Roosevelt's White House Legacy: The Public First Lady." *Presidential Studies Quarterly* XVIII(2): 331–45.

Winfield, Betty Houchin. 1994. *FDR and the News Media.* New York: Columbia University Press.

Winfield, Betty Houchin. 1994. " 'Madam President,' Understanding A New Type of First Lady." *Media Studies Journal* 8 (2): 59–71.

Witt, Linda, Karen M. Paget, and Glenna Matthews. 1994. *Running as a Woman: Gender and Power in American Politics.* New York: Free Press.

Women, Men and Media. 1994. "Arriving at the Scene: Women's Growing Presence in the News." April.

Yoder, Edwin W., Jr. 1995. "Douglass Cater's Rules of Journalism." *Washington Post* 20 September.

Young, Hugo. 1989. *One of Us.* London: Macmillan.

Zangrando, Joanna Schneider and Robert L. Zangrando. 1984. "ER and Black Civil Rights." In *Without Precedent: The Life and Career of Eleanor Roosevelt,* eds. Joan Hoff-Wilson and Marjorie Lightman. Bloomington: Indiana University Press.

Zoroya, Gregg. 1995. "Whither the Year of the Woman?" *Los Angeles Times* 23 August.

Index